Reforming Child Welfare in the Post-Soviet Space

This book provides new and empirically grounded research-based knowledge and insights into the current transformation of the Russian child welfare system. It focuses on the major shift in Russia's child welfare policy: deinstitutionalisation of the system of children's homes inherited from the Soviet era and an increase in fostering and adoption.

Divided into four sections, this book details both the changing role and function of residential institutions within the Russian child welfare system and the rapidly developing form of alternative care in foster families, as well as the work undertaken with birth families. By analysing the consequences of deinstitutionalisation and its effects on children and young people as well as their foster and birth parents, it provides a model for understanding this process across the whole of the post-Soviet space.

It will be of interest to academics and students of social work, sociology, child welfare, social policy, political science, and Russian and East European politics more generally.

Meri Kulmala holds a PhD in sociology and a title of docent in Russian and Eurasian Studies. She works as a university researcher and research coordinator of the Helsinki Inequality Initiative (INEQ) in the Faculty of Social Sciences at University of Helsinki, Finland. She works and publishes on issues of post-socialist welfare state and civil society development, women's activism, family and child welfare policy, and feminist research methods. She leads an international interdisciplinary research project on child welfare in Russia and is involved in a project exploring youth well-being in the Arctic region, with her focus being on the well-being of young care leavers, which she studies principally through participatory research methods.

Maija Jäppinen holds a PhD in social work and works as both a university lecturer in the Faculty of Social Sciences in University of Helsinki and a postdoctoral researcher in the Åbo Akademi University, Finland. Her research interests include Russian studies, gender violence, child welfare, social work practice research, social work with migrants, power asymmetries in social work encounters, migrant citizenisation, and human rights. Methodologically, she specialises in ethnographic research, qualitative research in different kinds of transnational settings, and feminist methodology.

Anna Tarasenko holds a PhD in political science. Her current research focuses on the non-profit sector development in Russia. She has accomplished empirical research on various types of non-profits and their involvement in social service provision as well as engagement in interest representation in contemporary Russia. She has worked as a researcher in several international research projects, including the UNRISD research project 'New Directions in Social Policy: Alternatives from and for the Global South' and the international research project based at the University of Helsinki entitled 'A Child's Right to a Family: Deinstitutionalisation of Child Welfare in Putin's Russia'.

Anna Pivovarova is a social anthropologist working on parenting, childhood, and kinship. She holds a master's degree in anthropology from the European University at St. Petersburg and works as a PhD candidate at the University of Helsinki focusing on adoptive and foster parenthood in today's Russia. She has conducted research and published on modern home birth practice and independent midwifery and participated in research projects on maternity health care, child welfare, and alternative family care in Russia. Her research interests include medical anthropology, new kinship studies, narrative analysis, invented traditions, rituals, and modern folklore.

Routledge Advances in Social Work

Forthcoming:

The International Development of Social Work Education
The Vietnam Experience
Edward Cohen, Alice Hines, Laurie Drabble, Hoa Nguyen, Meekung Han, Soma Sen and Debra Faires

International Perspectives on Social Work and Political Conflict
Edited by Joe Duffy, Jim Campbell and Carol Tosone

Asian Social Work
Professional Work in National Contexts
Edited by Ian Shaw and Rosaleen Ow

Critical Hospital Social Work Practice
Daniel Burrows

Challenges, Opportunities and Innovations in Social Work Field Education
Edited by Ronnie Egan, Nicole Hill and Wendy Rollins

The Challenge of Nationalist Populism for Social Work
A Human Rights Approach
Edited by Carolyn Noble and Goetz Ottmann

Reforming Child Welfare in the Post-Soviet Space
Institutional Change in Russia
Meri Kulmala, Maija Jäppinen, Anna Tarasenko and Anna Pivovarova

Women, Vulnerabilities and Welfare Service Systems
Edited by Marjo Kuronen, Elina Virokannas and Ulla Salovaara

For more information about this series, please visit: www.routledge.com/
Routledge-Advances-in-Social-Work/book-series/RASW

Reforming Child Welfare in the Post-Soviet Space

Institutional Change in Russia

**Edited by Meri Kulmala,
Maija Jäppinen, Anna Tarasenko,
and Anna Pivovarova**

Routledge
Taylor & Francis Group

LONDON AND NEW YORK

First published 2021
by Routledge
2 Park Square, Milton Park, Abingdon, Oxon OX14 4RN

and by Routledge
52 Vanderbilt Avenue, New York, NY 10017

Routledge is an imprint of the Taylor & Francis Group, an informa business

British Library Cataloguing-in-Publication Data
A catalogue record for this book is available from the British Library

Library of Congress Cataloging-in-Publication Data
A catalog record for this book has been requested

ISBN: 978-0-367-90424-1 (hbk)
ISBN: 978-1-003-02431-6 (ebk)

Typeset in Times New Roman
by Apex CoVantage, LLC

Contents

Figures

Tables

Contributors

Svetlana Biryukova is a leading researcher at the Centre for Comprehensive Social Policy Studies, National Research University Higher School of Economics (HSE) in Moscow, Russia. She received both BA and MA degrees at the Lomonosov Moscow State University, Faculty of Economics. Her doctoral research was held at the demography department of the same faculty, and Svetlana received her degree in 2013. Currently, Svetlana is involved in research projects examining issues of spatial distribution of poverty and inequality, effectiveness of pro-natal family policy and child welfare policy, as well as the interrelation of macroeconomic dynamics and individual demographic behaviour.

Zhanna Chernova is Professor in the Department of Sociology at the National Research University Higher School of Economics in St. Petersburg, Russia. She holds a PhD (Candidate of Sciences) in sociology and a doctorate from Saratov State Technical University. Her research interests include gender studies and family policy, and she has published two books and a number of articles examining family and parenting issues and the intersection between policy and everyday practices in Russia. She leads and participates in several international and Russian research projects on family policy and child welfare in Russia.

Anna Fomina holds a master's degree in sociology from European University at St. Petersburg, Russia, and works as a PhD candidate at the Aleksanteri Institute of the University of Helsinki, Finland. She participates in international projects on child welfare and alternative care in Russia, focusing on care leavers and aftercare. Her research interests include gender studies, qualitative methods in social science, childhood, parenting, and social policy.

Elena Iarskaia-Smirnova holds a PhD in social work and a doctoral degree in sociology. She works as a university professor at the Department of Sociology, is head of the International Laboratory of Social Integration Research, and is the Editor-in-Chief of the *Journal of Social Policy Studies* at the National Research University Higher School of Economics in Moscow. Her research interests include social policy, social work, sociology of professions, gender, family and children, disability studies, visual studies, and representations.

Methodologically, she specialises in qualitative research, textual analysis, and visual research methodology.

Maija Jäppinen holds a PhD in social work and works as both a university lecturer in the Faculty of Social Sciences in University of Helsinki and a postdoctoral researcher in the Åbo Akademi University, Finland. Her research interests include Russian studies, gender violence, child welfare, social work practice research, social work with migrants, power asymmetries in social work encounters, migrant citizenisation, and human rights. Methodologically, she specialises in ethnographic research, qualitative research in different kinds of transnational settings, and feminist methodology.

Rostislav Kononenko holds candidate degree in sociology and works as a university lecturer and is a docent at the Department of Sociology at the Higher School of Economics in Moscow, Russia. His research interests include sociology of culture, folklore, traditions and modernisation, social work, sociology of professions, family and children, disability studies, and representations. Methodologically, he specialises in qualitative research and textual analysis.

Olga Kosova holds an MA in sociology. She works as an independent researcher. Her research interests include social policy, sociology of social inequality, family and children, disability studies, and representations. Methodologically, she specialises in quantitative and qualitative research, content analysis.

Meri Kulmala holds a PhD in sociology and a title of docent in Russian and Eurasian Studies. She works as a university researcher and research coordinator of the Helsinki Inequality Initiative (INEQ) in the Faculty of Social Sciences at University of Helsinki, Finland. She works and publishes on issues of post-socialist welfare state and civil society development, women's activism, family and child welfare policy, and feminist research methods. She leads an international interdisciplinary research project on child welfare in Russia and is involved in a project exploring youth well-being in the Arctic region, with her focus being on the well-being of young care leavers, which she studies principally through participatory research methods.

Alla Makarentseva has a Russian degree of Candidate of Sciences in economics (equivalent to PhD) and works as a leading researcher in the Russian Presidential Academy of National Economy and Public Administration (Moscow). Alla's research interests are focused on demography and child welfare statistics, family, and social policy in Russia. She specialises in large-scale quantitative population surveys on well-being, reproductive behaviour, and parenting in Russia.

Anna Pivovarova is a social anthropologist working on parenting, childhood, and kinship. She holds a master's degree in anthropology from the European University at St. Petersburg and works as a PhD candidate at the University of Helsinki focusing on adoptive and foster parenthood in today Russia. She has conducted research and published on modern home birth practice and independent midwifery and participated in research projects on maternity health care, child welfare, and alternative family care in Russia. Her research interests include medical anthropology, new kinship studies, narrative analysis, invented traditions, rituals, and modern folklore.

Larisa Shpakovskaya holds PhD in sociology from National Research University Higher School of Economics in St. Petersburg, and works in research projects at the University of Helsinki. Her field of expertise is education, parenting, social movements, and social inequality. Her recent research projects are related to the issues of child welfare reforms, foster parenting and family placement, and social and educational trajectories of care leavers. She is the author of one book and more than 50 articles on education policy, social inequality, and parenting in Russia. She has led and participated in a number of international research projects on child welfare.

Anna Tarasenko holds a PhD in political science. Her current research focuses on the non-profit sector development in Russia. She has accomplished empirical research on various types of non-profits and their involvement in social service provision as well as engagement in interest representation in contemporary Russia. She has worked as a researcher in several international research projects, including the UNRISD research project 'New Directions in Social Policy: Alternatives from and for the Global South' and the international research project based at the University of Helsinki entitled 'A Child's Right to a Family: Deinstitutionalisation of Child Welfare in Putin's Russia' and others.

Preface

This book concludes years of scientific work and transnational collaboration on the topic of child welfare reform in Russia. We explore ongoing institutional change in the Russian child welfare system, which has developed within the context of global deinstitutionalisation policy trends. Inspired by neo-institutionalist scholarly discussions and debates, we are interested in understanding and explaining the changing institutional and everyday practices of the Russian child welfare system and in particular the consequences of this change.

Therefore, we hope that the volume will be interesting and useful not only to the readers interested in child rights, deinstitutionalisation, and recent policies related to them in Russia but also to those seeking new insights more broadly on social transformations and the developments of child welfare policy in the post-socialist space. Moreover, we believe that the volume offers an illustrative example of how international ideas travel and are implemented in different societal environments. We take the Russian case not as a unique or mysterious but as one with a specific context that is, all the same, doomed to follow global trends of deinstitutionalisation of care for children deprived of parental care and other groups of people that wider deinstitutionalisation processes seek to relocate. Our study demonstrates the similarities of the Russian case with the experience of other countries at the level of ideology, institutions, and everyday practices. What was instructive and striking was to find very inventive and progressive experts and practitioners in small towns and remote areas. In combination with other evidence, this finding demonstrated how close the Russian case is to other countries. On the other hand, our analysis also shows how much the political environment in which reforms are implemented matters.

The authors of this collective volume possess backgrounds in sociology, social work, social policy, anthropology, and political science, contributing to the collection of a unique combination of data. The reader can count on an analysis of interviews and diaries, as well as considerations of statistics and legislative changes. Despite the overall non-transparent context and restrained nature of communication within the system of government and public management, the authors were able to access this milieu and gain important insights. As a result, the authors made sense of how the new institutional design introduced by the reform is actually practiced, observing the meetings of officials and practitioners, visiting residential facilities in several regions, and talking to children deprived of parental care, as well as birth and foster parents, and NGO representatives. This enriched research experience produces highly relevant and sensitive findings, giving an impression of the main constraints and opportunities of all participants who involved in reform implementation.

The idea of scrutinising child welfare deinstitutionalisation emerged in the Centre of Excellence *Choices of Russian Modernisation* (2012–2017, Aleksanteri Institute, University of Helsinki) and particularly in its research group that focused on the welfare regime and its trajectories and transformations led by Professor Markku Kivinen. We are grateful to all the support and encouragement that we received in this inspiring research environment. Our interest in child welfare finally took the form of an interdisciplinary and international research project 'A Child's Right to a Family: Deinstitutionalisation of Child Welfare in Putin's Russia' (2016–2020) led by Docent Meri Kulmala.

As the project is coming to the end, we would like to thank the University of Helsinki, the KONE Foundation, and the Academy of Finland for funding our work. The University of Helsinki, more specifically the Aleksanteri Institute for Russian and Eastern European Studies and the Faculty of Social Sciences, provided a good environment for our activities. Important collaborating institutions for us, among others, have been the National Research University Higher School of Economics (Saint Petersburg and Moscow) and the European University of Saint Petersburg. We would like to thank also our partners and collaborations in other parts of Russia, especially in Nizhniy Novgorod, as well as in the United Kingdom and the United States for their contributions in earlier publications of the project.

Our warmest thanks go also to senior editor Claire Jarvis and editorial assistant Catherine Jones from the Routledge series in Social and Health Care for their support and trust in this book project, and to Matthew Blackburn for his patient, gentle, and very professional help with finalising the volume and its language. It is impossible to overestimate the contribution of many of our colleagues who served as anonymous reviewers, voluntarily devoting their time to comment and advise authors at the stage of work in progress. Finally, we want to thank all of our authors and all the research participants in the field of child welfare in Russia. Without them, this book would not have been possible.

Part I
Introduction

Part 1

Introduction

1 Introduction

Russian child welfare reform and institutional change

Meri Kulmala, Maija Jäppinen,
Anna Tarasenko, and Anna Pivovarova

Sadly, our country still has 130,000 children deprived of parental care. They have neither parents, nor guardians; they are denied of the most important thing – family warmth. We still have a long way to go to get rid of the 'abandoned children' notion. Child protection services (opeka) *must be directly focused on placing those children in families and helping foster families. There should be no 'unadopted' children in our country.*

Presidential Address to the Federal Assembly
of the Russian Federation (Medvedev 2010)

When it comes to the number of children deprived of parental care, Russia ranks among the top scorers across the world (2% of the total child population) (Kulmala et al. forthcoming). About 80% of these children have the Russian status of 'social orphan': children whose parents are alive but, for whatever reason, are not able to care for them. Approximately 20% are 'true' orphans in the English-speaking world's understanding: children whose parents have died.[1] In Russia, residential care has been the dominant form of alternative care.[2] Residential institutions have traditionally been large and segregated in the country (Khlinovskaya Rockhill 2010). For these reasons, among others, the Russian child protection system has been criticised for its inability to support families at risk and, as a result, has attempted to provide alternative care in large residential institutions (Kulmala et al. forthcoming). In the 2010s, President Medvedev's aforementioned annual address to the Federal Assembly in 2010 can be taken as a starting point, after which Russia began to fundamentally reform its child protection system and alternative care systems, mainly through dismantling the old system of children's homes inherited from the Soviet era and developing foster care, domestic adoptions, as well as community-based support services for birth families.

These reforms are based on the idea that every child has a right to grow up in a family. In the early 2010s, the Russian government set itself a target: nine out of ten children currently living in alternative care will move to live in families. This goal was to be achieved by promoting adoptions, increasing the number of foster families, and creating community-based family support services to prevent children from entering the alternative care system. In addition, the remaining residential institutions are to be drastically restructured into home-like environments, which would mean smaller apartment-like premises, less children in each of the units, and practices that resemble more family life than life in an institution.

These moves are all key elements of a global trend for deinstitutionalisation (DI), thus bringing Russia in line with global norms (An, Kulmala 2020). DI is a global policy which seeks to relocate residents in institutional care, including persons with disabilities and with mental illness, the elderly, and children deprived of parental care, the homeless, and criminal offenders to community-based housing, accompanied by the development of services that support participation in the community (Segal, Jacobs 2008). DI refers to the principle underlying the shift in the provision of care to various groups of people in need of support from institutional care to the 'living in the community' model. Integral to DI is the replacement of the paternalistic ethic with the interactive ethic and the recognition that human rights, as well as the dignity and autonomy of an individual, take precedence over their needs (An, Kulmala 2020). In the sphere of child welfare, this means the reduction of residential institutions for children deprived of parental care and the development of foster care and community-based support services for families at risk.

DI is internationally affirmed by several binding treaties, including the UN Conventions on the Rights of the Child (UN CRC 1989) and of Persons with Disabilities (UN CRPD 2006), both ratified by Russia. In their article on DI reforms in wider post-socialist space, Sofiya An and Meri Kulmala (2020) described how global deinstitutionalisation policy towards children's residential institutions finds its roots in the world wars and concerns about orphaned children who had survived these wars. The first attempts to set up a global legal framework resulted in the Geneva Declaration on the Rights of the Child (1924), which later became the non-binding UN Declaration adopted in 1948 and 1959. A binding global policy was only institutionalised when the UN Convention on the Rights of the Child was adopted in 1989. Although the UN convention does not specifically call for the dismantling of residential institutions, the Guidelines for the Alternative Care of Children (adopted in 2010) set clear expectations for DI in child welfare and obligations for member states to implement relevant national policies. The UN CRC was ratified by most newly independent post-Soviet states, including Russia as early as in 1990. The more recent UN Convention on the Rights of Persons with Disabilities (2006) explicitly recognises the right of disabled children to family life and requires that states provide services to prevent the segregation of people with disabilities. Russia ratified the CRPD in 2012.

The UN CRC has been integral to human rights and democratisation discourses involving global policy actors in post-socialist reforms (An, Kulmala 2020). Western child welfare experts' long-term consideration of the disadvantages of residential care was reaffirmed by the discovery of the terrible situation of children in institutions in the region, and reliance on institutional care was identified as the main challenge in the region (UNICEF 2003).

The dominance of institutional care dates back to the Soviet ideology of collective care and upbringing and the idea of the paternalist state as the primary caregiver. The Soviet child welfare model prioritised care in state residential facilities, which were seen to be a favourable environment for children to be brought up as good Soviet citizens (Stryker 2012). Apart from child welfare, other collective forms of education, such as work colonies and pioneer houses, also included living in an institutional setting (Kulmala et al. forthcoming). Moreover, Soviet child psychology focused on physical and cognitive functioning in contrast to the attachment and socialisation theories that led to the emphasis on family-type care in the West (Disney 2015). However, in reality, Soviet institutions provided children with only basic education and care and failed to meet children's developmental, health, and social needs (Kulmala et al. 2017). Institutionalisation led to very poor outcomes for graduates in their social adaptation who faced societal stigma (Khlinovskaya Rockhill 2010.)

Soviet-type residential care continued to serve as the dominant form until the 2010s – although DI had been somewhat on the policy agenda, thanks to new transnational collaborations of NGOs in the 1990s (Bindman et al. 2019; Kulmala et al. 2017). A few years after the ratification of the UN CRC, the first Russian Constitution from 1993 brought the national legislation in line with international child's rights commitments. The Constitution was followed by the new Family Code (in 1995), which, in principle, prioritised family forms of alternative care. In practice, residential care remained dominant still for more than a decade (Kulmala et al. forthcoming). The UN has repeatedly reminded Russia about the large number of children in institutions and its insufficient efforts to change the situation (An, Kulmala 2020).

At the same time, the turbulent transition of the 1990s led to an increasing need for care for children deprived of parental care. One cannot overestimate the social crisis in the 1990s that emerged as a result of this transition into a market economy. Increases in poverty, alcohol and drug abuse, and unemployment were dramatic indicators. They all contributed to the growing number of children deprived of parental care for socioeconomic reasons (Kulmala et al. forthcoming). Until now, a common risk factor for a child entering the alternative care system is their parents living in poverty and lacking proper housing, as many of the chapters of this volume indicate.

As of now, according to the Family Code of Russia, there are three main forms of family-based alternative care available: (1) 'adoption' (*usynovleniye*); (2) 'foster families' (*priemnye sem'i*); and (3) 'guardianship care' (*opeka i popechitel'stvo*) (Family code 1995). During the last decade, there has been a clear shift from institutional care to family forms of care, as Biryukova and Makarentseva show in Chapter 2 of this volume. In the current period, domestic adoption inside the Russian Federation is prioritised over international. In practice, the term 'foster family' (*priemnaya sem'ya*) is used as an umbrella term for all forms of family-based alternative care. Strictly speaking, however, foster care is differentiated into paid and non-paid form. The term 'foster family' (*priemnaya sem'ya*) describes paid foster care, while non-repayable custody is referred to as 'guardianship care' (*opeka i popechitel'stvo*) and is the most common form of foster care in the country.[3] Additionally, in some regions there are 'patronage families' (*patronat*).[4]

Thus, the emergence of trained foster families, who receive financial compensation for fostering children, has been an important change. To facilitate the professionalisation of family-based alternative care, candidates must complete a mandatory training course, with exceptions made only for the child's relatives. There is no unified teaching programme for the classes; however, normally they last for at least three months and are required to be focused on psychological, medical, and legal aspects of adoption and guardianship and include group training for candidates (Decree 2009). The need for this training is often explained by child welfare professionals as a matter of preventing situations where children are returned to an institution or replaced in another foster family. The courses do not provide special training targeted to different forms of family care, and prospective adopters and foster caregivers attend same classes following the same study programme. Foster families usually live on their own in separate accommodation, with the exception of the so-called 'children villages' (*detskaya derevnya*) in which several foster families often live together with many children (Chernova, Kulmala 2018).[5]

When none of the aforementioned family forms of care is possible, a child is placed in an institutional care. The existing institutions can be divided into three types. Firstly, there are former children's homes (*detskii dom*), which are now called 'family support centres' (*tsentr sodeystviya semeynomu vospitaniyu*). Their main function is to accommodate children temporarily, but they also provide services to birth and foster families and support those leaving care. Most of these are administered by the Ministry of Social Protection and Labour, though some keep an affiliation with the Ministry of Education and Science. Secondly, there are baby homes for children under the age of 3 (*dom rebenka*) that are part of the health care system. These two types of institutional care treat relatively healthy children and most of the analysis of this collective volume focuses on them. Thirdly, there are also additional forms of institutional care arranged for children with various disabilities.[6]

Thus, the global DI ideology with its emphasis on the family environment – either in birth, adoptive, or foster families or in family-like residential settings – and community-based preventive and supportive services is in conflict with the Soviet child welfare ideology that viewed residential institutions as the embodiment of an omnipotent and benevolent state taking care of its children (An, Kulmala 2020). The DI thus required a paradigm shift in the understanding of good care and in the institutional design of child welfare (Kulmala et al. 2017).

Russian economic growth in the 2000s led to wide investments in social policy, namely family policy (Kulmala et al. 2014), which laid the ground for the later DI reform. Since the early 2000s, the severe decline in population, the so-called demographic crisis, started to dominate the political agenda as the most severe threat to the Russian nation (Cook 2011), which created 'moral panic' surrounding family values and childhood (Kulmala et al. 2017). Since 2005, a strong family-centred ideology started to characterise policy programmes and a new conservative protection of the family became a key priority for the Russian government. Since the annual address to the 2006 Federal Assembly of President Vladimir Putin, numerous pronatalist measures were introduced, including increases in family and maternity benefits (Chernova 2013; Cook 2011; Kulmala et al. 2014; Rivkin-Fish 2010; Rotkirch et al. 2007). Finally, in the 2010s, the increasing attention towards Russian families also encompassed children deprived of parental care and rather rapidly led to a paradigm shift in Russian child welfare policy (Kulmala et al. 2017). Thus, the Russian DI reform discursively grew from the demographic crisis constructed as a threat to the nation and intertwined with President Putin's wider ideological project to revitalise the nation (Bindman et al. 2019; An, Kulmala 2020).

As often with paradigm changes (Khmelnitskaya 2015: 16–17), the Russian reform was triggered by an exogenous crisis. In 2008, a child adopted from a Russian orphanage to the United States died as a result of negligence by his American parents. The 'Dima Yakolev' case prompted a ban on the adoption of Russian children by US citizens in 2012, and importantly, drew attention to children living in institutions (Bindman et al, 2020). A number of abuse scandals in Russian children's homes furthered media and public interest in the topic, opening a 'window of opportunity' for Russian child welfare NGOs to put forward their proposals at an official level (Bindman et al. 2019; Kulmala et al. 2017).

The issue of children living in institutions was addressed as the government's top priority by President Medvedev in 2010 and was followed by several policy programmes designed with the involvement of Russian child welfare NGOs. A National Strategy (2012) was adopted which recommended that children's homes should be reorganised into 'family support centres' whose primary task was to return children to their biological families or place them in foster families. This important document articulated key alternatives to residential institutions and contained frequent references to international treaties. It took, however, several years to develop implementation mechanisms for these proposals, starting with the Presidential Decree #1688 (2012), which was passed on the same day that the ban on adoptions of children by US citizens was signed into law. It directed officials to work on fostering and adoption and added a specific criterion of the 'effectiveness' of regional governors by measuring the proportion of children placed in family care in their region, thus setting a strong top-down incentive to implement the reform in an increasingly undemocratic political environment. Moreover, in 2013, the presidential party, United Russia, established a nationwide programme called 'Russia Needs All Its Children'[7], which indicates the prioritised position of the issue and the demographic motivation behind the policy (Bindman et al. 2019; Kulmala et al. 2017). Finally, Government Decree RF#481 (2014) fundamentally altered the nature of care in residential institutions. Children's homes are now designated as 'family centres' working with birth and foster families, with the placement of children in a family home now made the ultimate goal. Such centres are designed to resemble a family-style environment: children live in small groups in apartment-type premises and go to local schools.

According to these new principles and goals, one would expect to see a new strong focus on community-based support services for birth families with a goal to prevent alternative care placements. Community-based services refer to support services accessible to families in their own everyday environment and in the least restrictive setting possible. These services can include, among others, financial support or assistance with housing, services at home, counselling from a psychologist or social worker, family therapy, family rehabilitation, support persons to children and/or parents, or access to peer groups. The key point here is that these services are provided to family members in order to keep them living together, without isolating the child from their birth family. Regardless of this, the major focus of the Russian reform has remained on alternative care; children are still placed outside their homes instead of resources being spent to keep birth families together (Kulmala et al. forthcoming). Socioeconomic factors, such as poverty and poor living conditions, are often seen as the key reasons why children cannot stay in their birth families and thus end up in alternative care. Despite this commonly accepted view, the reforms do not seem to deal much with the causes of these key problems and pay little attention to the resolution of such socioeconomic problems in living conditions, among others. However, unlike earlier, when residential institutions were extensively used, children are now more and more often moved to foster families. Nevertheless, there are still groups of children, who do not easily find their place in foster families, e.g. adolescents and children with disabilities or health issues, as analysed in several chapters of this book.

All in all, at the level of ideas and policies, a fundamental shift has no doubt taken place that should obviously lead to wide-scale changes in the institutional design and prevailing practices. The new ideas are being implemented throughout the country at a considerable scale and speed – and as a top priority of the government. Yet, as we show through the chapters of this volume, under such pressures in an increasingly authoritarian political environment and with the heavy legacy of residential care in large institutions, the reform is resulting in many tensions and multiple unintended, even paradoxical, consequences.

The research questions of the volume

DI reform takes place in the specific context of a deteriorating political regime, vanishing regional and local autonomy of governance as well as clear conservative turn and emphasis on conservative family values in elite's discourse and society at large. The reforms initiated by the federal government are expected to be implemented by regional authorities producing multiple tensions and resistance. Policy changes shift resources and responsibilities at the level of regional authorities, public and non-state organisations, as well as at the level of individual interactions of parents, children, public servants, and experts. The application and implementation of these new ideas set the research puzzle which the edited volume seeks to explain. The book analyses the implementation of the current reform, which echoes a fundamental change in the ideological premises of care for children deprived of parental care and thus has shifted the course of Russian child welfare policy. We ask how the reform is affecting the institutions and practices of child welfare, especially alternative care in Russia. What kind of institutional change has followed the shift in the ideals (i.e. ideational change)?

What are the intended and unintended consequences of the reform at the level of (institutional) practices and how can we explain them?

The neo-institutionalist framework

In this volume we explore ongoing institutional change in the Russian child welfare system brought about by the global DI policy. Inspired by neo-institutionalist scholarly discussions and debates (NI), we are interested in understanding and explaining real-world events and policy outcomes (Steinmo 2015: 183). In our case, this means examining the changing institutional and everyday practices in Russian alternative care and their consequences. As Elaine Weiner and Heather MacRae have pointed out (2017: xviii), NI is now several decades old and cannot be treated as something new. Back when this framework appeared, NI reaffirmed the key tenet of (old) institutionalism of political and social structures being normatively and historically embedded. However, NI is different from this old approach in three fundamental ways: firstly, by expanding exclusive focus on formal rules to both formal and informal conventions; secondly, in taking a more critical look on values and power and their functioning; and thirdly, in rejecting structural determinism in favour of structure–agency interplay in determining political outcomes (Weiner, MacRae 2017: xviii; Mahoney, Thelen 2010; Lowndes, Roberts 2013: 28). As Sven Steinmo (2015: 181) saw it, the central tenet of NI is that institutions are not neutral to policy outcomes: institutions define the rules of the political game, and as such they define who can play and how they play. Consequently, they ultimately can shape who wins and who loses. As Steinmo (2015: 181) commented: 'If politics is the study of who gets what, when, and why, then institutionalists argue that institutions should be at the heart of that study.'

Queries around the key themes of formal and informal institutions, institutional creation, continuity and change, structure and agency, and power sit in the analytical core of NI (Weiner, MacRae 2017: xviii). In our enquiry, we rely on B.G. Peters's definition of an institution as a structural feature of the society and/or the polity that may be formal, e.g. a legislature, an agency in the public bureaucracy, and a legal framework (Peters 1999: 18). This may also be informal, such as a network of interacting organisations or a shared set of norms (Krook, Mackay 2011: 11). NI permits a focus on processes and offers a conceptual toolkit that includes formal and informal institutions, critical junctures, and path dependencies of institutional change and logics of appropriateness, among others. It also invites consideration of the roles of ideas in determining the interests of actors operating in a specific institutional context (Lovenduski 2011: viii).

Despite their different interpretations of NI, the various schools of NI converge in their regard for institutions as 'relatively enduring features of political and social life – including rules, norms and procedures – that structure behaviour' (Mahoney, Thelen 2010: 4; cited in Weiner and MacRae 2017: xix). These features are not easily alterable. Yet, institutional change sometimes occurs. Indeed, for a long time, NI scholars deemed institutional change to be dependent on external shocks that incurred sudden reform. Increasingly, however, scholars tend to agree on a more continuous conception of institutional change that emphasises the subtle and organic nature of institutional evolution and its impetuses as endogenous and/or exogenous (Weiner, MacRae 2017: xix; Krook, Mackay 2011; Mahoney, Thelen 2010).

As Mona Lena Krook and Fiona Mackay (2011: 12) have stated, new institutions emerge rarely and often only in the context of crisis or great uncertainty. Nonetheless, institutions do change sometimes. Alongside the perhaps rarer case of 'punctuated equilibrium', in which long periods characterised by path dependence alternate with brief and dramatic turns of events (i.e. critical junctures), NI scholars have identified a model of more incremental change, endogenous 'institutional refinement', whereby institutions organically evolve (Avner, Laitin 2004). These scholars speak about 'institutional conversion' where existing institutions are directed to a new purpose (Streeck, Thelen 2005) or about 'institutional layering' where new institutional elements are added to older elements (Waylen 2011). Or they speak about 'nested newness' to capture the way in which a new institution relates to others, whose legacies and continuities with the past profoundly affect their operation (e.g. Mackay 2014; Chappell 2011). Institutional change can be shaped, modified, and constrained through the new institutions' interaction with these other institutions (Krook, Mackay 2011). Yet, due to path dependencies, i.e. a system's dependence on its former path of development, any reform process is associated with a risk of an institutional trap, i.e. inefficient yet stable norms of behaviour, which might even lead to a situation of lock-in (Polterovich 2008: 3088). As this volume shows, institutional change in Russian welfare reform contains all these layers from rapid change to more organic layering and lock-ins – at the different levels and loci of the reform.

Being very suitable for our multi-level and multi-cited analysis, NI allows an investigation of institutional change on different levels of social order (Novkunskaya 2020: 50–51). Moreover, state institutions are not monolithic but can be only understood when broken down into a number of institutional arenas or spaces (Krook, Mackay 2011: 13). As several of our previous investigations (e.g. An, Kulmala 2020; Bindman et al. 2019; Kulmala et al. 2017; Kulmala et al. forthcoming) have shown, a paradigm shift – a fundamental, ideational change in the understanding of good care for children at risk and left without parental – has taken place in the Russian child welfare policy in the 2010s. As Marina Khmelnitskaya (2015: 16) has pointed out, policy paradigms are defined as broad overarching ideas about means and aims of policy, whereas paradigmatic policy shifts are fundamental revisions of thinking about those aims and means within a particular policy field. Thus, in the ethos of NI, we see that ideas and how ideas change are important in comprehending how institutions change (Mätzke, Ostner 2010a, 2010b; Lovenduski 2011; Steinmo 2015).

Even if the ideas of DI had been on the agenda already for a longer period of time, no systematic change of the Russian child welfare system took place before the 2010s. It still required an exogenous shock – the aforementioned Dima

Yakolev case – to initiate the rapid changes at the level of policies which obviously started the institutional change at lower levels as well. In this volume, we focus on the outcome of this ideational change at the level of concrete institutions and daily practices. In the forthcoming sections, we analyse the practical implementations of the ideational shift and its effects and consequences at the level of the existing, transforming, and emerging institutions as well as at the level of the people – namely the children and young people themselves as well as their foster and birth parents. At those levels, instead of rapid changes, one can see different types of 'more organic' transformations, conversions, and layers – or even non-transformations and lock-ins due to severe path dependencies in both formal and informal institutions, including formal laws and more informal cultural norms.

Often the observed situations under our analytical treatment come close to what Kathleen Thelen (2003) labelled as 'bounded innovation' to characterise the boundaries between institutional reproduction and institutional creation as blurred. Employing a loose notion of path dependency, the author argues that periods of institutional reproduction overlap with moments of institutional creation in partial and often unpredictable ways and with unanticipated outcomes (Mackay 2011: 186). As such, institutional actors experience a combination of 'lock-in' and 'innovation' where already exiting institutional structures to some extent lock actors to certain paths. However, as the authors stated and seen in our empirical investigations, this does not preclude action and leaves scope for innovation. Old institutions are not just constraints but may act as strategic resources as well (Mackay 2011: 186). As we show in this volume, in the context of contemporary Russia and global DI policy in child welfare, these complex processes have brought along multiple unintended, even paradoxical consequences. Through our investigation, we aim to understand and explain these 'unintentions' and paradoxes.

Contents of the volume

The volume consists of four parts based on in-depth empirical investigations, each of which responds to the question of the daily application and practical implementation of these new ideas from different angles. After Part I, which is introductory, Part II, entitled, 'Changing numbers, shifting discourses', maps the changes at a more general level – from the viewpoint of numbers (statistics) and public images (media). Part III, 'Transforming institutions', analyses institutional change particularly from the angle of the changing roles and functions of the large number of residential institutions in the Russian child welfare system. Part IV, 'Foster and birth families under institutional change', focuses on the role of foster and birth families in the child welfare system. Part V, 'Children in care: social adaptation and aftercare', brings the well-being, life strategies, and agency of children with experience of living/having lived in alternative care into the front of the analysis. The empirical analyses reveal many tensions and unintended consequences and give evidence about the somewhat sporadic nature of the implementation of the new ideas. Part VI, 'Conclusions', contains the concluding chapter where the editors draw together these key findings and discuss and explain the main reasons for this fragmented outcome and sometimes unexpected by-products.

Part II paints a general picture of the institutional shift by discussing the different representations related to the reform in terms of numbers and discourses. This part opens with Chapter 2, Statistics on the deinstitutionalisation of child welfare in Russia, in which Svetlana Biryukova and Alla Makarentseva analyse and problematise statistics concerning children deprived of parental care in Russia from the early 2000s up until today. Using official numerical data, the authors discuss the dynamics of the key risks of children entering alternative care. They also analyse the share of foster family and institutional placements and the low prevalence of family reunions. They consider long-term institutionalisation for certain groups of children, including mentally or physically disabled children, as a major challenge of the system.

In Chapter 3, The 'last-minute children': where did they come from, where will they go? Media portrayals of children deprived of parental care, 2006–2018, Elena Iarskaia-Smirnova, Olga Kosova, and Rostislav Kononenko analyse how children involved in alternative care and child welfare reform are depicted in the Russian printed media. They focus on the discourses revolving around the new policies and images of children in care as well as of those agents which provide care, including residential institutions, foster and adoptive parents, and birth families. Along with describing images of child welfare system that appear in the discourse, the authors trace issues that tend to be absent from the public discussion such as lack of professional supervision of guardians providing care for children with special needs and inequality in support targeted to different types of families.

Part III moves to analyse the effects of the reform by focusing on its practical implementation at the level of care institutions. It discusses the new institutional design, forms, and practices which the change in the ideology resulted in. It asks what kind of institutional change resulted from the reform and with what kinds of consequences. Based on the number of expert interviews conducted in several regions of Russia, in Chapter 4, The ideal (re)organisation of care: child welfare reform as a battlefield over resources and recognition, Meri Kulmala, Larisa Shpakovskaya, and Zhanna Chernova examine the perceptions of how care for children deprived of parental care should be ideally arranged in the viewpoints of the experts located and positioned differently. The analysis of the ideal organisation addresses the questions: Who should ideally take care of children deprived of parental care? How, where, and with what resources? The chapter treats the reform as a playground (or an arena) in which different agents (players) with certain capabilities play to gain more resources to achieve their goals. The authors identify three major agents whose interests both coincide and compete and who seek for a maximally powerful position in the sphere.

In Chapter 5, Institutional variety rather than the end of residential care: regional responses to deinstitutionalisation reforms in Russia, Anna Tarasenko takes a political science perspective to describe and explain the different institutional responses of the Russian regional bureaucracies to the reform. The chapter shows how the new policy has been implemented at the level of residential care institutions in the Russian regions. The analysis reveals several factors and conditions which have driven the resistance to reform at the sub-national level of the Russian government.

In Chapter 6, 'One has to stop chasing numbers!' The unintended consequences of Russian child welfare reforms, drawing from neo-institutional theory and based on expert interviews conducted in 2018 in North-West Russia, Maija Jäppinen and Meri Kulmala explore the new forms and practices of the transforming institutions and argue that several of these forms and practices have emerged as an unintended consequence of the reform. Among others, the so-called children without status seems to end up living 'temporarily' in institutions for years, because it is in many ways beneficial for the system, even though this obviously violates the major principle of reforms demanding that every child must have a family. Also, the right of a foster parent to have a child seems to override the right of a child to have a family.

Part IV addresses the existing forms of care in families and discusses the perspectives of the foster and birth parents on the child welfare reform. In Chapter 7, 'Making' a family: the motives and practices of foster parenting, Zhanna Chernova and Larisa Shpakovskaya, based on autobiographies published by foster parents, analyse the motives, strategies, and justifications of parents for fostering that these parents address in their stories in the context of the wider public discussion on foster care. Asking how foster parents describe their experience as caregivers, and what practices they refer to when talking about fostering, the authors analyse what 'good' foster care means in today's Russia.

Chapter 8, No Longer Parents or Parents in Need of Support? Views of Child Welfare Experts on Birth Parents, by Maija Jäppinen, focuses on representations of birth parents of children in alternative care (either in foster families or institutions) by child welfare experts. Drawing on interviews with these experts in several regions of Russia, the chapter analyses the prevalent discourses on birth parents in discussions on their role in regard to children who are placed into alternative care, and thus suggests some key reasons that might hamper preventive work with birth families.

Part V focuses on the question of how the changes affect children in care. Chapter 9, The successful transition to foster care: the child's perspective, by Larisa Shpakovskaya and Zhanna Chernova, analyses the narratives of the fostered children who reflect on the changes that took place due to the separation from their birth family and adaptation to a foster family. The chapter is focused on the perspective of children on their transition, adaptation, and everyday life in foster families.

One of the aims of the reform was to improve the quality of care in order to promote the better social inclusion of this specific group of young people at the different stages of their life. In Chapter 10, Young adults leaving care: agency and educational choice, Meri Kulmala, Zhanna Chernova, and Anna Fomina focus on young adults' experiences of their transition from care to independent living. Based on a number of interviews with young adults in North-West Russia, the authors analyse these young people's decision junctures in education. Education is one of the key institutional pillars for later-life inclusion and well-being, because it obviously affects later-life trajectory, career, and income among other aspects. Through their conceptualisation of agency, the authors consider which modes of agency do care leavers exercise in their choices of education and which factors affect the modes. With the concept of subjective agency, the authors consider the resources and resilience of this vulnerable group of young people.

Part VI presents the concluding Chapter 11, which draws together the key findings of the previous chapters and discusses the current state of the art of child rights in Russia and the Russian child welfare system and the (institutional) outcomes of the reform. This is done through four conceptually inspired analytical lenses that in many and multi-layered ways explain the major challenges that the empirical analysis of the previous sections highlight. These analytical lenses are the following: (1) authoritarian political regime; (2) societal trust; (3) (child's) rights; and (4) a kinship/love-based understanding of care.

The contribution of the volume

The volume provides new empirically grounded research-based knowledge and insights regarding the current transformation of the Russian child welfare system, which implies a major paradigm change in Russia's child welfare policy (Kulmala et al. 2017). This process, which can be conceptualised as deinstitutionalisation, links Russia closely to the international trends of child rights–based child welfare systems (Bindman et al. 2019). Thus, analysing the reforms – which have fundamentally shifted the ideological premises behind Russian child welfare – is interesting not only as a detailed account of the recent developments in the particular Russian context, but also from the viewpoint of global trends in child welfare and how they travel transnationally and are adapted locally (An, Kulmala 2020). In other words, the analysis addresses the question of how global becomes (g)local – and what kinds of consequences emerge from this.

What makes the Russian case specific is that the ongoing reorganisation of the institutional design according to the new ideas is being implemented throughout the country at a considerable scale and speed – and as a top priority of the government. In the current political environment, the reforms, as one of the top priorities of the Russian government in the sphere of social policy (Kulmala et al. 2017), are creating a strong impetus for regional-level governments and locally operating institutions to further implement these new principles. Such top-down modes of reform definitely create many tensions in the implementation at the lower levels. Under such pressures in the current increasingly authoritarian political environment and with the heavy legacy of residential care in large institutions, the reform is resulting in multiple unintended, even paradoxical, consequences of 'good intentions'.

As we have shown earlier (e.g. Kulmala et al. 2017), the shift in the ideal of care is real and has happened at the policy and programme level. However, based on the analysis in this volume, we argue that the overall execution of the deinstitutionalisation reform in Russia remains sporadic and fragmented – far from being a coherent and comprehensive process. Many flaws and drawbacks – such as lack of resources, skills, common understanding, and competing interests – hinder the implementation of new ideas and ideals, as shown by the empirical chapters. We do not claim that there are no good intentions to genuinely reform the system. Instead, we argue and show that good intentions have in many places led to unintended consequences for many reasons, some of which are somehow path dependent in their nature. We argue that there are a few major issues that play a crucial role in slowing down and hampering the realisation of the new ideology into practice.

Based on our exploration, we argue that the political regime has a major influence on the reform processes. Russia's undemocratic political regime creates a lot of pressure for regional and local authorities, which make things happen but most of all push them to show good results – sometimes, unfortunately, faked ones. A strange combination of neo-liberally oriented aims of cost-effectiveness and other new public management with Soviet-type governing principles seems to produce path dependency, i.e. practices that are self-supporting and self-reinforcing, which hinder the development of preventive support and community-based services that should be in the essence of the reform. Incentives created by the political system produce unintended consequences and adoptive strategies, which sometimes contradict main goals of the reform. In addition, the low level of societal trust is a severe obstacle. Mistrust seems to be present everywhere and at each level: parents do not trust officials, professionals, or institutions; officials and practitioners (including NGOs) and larger public do not trust parents; care leavers trust hardly anyone. Moreover, even if the reform stems from a movement to international child's rights, it seems that, despite the official declarations of working in the child's best interests, it is sometimes everyone else's rights and interests that matter more. Finally, the kinship/love-based understanding of care relations is a challenge for the development of professional alternative care system as it imposes unrealistic expectations addressed to both caregivers and those who are in care. All these elements are brought together in the final chapter to evaluate the (institutional) outcomes of the reform.

Notes

1 In this volume, we avoid the concept 'orphan', as we find it misleading in the international context, and prefer the term 'children deprived of parental care'.
2 With the term 'alternative care', we refer to all forms of care for those children who have been left without parental care, including residential care and foster care. In addition, adoption is considered to be part of the alternative care system in Russia and is sometimes taken to be almost parallel to foster care, as many of the chapters of this volume show.
3 Foster family care and guardianship are established on the basis of a temporary agreement between caregivers and guardianship authorities. Both foster caregivers and guardians receive a child allowance, and in the case of the compensated care that are foster families (*priemnaya sem'ya*) and patronage families (*patronatnaya sem'ya*), one or two foster parents (usually spouses) receive a monthly payment for their work as caregivers. The minimum monthly payment is defined by the federal state, while the

actual amount of the compensations to be paid depends on the region in which the family resides.

4 *Patronatnaya sem'ya* (patronat family) is made up of parents who enlist as working by contract in the social services and receiving payment and necessary services for upbringing the child(ren). In some cases, these *patronat* parents are recruited among the leading specialists in care institutions. *Patronatnoye vospitanie* (patronat upbringing) exists in 42 regions where the local law supports it: www.usynovite.ru/adoption/patronage/patronat/chapter4/

5 Internationally, children villages are usually associated with the worldwide SOS children villages (www.sos-childrensvillages.org/), but in Russia there are also many other non-profit organisations that have their villages (https://sos-dd.ru).

6 There are various types of rehabilitation, medical, and correctional programs implemented in institutional care that are divided according to specific child's illnesses. A range of residential facilities implement these programs. Firstly, correctional children's homes (*korrektsionnyi detskii dom*) house children with severe physical and mental disorders. These correctional homes can, depending on the region, fall under the remit of the social protection agencies or the health care system. Secondly, similar to these correctional children's homes, there are also *doma-internaty*: special residential facilities for disabled children 4–18 years old. These facilities may also include children with disabilities who still have parents. Thirdly, there are boarding schools (*shkola-internat*) which fall under the Ministry of Education and Science and house not only children deprived of parental care and children with parents but, unlike correctional children's homes, also children who partly live at home with their own family (Sirotstvo 2011; see also Kulmala et al. forthcoming). Parents of children with disabilities tend to place their children for several days in these residential facilities due to the absence of any special correctional programmes in ordinary elementary schools. This is especially typical for remote areas of Russia. The main trend is for these types of institutional care for children to be transferred to Family support centres as a part of the social protection system.

7 Available at http://council.gov.ru/media/files/41d49b8a57474a8ca104.pdf

References

An, S., Kulmala, M. 2020. Global Deinstitutionalisation Policy in Post-Soviet Space: A Comparison of Child-Welfare Reforms in Russia and Kazakhstan. *Global Social Policy*, OnlineFirst (May 19, 2020): 1–24. Available at: https://doi.org/10.1177%2F1468018120913312.

Avner, G., Laitin, D. 2004. A Theory of Endogenous Institutional Change. *American Political Science Review* 98 (4): 633–652.

Bindman, E., Kulmala, M., Bogdanova, E. 2019. NGOs and the Policy-Making Process in Russia: The Case of Child Welfare Reform. *Governance: An International Journal of Policy, Administration, and Institutions* 32 (2): 207–222.

Chappell, L. 2011. Nested Newness and Institutional Innovation: Expanding Gender Justice in the International Criminal Court. In: M. Krook, F. Mackay (eds.), *Gender, Politics and Institutions Towards a Feminist Institutionalism*. Basingstoke: Palgrave Macmillan: 163–180.

Chernova, Z. 2013. *Sem'ia kak politicheskii vopros. Gosudarstvennyi proiekt i praktiki privatnosti* [The Family as a Political Question: State Projects and Practices of Privacy]. Saint Petersburg: European University at Saint Petersburg.

Chernova, Z., Kulmala, M. 2018. *'Po slozhnosti – eto rabota, po sostoyaniyu dushi – sem'ya': professionalizatciya premenogo roditel'stva v sovremennoi Rossii* ['In Its Complexity: It's Work, in Its Soul: It's Family': The Professionalisation of Foster Parenthood in Contemporary Russia]. *Zhurnal sotciologii i sotcial'noi antropologii* [Journal of Sociology and Social Anthropology] 21 (3): 46–70.

Cook, L. 2011. Russia's Welfare Regime: The Shift Toward Statism. In: M. Jäppinen, M. Kulmala, A. Saarinen (eds.), *Gazing at Welfare, Gender and Agency in Post-Socialist*. Newcastle upon Tyne: Cambridge Scholars Publishing: 14–35.

Decree #423. 2009. Decree of the Government of the Russian Federation of May 18, 2009 No. 423 'On Certain Issues of the Implementation of Guardianship and Trusteeship in Relation to Minor Citizens' (*Postanovlenie pravitel'stva Rossijskoj Federacii ot 18 maja 2009 g. N 423 'Ob otdel'nyh voprosah osushhestvlenija opeki i popechitel'stva v otnoshenii nesovershennoletnih grazhdan'*). Available at: https://rg.ru/2009/05/27/opeka-dok.html (accessed 3/04/2020).

Decree #481. 2014. Decree of the Government of the Russian Federation of May 24, 2014 No. 481 'On the Performance of Organizations for Orphanned Children and Children without Parental Care, and on Placement of Children in these Organizations' (*Postanovlenie Pravitel'stva Rossijskoj Federacii ot 24 maja 2014 g. N 481 g. Moskva 'O dejatel'nosti organizacij dlja detej-sirot i detej, ostavshihsja bez popechenija roditelej, i ob ustrojstve v nih detej, ostavshihsja bez popechenija roditelej'*). Available at: http://static.government.ru/media/files/41d4e0dc986dd6284920.pdf (accessed 30/03/2020).

Decree #1688. 2012. Presidential Decree of December 28, 2012 No. 1688 'On Measures to Implement State Policy in the Field of Protecting Orphans and Children Living without Parental Care' (*Ukaz Prezidenta RF ot 28 dekabrja 2012 N 1688 'O nekotoryh merah po realizacii gosudarstvennoj politiki v sfere zashhity detej-sirot i detej, ostavshihsja bez popechenija roditelej'*). Available at: www.kremlin.ru/events/president/news/17234 (accessed 30/03/2020).

Disney, T. 2015. The Role of Emotion in Institutional Spaces of Russian Orphan Care: Policy and Practical Matters. In: M. Blaze, P. Kraftl (eds.), *Children's Emotions in Policy and Practice: Mapping and Making Spaces of Childhood*. Basingstoke: Palgrave Macmillan: 17–33.

Family Code. 1995. Family Code of the Russian Federation. Code of the Russian Federation of December 29, 1995, No. 223-FZ (*Semejnyj kodeks Rossijskoj Federacii. Kodeks Rossijskoj Federacii ot 29.12.1995 # 223-FZ*). Available at: www.kremlin.ru/acts/bank/8671 (accessed 3/04/2020).

Khlinovskaya Rockhill, E. 2010. *Lost to the State: Family Discontinuity, Social Orphanhood and Residential Care in the Russian Far East*. New York: Berghahn Books.

Khmelnitskaya, M. 2015. *The Policy-Making Process and Social Learning in Russia: The Case of Housing Policy*. Basingstoke: Palgrave Macmillan.

Krook, M.L., Mackay, F. 2011. Introduction: Gender, Politics, and Institutions. In: M.L. Krook, F. Mackay (eds.), *Gender, Politics and Institutions Towards a Feminist Institutionalism*. Basingstoke: Palgrave Macmillan: 11–20.

Kulmala, M., Jäppinen, M., Chernova, Z. Forthcoming. Reforming Russia's Child Protection System: From Institutional to Family Care. In: J.D. Berrick, N. Gilbert, M. Skivenes (eds.), *Oxford International Handbook of Child Protection Systems*. Oxford: Oxford University Press.

Kulmala, M., Kainu, M., Nikula, J., Kivinen, M. 2014. Paradoxes of Agency: Democracy and Welfare in Russia. *Demokratizatsiya: The Journal of Post-Soviet Democratization* 23 (4): 523–552.

Kulmala, M., Rasell, M., Chernova, Z. 2017. Overhauling Russia's Child Welfare System: Institutional and Ideational Factors behind the Paradigm Shift. *The Journal of Social Policy Studies* 15 (3): 353–366.

Lovenduski, J. 2011. Foreword. In: M.L. Krook, F. Mackay (eds.), *Gender, Politics and Institutions Towards a Feminist Institutionalism*. Basingstoke: Palgrave Macmillan: vii–xi.

Lowndes, V., Roberts, M. 2013. *Why Institutions Matter: The New Institutionalism in Political Science*. Basingstoke: Palgrave Macmillan.

Mackay, F. 2011. Conclusion: Towards a Feminist Institutionalism? In: M.L. Krook, F. Mackay (eds.), *Gender, Politics and Institutions Towards a Feminist Institutionalism*. Basingstoke: Palgrave Macmillan: 181–196.

Mackay, F. 2014. Nested Newness, Institutional Innovation, and the Gendered Limits of Change. *Politics and Gender* 10 (4): 549–571.

Mahoney, J., Thelen, K. 2010. A Theory of Gradual Institutional Change. In: J. Mahoney, K. Thelen (eds.), *Explaining Institutional Change: Ambiguity, Agency, and Power*. Cambridge: Cambridge University Press: 1–19.

Mätzke, M., Ostner, I. 2010a. Introduction: Change and Continuity in Recent Family Policies. *Journal of European Social Policy* 20 (5): 387–398.

Mätzke, M., Ostner, I. 2010b. Postscript: Ideas and Agents of Change in Time. *Journal of European Social Policy* 20 (5): 468–476.

Medvedev, D. 2010. *Presidential Address to the Federal Assembly of the Russian Federation of 30 November 2010*. Available at: http://en.kremlin.ru/events/president/news/9637 (accessed 20/06//2017).

National Strategy. 2012. Presidential Decree of June 1, 2012 No. 761 'On the National Strategy to Promote the Interests of Children in 2012–2017' (*Ukaz Prezidenta RF ot 01.06.2012 N 761 'O Nacional'noj strategii dejstvij v interesah detej na 2012–2017' gody*). Available at: http://static.kremlin.ru/media/acts/files/0001201206040004.pdf (accessed 30/03/2020).

Novkunskaya, A. 2020. *Professional Agency and Institutional Change: Case of Maternity Services in Small-town Russia*. Helsinki: University of Helsinki.

Peters, B. 1999. *Institutional Theory in Political Science: The New Institutionalism*. London: Pinter.

Polterovich, V. 2008. Institutional Trap. In: S. Durlauf, L. Blume (eds.), *The New Palgrave Dictionary of Economics*. London, UK: Palgrave Macmillan: 3087–3092.

Rivkin-Fish, M. 2010. Pronatalism, Gender Politics, and the Renewal of Family Support in Russia: Toward a Feminist Anthropology of 'Maternity Capital'. *Slavic Review* 69 (3): 701–724.

Rotkirch, A., Temkina, A., Zdravomyslova, E. 2007. Who Helps the Degraded Housewife? Comments on Vladimir Putin's Demographic Speech. *European Journal of Women's Studies* 14 (4): 349–357.

Segal, S., Jacobs, L. 2008. Deinstitutionalization. In: T. Mizrahi, L. Davis (eds.), *The Encyclopedia of Social Work*. Washington, DC, New York: NASW Press, Oxford University Press.

Sirotstvo. 2011. *Sirotstvo v Rossii: Problemy i Puti Ikh Reshenia* [Orphanhood in Russia: Problems and Paths to Their Resolution]. Available at: www.psychologos.ru/images/ZCKti9UQHD_1431501427.pdf (accessed 18/02/2020).

Steinmo, S. 2015. Institutionalism. In: D. Wright (ed.), *International Encyclopedia of the Social & Behavioral Sciences*, 2nd edition, Volume 12. London: Elsevier Health Sciences: 181–185.

Streeck, W., Thelen, K. 2005. Introduction: Institutional Change in Advanced Political Economies. In: W. Streeck, K. Thelen (eds.), *Beyond Continuity: Institutional Change in Advanced Political Economies*. Oxford: Oxford University Press.

Stryker, R. 2012. Emotion Socialization and Attachment in Russian Children's Homes. *Global Studies of Childhood* 2 (2): 85–96.

Thelen, K. 2003. How Institutions Evolve: Insights from Comparative Historical Analysis. In: J. Mahoney, D. Rueschemeyer (eds.), *Comparative Historical Analysis in the Social Sciences*. Cambridge: Cambridge University Press: 208–240.

UN CRC. 1989. *Convention on the Rights of the Child*. United Nations. Geneva, Switzerland.

UN CRPD. 2006. *Convention on the Rights of Persons with Disabilities*. Geneva, Switzerland.

UNICEF. 2003. *Changing Minds, Policies and Lives: Improving Protection of Children in Eastern Europe and Central Asia*. Concept paper. UNICEF Innocenti Research Centre, Florence, Italy.

Waylen, G. 2011. Gendered Institutionalist Analysis: Understanding Democratic Transitions. In: M.L. Krook, F. Mackay (eds.), *Gender, Politics and Institutions Towards a Feminist Institutionalism*. Basingstoke: Palgrave Macmillan: 147–162.

Weiner, E., MacRae, H. 2017. Introduction. In: H. MacRae, E. Weiner (eds.), *Towards Gendering Institutionalism: Equality in Europe*. London: Rowman & Littlefield International: xv–xxxi.

Part II
Changing numbers, shifting discourses

2 Statistics on the deinstitutionalisation of child welfare in Russia

Svetlana Biryukova and Alla Makarentseva

Introduction

Overall, Russia remains a country with one of the highest proportions of children deprived of parental care and a still relatively high level of residential care among such children. Although both Russian officials and society acknowledge the importance of this problem, we still know very little about the dynamics of the number of children deprived of parental care, their characteristics, or how forms of alternative care are developing in Russia. Data on the number of children deprived of parental care is often incomplete and sometimes contradictory (Ovcharova, Iarskaia-Smirnova 2010; Biryukova, Sinyavskaya 2017).

The national legislative framework introduced by deinstitutionalisation (DI) reforms takes family-based care as the ideal choice and aims at providing all children deprived of parental care with conditions as close as possible to this ideal. Within this research, we trace the dynamic of three components of deinstitutionalisation reforms in order to understand whether the proposed ideal of care translates into changes in children's placement and the transformation of alternative care. Firstly, we follow changes in primary risk of placement and compare dynamics in the limitation and termination of parental rights in pre-reform and post-reform periods. Secondly, we study the dynamics and particularity of institutional placement, and examine how it correlates with the policy ideal of shrinking the scope of institutional roles. Thirdly, we scrutinise the difference in the scope of family placements to consider whether the ideal of family environment finds support in practice.

To address this goal, we track shifts towards deinstitutionalisation after the 2006 Presidential Address and change of the institutional care model defined within Decree #481 in 2014 (Decree 2014). We aim to trace the dynamics of the primary risk of placement to alternative care, the prevalence of family reunions, as well as foster family–based and residential institutional placements, especially for children with disabilities. Additionally, we consider whether existing national statistics evolve in line with new management challenges.

The chapter consists of five sections. The first section describes the starting point of the deinstitutionalisation reform and its general track, suggesting neo-institutionalist perspective as a wide theoretical framework for the analysis. The second section is methodological; it discusses the sources of statistical data on children in alternative care and its limitations in Russia. The third section considers recent tendencies in primary risk of placement to alternative care. The fourth section provides an analysis of changes to institutional placements occurring amid reforms in child welfare carried out over the last two decades. Finally, the fifth section examines tendencies in family placements of children.

This chapter is predominantly a descriptive analysis. We aim at studying all the available statistics on alternative care for children, assessing dynamics and tracing any changes before and after the DI reform. The analysis that follows also reveals the limitations of the available official statistical data for monitoring the transformations taking place in the child welfare system.

The trend towards deinstitutionalisation

Social policy for children deprived of parental care is implemented in the same field of ideas as the state family policy in general. In Russia, the latter incorporates mutually exclusive ideas and concepts regarding how the family and the state should share the care for children, and what position the state takes regarding family autonomy. On the one hand, the state relies on pro-natalist policies, proclaiming the upbringing of several children in the family as the key to the country's prosperity (Presidential Address 2020).[1] On the other hand, state rhetoric and policies increasingly concentrate on paternalistic assistance to financially disadvantaged families with children, almost completely ignoring wealthy and untroubled families. Similarly, the state shares with families the duty of care, and it becomes the guardian for children from dysfunctional families or children deprived of parental care.

In this chapter, we rely on the neo-institutional approach, which recognises the dependence of the present system of institutions on its past image due to non-zero transformation costs, and also postulates the impossibility of transforming institutions or organisations without replacing existing norms and rules or introducing new ideas (Meyer, Rowan 1977; Suddaby, Greenwood 2009). In this context, we partially regard existing contradictions as a legacy of previous periods in the development of the childcare system.

While being implemented, the ideas and ideals of childcare system undergo transformation at least twice. Firstly, at the moment of their definition in the paradigm or legislative framework of a reform, and then, again, while being adapted by social and economic institutions. As has already been stated, the ideal of childcare reform in Russia is the realisation of the right of every child to live and be raised in a family. It turns out that it at the stage of formulating reform objectives this ideal is determined by the state, which clearly pictures the image of an ideal or a suitable family; for example, a native family not from a foreign state, or a family living in decent housing. Additionally, the state retains the right to intervene in families. Thus, familistic and liberal discourses come into a conflict with that of state paternalism which is already embedded at the level of ideas. During the process by which ideas are assimilated by institutions, contradictions become even more pronounced. Thus, the idea of the need for a private apartment-type living, even outside the family, cannot be fulfilled within the existing system of institutions which were built in compliance with completely different ideas and goals in the field of childcare.

The inertia of the entire institutional system significantly affects social policy regarding children deprived of parental care in Russia. The theory of path dependency (David 1985; Arthur 1989) states that social institutions and organisations largely inherit patterns and logic of functioning developed in past periods, even though the environment and circumstances might change dramatically in time. In Russia, the shift towards family-based care started with an almost universally spread institutional care for children without parental care.[2] Historically, the Soviet system started to take shape in the 1920s, when the previous system of care for children deprived of parental care based on the charity of the wealthiest citizens collapsed (Tyapkina 2015). A few years later, in the 1930s, due to hunger and massive repressions, the Russian society faced further growth in the number of children deprived of parental care. Another decade later, the Second World War caused extremely high growth rates in the number of children deprived of parental care in Russia, which had the greatest impact on the development of the institutional care system (Dementieva 1991: 72).

During the war and the early post-war years, the state made its first attempts to introduce contractual patronage (guardianship care: *opeka i popechitel'stvo*), but they were not widespread, and in 1968 this type of alternative care was eliminated (Besschetnova 2011: 106). In later Soviet years, during the second half of the twentieth century, the consequences of evacuation and re-evacuation together with specifics of population resettlement (i.e. the long distances between cities) and post-war parsimony in state spending shaped childcare institutions. Besides that, the Soviet regime tended to isolate socially disadvantaged citizens, which at that moment included children without parental care and children with disabilities. Eventually, the system of care for children without parental care ended up taking the form of large institutions hosting several hundred children simultaneously, which were often located outside of large cities, and were completely isolated from external social infrastructure. Residing children received their education, care, and leisure activities within such institutions. Thereby, in the second half of the twentieth century, until the collapse of the USSR, institutions for children deprived of parental care carried, first of all, the function of ensuring the survival of residing children and preparing them for independent life, which mostly meant training to be low-qualified workers.

However, after the transition from a socialist regime, new ideas on the child welfare system generally and on children without parental care in particular were introduced into the national social policy agenda. In Russia, ideological changes were necessary prerequisites for reforms, while the key driving forces included political factors and the presence of political will (Kulmala et al. 2017). Such complicated reforms take time; sometimes decades can pass before successful implementation. In Russia, the situation is complicated by inconsistency in social policies, which often put the very same issues under jurisdiction of many actors, often demonstrating weak cross-administrative cooperation.

The presented theoretical framework and reliance on the theory of path dependency explains our hypothesis regarding the process of deinstitutionalisation. Namely, we expected to see a continuing fall in the number of children in alternative care, especially in residential care. However, we did not expect to see any serious progress in the transformation of the institutions themselves, especially with regard to the correctional institutions for children with disabilities. This is because with regard to institutional transformation, we expected to see inertia. Previous research on the topic demonstrated that the results of the reforms were less promising for children with disabilities in comparison to healthy children (Biryukova, Sinyavskaya 2017; Avdeeva, Rusakova 2017). We expected the following tendencies to be still present: (1) less opportunity for disabled children to end up in alternative care; and (2) less progress in carrying out the reforms in special and correctional institutions in comparison to regular ones. As a result, we expected to observe a growing share of disabled children among those residing in institutional care.

Methodology: available statistical data and its major limitations

The Russian child welfare system includes many actors operating at the federal, regional, and local levels and under different administrative branches. Data providers are also divided under the responsibility of different ministries, and the Russian Federal State Statistics Service (*Rosstat*) gathers data from the Ministry of Healthcare, the Ministry of Labour and Social Protection, and the Ministry of Education. Due to this reason, the available statistical data on the children without parental care has some shortcomings.

Firstly, the plurality of data providers sometimes produces inconsistencies. Over last decades, the total number of children without parental care was annually calculated and announced by *Rosstat*, but this estimate did not agree with the aggregated data of the ministries (Ovcharova, Iarskaia-Smirnova 2010: 20). Moreover, in recent years, *Rosstat* replaced this indicator with the rate of decrease in the total number of children without parental care as a percentage of the previous year. Meanwhile, in line with the current *Rosstat* methodology, this number includes adopted children. As, according to the national law, adopted children are equal to biological children in terms of rights, they cannot be categorised as children without parental care. Therefore, experts used to reduce the estimate of total number of children without parental care by the size of this group. Unfortunately, after the introduction of a new indicator (the rate of decrease), such corrections are no longer available, which makes the official statistics less informative.

Secondly, some important processes are not reflected in the statistics due to the complexity of their measurement. In particular, a major problem is the inability to estimate the number of children in residential care whose birth parents' parental rights have not been terminated, i.e. children 'without status' (see Jäppinen, Kulmala in this volume). These children cannot be considered for family placements while having birth parents with their parental rights in force. Among them might be the children of those temporarily imprisoned or children with severe disabilities placed temporarily, but not necessarily for a short period of time, in institutions at the request of their parents. According to the formal definition, these children are not without parental care and are not included in the relevant statistics. However, they may in fact stay in institutions without any contact with their relatives for a long time, forming an invisible or latent sector of social orphans.[3] The different justifications for this are analysed later in this volume (Jäppinen, Kulmala).

Next, the methodology for calculating the same indicators sometimes may vary not only between ministries but also between different statistical reports within one ministry.[4] For example, statistical form F-19 '*Information on Children with Disabilities*', issued by the Ministry of Health, contains data on the total number of children with disabilities in residential care (boarding school – *shkola-internat*), but only together with children having parents or families without any limitations in their parenting rights who were temporary placed into a boarding school in order to get education. Furthermore, statistical form NOO-1 issued by the Ministry of Education provides information on both the number of disabled children and the number of children deprived of parental care studying in special educational institutions. However, this data source does not contain estimates of the overlap between these two categories of pupils. Another statistical form issued by the same ministry, D-13, gives information on the number of disabled children living in the institutions for children without parental care; however, information given in other sections of this form indicates that not all of these children have the official status of 'child deprived of parental care' (similar to the shortcomings in the form F-19 by the Ministry of Health). In addition to that, in 2014 and 2015, some of the institutions working with disabled children changed their jurisdiction, which caused serious (although temporary) losses in statistics. Finally, even existing estimates of disabled children staying or studying in institutions are not differentiated by disability group or causes of disability (type of health limitation) in the statistics. The only data source that has some information on health status of children deprived of parental care is summary report 103-RIK; however, it is incomplete.

Another source of data to be mentioned is the federal database on children deprived of parental care,[5] created to provide information to potential alternative parents. This data source is broadly used by the media; however, it is not reliable for expert or statistical monitoring, because a certain number of children identified as children deprived of parental care never appear in this databank; namely those children who are quickly taken into alternative family-based care. Nevertheless, this data source might be seen as useful for getting some data on disabled children, because the available information referring to this group is generally very scarce.

Despite the indicated shortcomings, an analysis of the existing statistics allows us to track the dynamics in the sphere of alternative care, namely dynamics of the primary risk of placement to alternative care, prevalence of family reunions, as well as foster family–based and residential institutional placements. Within the analysis presented in this chapter, we use the following data sources:

- data provided by the Ministry of Education: yearly federal statistics on the identification and placements of children and adolescents deprived of parental care (103-RIK statistical form); yearly federal statistics on institutions for children deprived of parental care (D-13 statistical form)

- data on the number of disabled children in Russia provided by the Ministry of Healthcare (statistical form F-19)
- data withdrawn from the federal database on children deprived of parental care (usynovite.ru)
- aggregated data from the Federal State Statistics Service (*Rosstat*) on topics for which raw statistical forms and administrative data are not publicly available

Children taken from families: declining numbers

Less children taken from families

According to the *Rosstat* data, the total number of children deprived of parental care, which includes children in residential care, as well as children in family-type placements, has been shrinking since 2005 (see Figure 2.1). In the years from 2005 to 2017, the number of children deprived of parental care increased only once, in 2007, by 500 children over the previous year. This tendency set in after a period of steady growth of this indicator, spanning from the early 1990s until the mid-2000s, a period which was marked at the beginning by a highly volatile macroeconomic situation and a decline in living standards, as well as improvements in the system for identifying troubled families by the end of this period.

Most children out of those without parental care in Russia are social orphans – meaning they have at least one living parent, although they have been placed into alternative care. For example, according to the most recent data, 48,300 children were identified as children deprived of parental care in 2018; of these, only 3200 children were left by their mothers at birth.

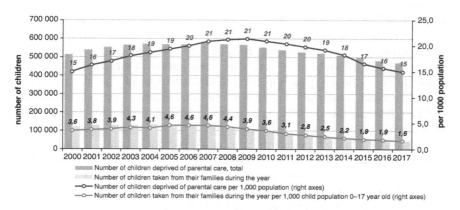

Figure 2.1 Children deprived of parental care, 2000–2017.

Source: Statistical form 103-RIK, *Rosstat* data.

More than a half of children identified as being out of parental care are of school age (6 years old) or older. In the last decade, the number of children younger than 7 years of age as a percentage of all children identified during a calendar year has fluctuated between 40% and 45% and has not shown any tendency to grow (see Figure 2.2). At the same time, both Russian (Biryukova, Sinyavskaya 2017) and international experiences show that older children represent one of the 'hardest to place' groups (Fenyo et al. 1989).

Generally, the dynamics of the main indicators already described allows predicting further decline, both in the total number of children without parental care and in the number of institutionalised children in the coming years.

Terminating or limiting parents' rights? An essential decision

The dominant legislative measure used when taking children from their families in Russia is terminating parental rights, which is a very tough measure, narrowing the possible scope of further efforts to reunite families. In 2018, the parents of 35,707 children had their parental rights terminated, whereas the option of limiting parental right was applied to parents of 10,191 children. However, the share of children whose parents' rights were limited in total number of children taken from families grew from 5.7% in 2002 up to 22.2% by 2018 (Figure 2.3).

In recent years, the number of children placed in families during the year has been exceeding the number of children identified as deprived of parental care (see Figure 2.4). Due to this, the number of institutionalised children has been gradually declining. However, because we do not have any data on the length of stay in the institutions, we can only guess that children who were recently put into the system mostly drive this dynamic. Thus, we assume that for now the contingent of children in residential care is likely to fall into two parts – children institutionalised for a short period of time who are quickly taken to foster families

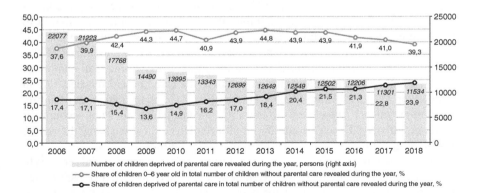

Figure 2.2 Orphans (children with no living parents) and children deprived of parental care under 7 years old, 2006–2018.

Source: Statistical form 103-RIK.

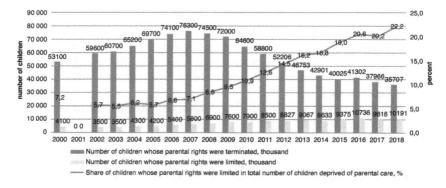

Figure 2.3 Prevalence of termination and limitation of parental rights, 2000–2018.
Source: Statistical form 103-RIK.

(usually they are infants and/or relatively healthy children) and permanently institutionalised children living in institutions for several years or even lifelong (such
as children with severe health limitations, or siblings that entered the system at
school age). A problem arising from this situation is an emerging group of children who, according to their characteristics, meet the first category, but have a
sibling from the second category, often residing in different institution. Currently,
any family placement of children apart from their siblings is actually prohibited,
which naturally has a positive effect for some children and negative for others.

However, the problem is not only in the low proportion of parental rights limitations but also in the weak or absent work with the birth families after that.
In recent years, work with birth families aimed at achieving family reunions is
receiving more and more attention. This tendency is reflected in the statistical
monitoring; thus, since 2018, the 103-RIK form provides more complete information on family reunions. For example, the number of children transferred to
the birth parents from institutions is given in a separate row, while previously it
was absent from the form. In 2018, this group counted 3,200 children or 18.2%
of all children returned to biological families during the year; the total number of
children reunited with biological families over the same period reached 17,500
children or 24% of all children placed in families. To track the dynamics of family
reunion prevalence, we have to follow the indicator which does not account for
children transferred from institutions, and it remains almost unchanged over the
last six years: about 20% of all children placed in families.

The problem of reuniting children with birth families requires social services to
be versatile in their methods. The system of temporary (short-term) institutional
placements recently introduced for parents, who cannot perform their parental
duties for good reasons,[6] was aimed at preserving biological families. However,
as has already been mentioned, this policy produced both positive and negative
effects for children and families. For temporary placements to really serve their

purpose, it is necessary to limit the possibilities of its extension, on the one hand, and to conduct active social rehabilitation of the birth family during this period, on the other. In addition, for children with a high chance of returning to birth family, it is possible to organise temporary placement in professional foster families. This may be a separate category of alternative care families receiving additional payments and working with this group of children only.

Thus, although the introduction of thorough work with birth families is postulated as one of the key goals of the child welfare policies, it has been implemented rarely so far. Whereas such options as the right to voluntarily submit one's child for alternative care are available for families, they do not receive any support aimed at family reunion.

Child placements into residential care

Types of residential care institutions and general dynamics of placements

As already noted, residential care is subordinated to different Ministries. This practice was established in the Soviet years, and it separated institutions depending on the age and health status of the pupils. Special children's homes for 0–3 year olds (baby homes, *dom rebenka*) are under the responsibility of the Ministry of Healthcare, which historically meant that these children were in need of medical and everyday care but not yet of education. All children's homes (*detskii dom*) for older children are administered by the Ministry of Education, which reflects the leading function of education in these institutions, and at the same time implies that children live and study in one place, that is, they are in an absolutely closed territory. Finally, children's homes for disabled (*korrektsionnyi detskii dom*) are very special institutions for disabled children deprived of parental care. They are administered by the Ministry of Labour and Social Protection, and this again implies that children with mental disabilities (the main contingent of these houses) are not trained and do not need education, but only everyday care.

However, now such divisions have become outdated; in particular, children with intellectual disabilities have long been recognised as able to study. Moreover, this division increasingly tangles the progress of the deinstitutionalisation reform. The separation by type and department not only carries direct negative effects for children placed within the system, such as the separation of siblings or transfers from one institution to another as they grow older or change health status, but also means different levels of budgetary provision and quality of care in these institutions.

Some steps towards unification of the institutions have been taken in the recent years. For example, the Decree #588n (2015) issued by the Russian Ministry of Labour and Social Protection on 9 September 2015 states that institutions for children without parental care operating under different ministries are still providing identical treatment and educational services. Additionally, the reform of institutions for children deprived of parental care aims at providing joint care for children of different age and health status.[7] Thus, it is proposed to bring all such organisations into a unified form, as, for example, Deputy Chairman of the Government of the Russian Federation on social policy Tatyana Golikova (Government.ru 2019) declared in her official speech at a meeting of the *Committee for Guardianship in the Social Sphere* on 1 February 2019.[8]

The share of children put into residential care out of the children taken from their families during the year also decreased, going from 26.9% in 2000 to 18.8% in 2015; and then it stabilised. In other words, children taken from their families now more often bypass institutional care and immediately go to family-based alternative care. However, the main decline in this indicator occurred in the period of 2012–2014.

The dynamics of the rank order of the placement options used for children without parental care clearly reflects the process of deinstitutionalisation taking place in Russia since the mid-2000s. In 2017, the total number of children without parental care in Russia reached 572,600, and about 45,000 of them were residing in various institutions.[9] However, in 2000, the number of institutionalised children without parental care was 180,000. Legislation prioritises family placements over residential care, and the statistics clearly reflects this priority: in 2000–2017, the share of children placed at children's homes and other residential care facilities declined by almost three quarters, from 27% to 6.7%. Moreover, by now institutional placements have become the least popular, although before 2007 institutions were almost the most often used option, second only to guardianship (Figure 2.4).

The general decline in the number of institutionalised children without parental care was accompanied by changes in their distribution across institutions of different types (see Table 2.1). The observed proportion of children living in children's homes for 0–3 year olds is quite stable and strongly depends on the age

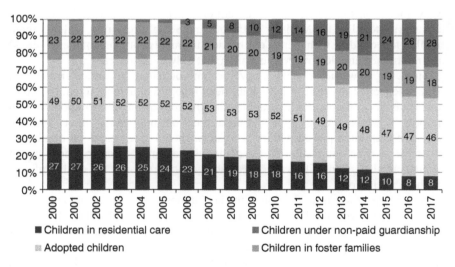

Figure 2.4 Structure of children placements, 2000–2017.

Source: Rosstat, statistical form D-13.[10]

Table 2.1 Structure of residential care, number, and percentage

	2000	2010	2015	2016	2017
Children in residential care, total number	180,295	119,860	58,918	47,154	44,941
Special children's homes for 0–3 year olds, % (*dom rebenka*)	7.8	10.6	9.2	8.8	7.9
Children's homes, % (*detskii dom*)	37.5	41.1	39.5	43.5	41.7
Children's homes, schools, %	5.4	4.2	2.8	2.3	1.7
Boarding schools for children deprived of parental care, % (*shkola-internat*)	12.9	7.3	4.7	5.2	4.8
Boarding schools for all children, %	5.1	3.3	1.2	n/a	n/a
Boarding schools for disabled children, % (*korrektsionnyi detskii dom*)	22.7	21.7	22.0	n/a	n/a
Children's homes for disabled, % (*doma-internaty*)	8.5	11.7	20.5	23.4	28.7

Source: Rosstat.

structure of the population. The most evident changes are seen in the share of residents in children's homes for disabled: it grew from 8.5% in 2000 up to 28.7% in 2017. At the same time, the number of children corresponding to these figures barely changed (15,300 children in 2000 and 12,900 children in 2017), whereas the number of children residing in all other types of institutions has been rapidly declining during this period. These dynamics clearly reveal a failure in the implementation of the ongoing deinstitutionalisation reform within children's homes for disabled.

Apart from that, we observe a decline in the share of children staying in boarding schools, from 12.9% in 2000 down to 4.8% in 2017, which goes in line with one of the goals of the reform, i.e. putting all schooling and educational activities out of the institutions where children reside. The share of children residing in boarding schools for disabled children went down to approximately 12.5% in 2017 from 22.0% in 2015. Indeed, the proportion of children getting an education in schools outside institutions of their residence has slightly increased: in 2014, 11.1% residents were studying outside, and in 2018 this rose to 17.8%. Basically, this growth is attributed to the changes within the regular boarding schools, where this share increased from 15.4% to 27.6%; while within special (correctional) institutions for disabled or troubled children, we observe practically no changes.

Children with disabilities in residential care

Many of children residing in institutional care are children with disabilities, and we believe it is essential to consider their situation within this chapter separately. In 2018, over 60,000 disabled children resided in all kinds of residential institutions (Table 2.2), although it is impossible to estimate the number of children without parental care among them. Based on the estimates extracted from the federal database, we can count 18,500 disabled children with no parents alive or without parental care. Over the three years between 2015 and 2018, the proportion of disabled children residing in institutions for children without parental care increased from 15% to 20.8% (see Table 2.3). In special (correctional) residential institutions, more than half of the children in 2018 had a disability.

Table 2.2 Number of disabled children in Russia, 2018

Age	Number of disabled children		Among them: children living in institutions*			
	Total number	Among them: children with no parents alive*	Administered by the Ministry of Health	Administered by the Ministry of Education	Administered by the Ministry of Labour	Total number
0–4 years old	86,316	486	1,428	357	245	2,030
5–9 years old	186,590	2,078	26	10,606	3,302	13,934
10–14 years old	199,743	3,979	–	21,421	6,550	27,971
15–17 years old	114,206	2,935	–	11,909	4,981	16,890
Total	586,855	9,478	1,454	44,293	15,078	60,825
	Percentage					
0–4 years old	100.0	0.6	1.7	0.4	0.3	2.4
5–9 years old	100.0	1.1	0.0	5.7	1.8	7.5
10–14 years old	100.0	2.0		10.7	3.3	14.0
15–17 years old	100.0	2.6		10.4	4.4	14.8
Total	100.0	1.6	0.2 (2.4)	7.5 (72.8)	2.6 (24.8)	10.4 (100.0)

Source: Statistical form D-19 issued by the Ministry of Health.

*Not all of residents officially labelled as children deprived of parental care (see the preceding sections)

Table 2.3 Share of disabled children in residential care in the total number of disabled children in Russia, %, 2015 and 2018[11]

	2015	2018
In all types of residential care	15.0	20.8
Among them: children's homes (*detskii dom*)	10.0	15.6
Including: regular	6.3	10.2
sanatoriums	12.6	10.5
special (correctional)	37.3	56.4
Boarding schools for children deprived of parental care *(shkola-internat)*	4.8	9.2
Special (correctional) boarding schools for children deprived of parental care (*korrektsionnyi detskii dom*)	32.7	39.6
Other children's homes – schools	4.7	4.9
Non-governmental institutions	2.7	9.4

Source: Statistical form D-13 issued by the Ministry of Education.

With regard to disabled children, the question of deinstitutionalisation is closely intertwined with the territorial availability of inclusive schools or special educational organisations for those living in families. Most children with disabilities reside in institutions administered by the Ministry of Education, while approximately a quarter of them permanently reside in special children's homes for disabled administered by the Ministry of Labour (Table 2.2). The latter should be closely studied in the context of the deinstitutionalisation reform. These special homes can take two forms: one which accepts children with mental disabilities, and the other with physical disabilities. In both cases the residing children are in constant need of caregiver assistance due to partial or complete loss of the ability to look after themselves. Based on this definition, one could expect that almost all of such residents would have severe disabilities. However, this is far from true: children with relatively light mental and physical deviations, caused by deprivation due to living outside the family or pedagogical neglect, end up living in these institutions (Allenova 2018). Local experts working in the non-governmental sector such as N. Federmesser (Presidential Council 2019[12]) note that special homes for disabled children remained almost unchanged during the deinstitutionalisation reform, and they should be addressed at the next stage of the state intervention, together with psychoneurological boarding homes for adults.

Are institutions changing?

The current stage of the reform suggests not only increasing the proportion of children living in family-based alternative care but also reorganising the institutions themselves. Firstly, they should transform into family-type institutions, which, among other things, includes a shift towards an apartment-type living conditions for children. Secondly, the institutions should gradually become more open to the society and external environment, which involves educating children outside the institution they reside.

The most important characteristic of institutional placements for children without parental care is the size of institutions and the number of children in a group handled by a single caregiver. It is generally believed that small groups and small-sized children's homes are better for forming a stable relationship with a caregiver (Williamson, Greenberg 2010), and this thinking is reflected in the key points of Decree 481 (Decree 2014) which emphasises family-type care in children's homes.[13] It is necessary to highlight that the total number of children in an institution and the number of biological orphans and children deprived of parental care in an institution are not equal. The data presented in Table 2.4 shows that these indicators differ significantly. The official methodological recommendations provided for the national statistical forms do not offer a clear definition of such inconsistencies. We assume that, first of all, this indicator includes 'family' children[14] enrolled in boarding schools during the school year; these might be, for example, children with disabilities who need a certain type of educational institution and who do not have the opportunity to study in an inclusive classroom

Table 2.4 Average number of children in residential care, in a group, and in an institution, 2010 and 2018

	Average number of children in a group			
	Residents		*Among them: children deprived of parental care*	
	2010	*2018*	*2010*	*2018*
Total number of children	9.1	7.7	8.6	5.7
Children's homes, regular	8.5	6.9	8.4	5.8
Children's homes, special (correctional)	8.6	6.9	8.5	5.9
Boarding schools, regular	8.5	6.4	8.4	6.1
Boarding schools, special (correctional)	8.4	7.3	8.1	5.1
	Average number of children in an institution			
	Residents		*Among them: children deprived of parental care*	
Total number of children	59.3	45.1	56.3	33.5
Children's homes, regular	47.7	36.8	47.0	30.6
Children's homes, special (correctional)	46.3	35.1	45.8	29.7
Boarding schools, regular	77.4	57.2	76.5	55.2
Boarding schools, special (correctional)	51.0	55.4	49.0	38.4

Source: Statistical form D-13.

or the school nearest to their place of family residence. Secondly, it is likely that children temporarily placed in residential care at the request of a parent are also included in this category ('children without status'). This may explain the growth in the size of this group of children observed in statistics after 2014. As for now, when a family is acknowledged as troubled by the social service, the state gives parents the opportunity to temporarily place their child or children in residential care. At that, parents are not deprived of parental rights or limited in them, and they can take the child home at any time. Such children make up to 30% of children in institutional care.[15]

The Ministry of Health provides very few data about operating special children's homes for 0–3 year olds (Table 2.5). Over the observed period, 2011–2018, the average number of children 0–3 year olds in residential care decreased significantly, from almost 75 to 52, while the total number of residents fell twice, from 16,300 to 7,500 children. At the same time, the proportion of residents not officially labelled as children deprived of parental care has increased inexplicably, from 27.6% to 53.4%.

The reduction in the number of children without parental care should lead to a decline in the number of institutional care units. Conversely, a shift to the family-type institutional care stated within the framework of the ongoing reform and, as a result, reduction in the average number of residents should boost the number of institutions. Statistics show that the total number of institutions for children

Table 2.5 Special children's homes for 0–3 year olds, 2011–2016

	2011	2012	2013	2014	2015	2016	2017	2018
Number of special children's homes for 0–3 year olds (at the end of the year)	218	207	194	176	166	161	154	145
Number of residents	16,296	15,993	13,977	11,530	10,245	8,575	7,774	7,524
Among them: children deprived of parental care	11,803	11,145	9,333	6,892	5,439	4,170	3,543	3,504
Average number of children residing in one institution	74.8	77.3	72.0	65.5	61.7	53.3	50.5	51.9
Share of children without orphan/ without parental care status among all residents of institutions	27.6	30.3	33.2	40.2	46.9	51.4	54.4	53.4

Source: Fedstat 2019.

Table 2.6 Number of institutions for children deprived of parental care, 2010–2018[16]

	2010	2015	2017	2018
	Number of organisations			
All children's homes	1,048	720	613	621
Children's homes, regular	871	637	557	568
Children's homes, special (correctional)	151	73	50	48
Boarding schools, regular	90	46	45	42
Boarding schools, special (correctional)	193	145	118	122
Special children's homes for 0–3 year olds	227	166	154	145
Children's homes for disabled	143	144	251*	228*

Source: Statistical form D-13, *Rosstat* Table 7.13 of 'Social status and standard of living of the Russian population.'[17]

*Until 2017, indicator of 'Children's homes for disabled' did not include 'other organisations providing residential social services'; in a comparable methodology, there were 112 institutions in 2017 and 109 in 2018.

without parental care has been shrinking until recently (see Table 2.6). The sharpest drop in this number occurred between 2010 and 2015, which is mostly before 2014, i.e. before Decree #481 which marked a turning point in the institutional design. Then, due to the overlap with the reorganisation process, these dynamics slowed down. Moreover, in 2018, the number of institutions even slightly increased. However, it seems that the reorganisation process has yet come to full force. Thus, according to data on institutions of the Ministry of Education, in 2018, only 4% or 32 out of 800 institutions working under jurisdiction of this ministry were reorganised. In general, statistics regarding institutions indicate that reform is being gradually implemented, but the pace remains slow and uneven for different types of institutions.

Family placements: changing priorities?

The dominant family placement option during the entire period under review was guardianship, which is a placement into a family up to the age of 18 years. This family might be relative (grandparents, aunt and uncle, etc.) or non-relative, and it might receive some payments or benefits for the provided care or not, depending on the type of a contract it signs with the social services. In 2001–2011, these placements accounted for more than half of all family placements. In recent years, this share shrank, albeit insignificantly: in 2017, 45.7% of all children without parental care were placed with guardians (Figure 2.5). Currently, the most dynamically developing form of family placement for children without parental care are foster families. In 2005–2017, the share of children placed with foster families grew from 2% to 28.2%. This rise was promoted, inter alia, by a Federal Law (48-FZ 2008) adopted in 2008. There are several separate trends underpinning the spread of fostering. Firstly, it is crucial to note transformations of social values and public mood that followed the change in the state's attitude to children in state care in the early 2000s, emphasising their vulnerability, rather than deviance. Secondly, it is the gradual development of the institution of foster families, including the creation of schools for them and the system of their selection and assistance to them. And thirdly, the increase in the number of children raised in foster families is partially explained by the fact that some guardians made new official arrangements, in order to gain access to services and benefits provided by Federal Law 48-FZ, such as professional support and financial assistance, including foster parents' salaries and money allowances for food, clothes, and other child-related expenditures.

Given these tendencies, since 2006, the share of adoptions in the placement options for children without parental care has been slightly declining. In 2000–2006, about 22% were being adopted, and then this figure went down to 18–20%, remaining at this level ever since. In addition, adoption and gratuitous (non-paid) guardianship provided by non-relatives are relatively more common with infants (see Table 2.7); the chances to be adopted fall sharply for children over 1 year old. In 2018, 93.2% of adopted children were adopted by Russian citizens. On the eve of the adoption of the so-called Dima Yakovlev law, it was noted that in 2007–2011, among adopted children, about 30% of cases were foreign adoptions, and only 70% were adopted by Russian citizens (Foundation 2012).

As noted at the beginning, there is no data on total number of children with disabilities in alternative care; however, we have information on the transfer of children with disabilities to guardianship and adoption for each year (see Table 2.8). In recent years, children with officially established disabilities accounted for 7–10% of all children transferred to foster families, and the peak of the family placements of children with disabilities was registered in 2016. Generally, disabled children

Table 2.7 Distribution of family placements by age of a child, % by row, 2018

	Infants (under 1 years old)	1–3 years old	3–7 years old	7 years old and older
Non-paid guardianship	6.1	11.0	22.5	60.4
among them, provided by non-relative caregivers	16.2	20.1	23.8	39.8
Paid guardianship (foster families)[18]	3.4	10.4	24.1	62.1
Adoption	46.8	21.3	18.3	13.6

Source: Statistical form 103-RIK.

Table 2.8 Placements of disabled children, 2013–2018

	2013	2014	2015	2016	2017	2018
Number of children						
Non-paid guardianship	686	580	601	656	495	502
Paid guardianship (foster families)	715	963	1,158	1,001	740	570
Adoption (by Russian citizens)	132	123	144	136	134	117
Total	1,533	1,666	1,903	1,793	1,369	1,189
% of the total number of children placed in every type of residence						
Non-paid guardianship	2.0	1.5	2.0	2.3	2.0	2.2
Paid guardianship (foster families)	3.6	4.1	5.1	5.1	4.3	3.9
Adoption (by Russian citizens)	1.6	1.9	2.4	2.8	3.0	3.0
Total	7.2	7.4	9.6	10.1	9.4	9.0

Source: Statistical form 103-RIK.

are more likely to be placed in paid alternative families compared to all other children. In 2018, among all children transferred to alternative families, 35.9% went to paid forms and 54.6% to non-paid forms; among disabled children, this ratio was 47.9% and 42.2%, which might point to the fact that the development of a paid form of guardianship has some positive effect for disabled children.

A separate issue in the context of alternative care is the prevalence of children returning to residential care. Although the total number of cases when children were returned from alternative families to institutions has been declining since 2010, the statistics for 2018 shows 5,268 cases; 3,522 of them were initiated by host families themselves. Forty-two per cent of the aforementioned cases referred to non-relative alternative families, while the remaining 58% were returns from relative caregivers, which stresses lack of training provided for potential caregivers coming from birth family. Preventing repeating placements to the residential care is one of the key tasks of the child protection services because this can seriously traumatise the child and lead to the child being placed at an institution permanently due to difficulties in finding new family placements for children with such histories. Mechanisms to prevent repeat placements to residential care include the development of a system of professional and psychological training for potential caregivers, which would continue to be available for them after they take in a child, as well as improving the system of complex support for families and applying an individualised approach to working with families and children.

The observed evolution of family-based alternative care reflects the state's perception of the ideal form of alternative care. We can see that professional family-based alternative care in Russia is supported weakly and inconsistently. For example, the SOS village programme, which was first introduced in the country in the mid-1990s, did not receive strong government support and had only limited spread throughout Russia (only six villages work now.)[19] Foster families, which are one of the forms of paid guardianship in Russia, never developed into a professional care and differ from other forms of alternative family care only in slightly higher state financial support and stricter paperwork.

Generally, it seems that the state has the idea that a family providing alternative care is a family, which simply receives a little more monetary benefits than a family parenting only birth children. This emphasis on the financial aids fits into the general mainstream of the modern monetary-oriented social policy in Russia rather than meeting the specific needs of alternative care system. It is particularly important that educational programmes and continuous support for foster families are quite limited: virtually the only available options are a short-term school for foster parents and a number of support programmes provided by non-government organisations. As a result, there are no professional families that would provide temporary custody instead of temporary institutional placement, and severely disabled children, as well as siblings and teenagers, are still relatively rarely placed into long-term family-based alternative care.

Conclusions and discussion

Generally, we can state that the adoption of Decree #481 has marked a new stage in the evolution of the Russian child welfare system. The Decree highlighted the temporary character of the residential care and set new standards for the functioning of the institutions, which produced a strong impulse for transformation of the system. As time passed, it became clear that the implementation of this reform is challenged by legislative, administrative, and financial constraints, which became particularly explicit due to the recent economic downturn and ensuing budget cuts that made it impossible to finance core changes to the child welfare system implied by the reform. What is more, the inertia of the entire institutional system slows down changes in social policy regarding children deprived of parental care in Russia. This first impulse given by the legislative changes and designated political will has gradually faded away, and now a new increase in public attention to the problem of child welfare is required.

The first component of the deinstitutionalisation process in Russia is the shrinking of institutional placement and transformation of institutions. The data reveals stable positive dynamics: the total number of children without parental care is gradually declining as well as primary risk placement. The statistics show that children are more likely to be placed in families and the number of institutions is decreasing. In accordance with the goal of the reform, the average number of children living in one institution has dropped. Unfortunately, the statistics do not reflect an average size of the children groups, as well as the organisation of their everyday routine. For example, we cannot track whether the children from different groups spend all their time during the day within one common room or not (Allenova 2018).

The reorganisation proceeds faster in regular institutions and, on the contrary, lags behind in those for disabled children. This situation is connected with both the health and educational status of residents and their location; in Soviet times, such institutions were often built far from settlements and designed to be very large, which now produces barriers for their reorganisation. By now, the children residing in institutions can be divided into two groups: those who move quickly into family-based care and those who live there for a long time, virtually permanently. The second group is more and more represented by children with disabilities.

The second element of the deinstitutionalisation process is the development of family-based alternative care, including professional ones. As for now, it is based on promoting placements into non-relative families with state support, mainly in the form of cash benefits. The development of paid family-based alternative care in Russia has brought many fruits, including an increase in prevalence of family placements among deprived groups of children. However, currently, we see very little initiative coming from the child welfare authorities in promoting the search for foster families among relatives or adults familiar to the child. In addition to that, there is evident lack of professional foster families for temporary placements of children with high chances of family reunion or of permanent family-based placement (to avoid even temporary institutional placements). Finally, professional foster families for special groups of children, such as severely disabled, whose placement in an unprofessional family is unlikely, are also scarce.

The third element of deinstitutionalisation is the prevention of social orphanage and work with birth families in difficult life situations. In fact, in Russia it is limited to the possibility of temporary placement of a child into institutional care, which might have more drawbacks than positive effects for the child. Social support programmes for troubled families are appearing in Russia, but are not yet widespread. As a result, of the number of children going to family placements, only a little less than a quarter returns to birth families. However, a more obvious indicator of the lack of work with birth families is the growing share of children staying in organisations at the request of their parents. As a matter of priority, the state should track the number of renewed requests and limit the possibility of multiple renewals, as well as require such families to be included in social support programmes.

Generally, the observed dynamics of the main statistical indicators shows that the institutions are being reorganised, but unevenly and sometimes formally, without changing the living conditions of children, for example, without any shift towards apartment-type accommodation. As for child placements, the prevalence of alternative family-based care is growing, but birth family reunions remain relatively rare. In other words, the goals of the childcare reform are being fulfilled only partially.

As it was stated in the introductory part of the chapter, one of the goals of our research is to find out whether national statistics evolves in line with the new management challenges. Summing up the analysis presented on the data quality, we conclude that existing statistics on children deprived of parental care has slightly changed over the recent years; however, in most parts it serves poorly to evaluate the outcomes of the ongoing reform, and we can still see numerous gaps in the data. In general, it is necessary to introduce targets for each goal of the reform; where there are none, their monitoring is not possible.

Based on the conducted analysis, we can name several strong shortcomings of the existing statistical data. Firstly, the statistics for different types of institutions is not unified, which is crucial for proper monitoring of the reform, until the rudimentary separation itself is eliminated. Secondly, in the context of the current reform goals, limited statistics on transfers between different types of residential institutions (for example, on transfers from children's homes to boarding schools for children with disabilities, etc.) means that the frequency of the changes in children's environment is unknown. Thirdly, the distribution of brothers and sisters by residential institutions as well as their share among residents is not monitored in any way. In the context of the deinstitutionalisation goal, this group is of great interest due to the complexity of placing such children in one family. Additionally, it is impossible to relate the statistics of different departments with regard to the state of health and the spread of disability among children in alternative care, as well as undisclosed data on infant mortality in institutions. Next, because staying outside the family should be just a temporary phenomenon for each child, the reduction of the time spent in an institution could and probably should be the goal of the state policies in the field. However, there is no such indicator in the official statistics on alternative care at the moment. Finally, the absence of statistics of refusals given to potential foster parents and families, including refusals given after signing the agreement, makes impossible to reveal the unlawful behaviour of child protection service officers (*opeka*).[20] More widely, the complete absence of statistics on the performance of social services reflects the fact that they still stick to the old model, responding to requests from alternative parents, not children, something Jäppinen and Kulmala also argue in this volume.

Generally, we can conclude that existing statistics serves administrative but not social policy goals. That is, existing data are collected to maintain the routine of the established system, and its structure and contents do not allow to improve the system of alternative care or to thoroughly monitor the ongoing reform, even though some new data appeared in statistical forms.[21]

Notes

1 Presidential Address 2020 posted on the official website of the president of Russia. Available at: http://kremlin.ru/events/president/news/62582

2 This chapter uses a narrow definition of institutions as organisations where children deprived of parental care reside temporarily or permanently. They form the core of the entire institutional system of child care; in addition to them, there are actors such as social services, government bodies, and non-profit organizations.

3 Children whose parents are alive but, for whatever reason, are not able to care for them.

4 The various statistical forms (103-RIK, D-13, NOO-1) mentioned in this chapter are not available online and were provided by the ministries to the authors after requests were made.

5 The Federal database on children deprived of parental care is available at usynovite.ru.

6 This right is given by Part 1 Article 13 of Federal Law N 48-FZ (24/042008) 'On guardianship and fostering' (*'Ob opeke I popechitel'stve'*), and the definition of *good reasons* is not given.

7 Paragraph 34 of Decree of the Government of the Russian Federation (2014) *O deyatel'nosti organizatsiy dlya detey-sirot i detey, ostavshikhsya bez popecheniya roditeley, I ob ustroystve v nikh detey, ostavshikhsya bez popecheniya roditeley* [On the Activity of Organizations for Orphan Children and Children without Parental Care and on Placement of Children without Parental Care in Them] N 481 from 24.5.2014.

8 These changes have already been introduced into the Draft of the Decree of the Government of the Russian Federation *O vnesenii izmenenij v Polozhenie o deyatel'nosti organizacij dlya detej-sirot i detej, ostavshihsya bez popecheniya roditelej, i ob ustrojstve v nih detej, ostavshihsya bez popecheniya roditelej* [On Amending the Regulation on the Activities of Organizations for Orphans and Children Deprived of Parental Care, and on the Placements of Children Deprived of Parental Care] from 24.5.2019. Available at: https://regulation.gov.ru/p/91602.

9 In addition to that, the Ministry of Education estimates the number of children deprived of parental care residing in boarding schools for children with parental care as 847 in 2017 and 1,123 in 2018. However, because there is no regular statistics on these children, and the given statistics exists only for these two years, in the following analysis we do not take this data into account.

10 *Rosstat* estimates of the total number of children deprived of parental care for 2016–2017 does not contain data on such children residing in other special (correctional) boarding schools. We adjust these estimates using the data from the Ministry of Education (the statistical form D-13).

11 The given statistics refers to all children, not only those labelled as children deprived of parental care.

12 See the speech of Nyuta Federmesser at the special meeting of the Russian Human Rights Council on the observance of human rights in psychoneurological boarding homes on 25 June 2019. Available at: http://president-sovet.ru/presscenter/news/read/5612/

13 Similar reform is meant to be introduced for psychoneurological boarding schools (PNI); right now the relevant legislative documents are being processed. Although psychoneurological boarding homes for children generally fall into the jurisdiction of the Decree #481, its transformation is handled much more poorly (see report of Elena Alshanskaya at the special meeting of the Presidential Council for the Development of Civil Society and Human Rights on 24 June 2019. Available at: https://philanthropy.ru/news/2019/06/27/77461/)

14 These are children whose parents voluntarily put them into a boarding school for education, but keep their parental rights and continue to fulfil their parental responsibilities. This decision might be due to the small size of the settlement and the lack of schools in it, special needs of the child, or lack of inclusive schools nearby.

15 The estimate was announced by Deputy Chairman of the Government of the Russian Federation on social policy Tatyana Golikova at a meeting of the *Committee for guardianship in the social sphere* on 1 February 2019.

16 Here and later on we do not track separately the rarest institutions, such as children's homes – schools, non-government children's homes, and some others.
17 The *Rosstat* data are used to estimate the number of special children's homes for 0–3 year olds (initially, the statistics comes from the Ministry of Health and gathered within the statistical form No. 47; however, this is not publicly available).
18 Non-paid guardianship stands for families who take children for care and receive benefits assigned for children themselves, but no payments for their care services; while in paid guardianship, which might take different forms in Russia, families receive payments for their care services and have to some extent stricter scheme of reporting to social services. Although in Russia, these families are not necessarily professionally trained carers, children often stay with them permanently (up to 18 years old), not temporarily; further in the text we will be calling all types of paid guardianship *foster families*.
19 Official website of the Russian SOS-villages is https://sos-dd.ru/
20 This refers to the cases when transfer to family-based alternative care is being blocked for children with disabilities. One of the motives for such a practice is the will to keep the money within the system. There are a number of scandalous cases when five or more candidates were denied one after another on the most far-fetched reasons. As for now, it seems that it does not cause any reaction from the authorities; for example, www.pravmir.ru/ustinya-kak-budto-ponyala-mamyi-ne-budet-pochemu-organyi-opeki-otkazyivayut-vsem-potentsialnyim-roditelyam/.
21 Acknowledgements: This work is an output of a research project implemented as part of the Basic Research Program at the National Research University Higher School of Economics (HSE) and the state assignment by the RANEPA under the President of the Russian Federation, 2020.

References

In this volume

Chapter 6: Jäppinen and Kulmala

Allenova, O. 2018. *Uzniki internatov: o problemah regional'nyh detskih domov dlya detej s mental'noj invalidnost'yu* [Prisoners of Boarding Schools: On the Problems of Regional Orphanages for Children with Mental Disabilities]. *Ogonek* [Journal] 11: 20, published 26.03.2018.
Arthur, W.B. 1989. Competing Technologies, Increasing Returns, and Lock-In by Historical Events. *Economic Journal* 99 (394): 116–131.
Avdeeva, V.P., Rusakova, M.M. 2017. *Teoreticheskie osnovaniya i rezul'taty issledovaniya social'noj politiki v otnoshenii detej-sirot i detej, ostavshihsya bez popecheniya roditelej, v postsovetskih stranah* [Theoretical Foundations and Results of Studies of Social Policy in Relations between Orphans and Children without Parental Participation in Post-Soviet Countries]. *Peterburgskaya sociologiya segodnya* [Petersburg Sociology Today] 8.
Besschetnova, O. 2011. *Sirotstvo v Rossii: ot prizreniya k deinstitucionalizacii* [Orphanhood in Russia: From Surveillance to Deinstitutionalization]. *Sociologicheskie issledovaniya* [Social Studies] 11: 102–110.
Biryukova, S., Sinyavskaya, O.V. 2017. Children without Parental Care in Russia: What We Can Learn from the Statistics. *Journal of Social Policy Studies* 15 (3): 367–382.
David, P.A. 1985. Clio and the Economics of QWERTY. *American Economic Review* 75: 332–337.

Decree #481. 2014. Decree of the Government of the Russian Federation of May 24, 2014 No. 481 'On the Performance of Organizations for Orphanned Children and Children without Parental Care, and on Placement of Children in these Organizations' (*Postanovlenie Pravitel'stva Rossijskoj Federacii ot 24 maja 2014 g. N 481 g. Moskva 'O dejatel'nosti organizacij dlja detej-sirot i detej, ostavshihsja bez popechenija roditelej, i ob ustrojstve v nih detej, ostavshihsja bez popechenija roditelej '*). Available at: http://static.government.ru/media/files/41d4e0dc986dd6284920.pdf (accessed 30/03/2020).

Decree #588N. 2015. Decree of the Ministry of Labour of Russia of September 1, 2015 No. 588N 'On the Establishment of the Identity of Professional Activities Carried Out in Educational Organizations, Organizations Providing Social Services, and Medical Organizations in Which Orphans and Children Deprived of Parental Care Are Placed under Supervision' (*Prikaz Ministerstva truda i social'noj zashhity Rossijskoj Federacii ot 01.09.2015 No. 588N 'Ob ustanovlenii tozhdestvennosti professional'noj dejatel'nosti, vypolnjaemoj v obrazovatel'nyh organizacijah, organizacijah, okazyvajushhih social'nye uslugi, i medicinskih organizacijah, v kotorye pomeshhajutsja pod nadzor deti-siroty i deti, ostavshiesja bez popechenija roditelej '*). Available at: https://rusdocs.ru/pravovye-akty/mintrud-rossii/1201512010019-pravovye-akty- ministerstv-i-vedomstv (accessed 30/03/2020).

Dementieva, I. 1991. *Deti-siroty: problema vyzhivaniya* [Children without Parental Care: The Problem of Survival]. *Sociologicheskie issledovaniya* [Social Studies] (9): 72–77.

Draft of the Decree of the Government of the Russian Federation. 2019. *O vnesenii izmenenij v Polozhenie o deyatel'nosti organizacij dlya detej-sirot i detej, ostavshihsya bez popecheniya roditelej, i ob ustrojstve v nih detej, ostavshihsya bez popecheniya roditelej* [On Amending the Regulation on the Activities of Organizations for Orphans and Children Deprived of Parental Care, and on the Placements of Children Deprived of Parental Care] from 24.05.2019. Available at: https://regulation.gov.ru/p/91602 (accessed 30/03/2020).

Federal Law #48-FZ. 2008. Federal Law of April 24, 2008 No. 48-FZ 'On Custody and Guardianship' (*Federal'nyj zakon ot 24 aprelja 2008 goda No. 48-FZ 'Ob opeke i popechitel'stve '*). Available at: http://kremlin.ru/acts/bank/27263 (accessed 30/03/2020).

Fedstat. 2019. The Data from the Federal Statistical Services of Russian Federation for 2010, 2015, 2017, 2018 'On the Number of Childen's Homes' (*Chislo domov rebenka*). Available at: https://gks.ru/bgd/regl/b19_34/IssWWW.exe/Stg/03-04.doc (accessed 30/03/2020).

Fenyo, A., Knapp, M., Baines, B. 1989. Foster Care Breakdown: A Study of a Special Teenager Fostering Scheme. In: J. Hudson, B. Galaway (eds.), *The State as Parent*. NATO ASI Series (D: Behavioural and Social Sciences), Volume 53. Dordrecht: Springer: 315–329.

Foundation to Support Children. 2012. Report 'Children in Difficult Life Situations: Overcoming the Social Exclusion of Children Deprived of Parental Care', 2012 (*doklad 'Deti v trudnoj zhiznennoj situacii: preodolenie social'noj iskljuchitel'nosti detej-sirot', 2012*). Available at: www.aksp.ru/work/activity/nac_strateg/files/dokl.pdf (accessed 30/03/2020).

Government.ru. 2019. Speech of Deputy Chairman of the Government of the Russian Federation on Social Policy Tatyana Golikova at a Meeting of the Committee for Guardianship in the Social Sphere on February 1st. Available at: http://government.ru/news/35604/ (accessed 30/03/2020).

Kulmala, M., Rasell, M., Chernova, Z. 2017. Overhauling Russia's Child Welfare System: Institutional and Ideational Factors behind the Paradigm Shift. *The Journal of Social Policy Studies* 15 (3): 353–366.

Meyer, J.W., Rowan, B. 1977. Institutionalized Organizations: Formal Structure as Myth and Ceremony. *American Journal of Sociology* 83 (2): 340–363.

Ovcharova, L., Iarskaia-Smirnova, E. (eds.). 2010. *Faktory semeynogo neblagopoluchiya i mekhanizmy profilaktiki sotsial'nogo sirotstva: rezul'taty analiza i rekomendatsii* [Factors of Family Problems and Mechanisms of Prevention of Child Abandonment: Results of the Analysis and Recommendations]. Moscow: IISP.

Presidential Address. 2020. *Poslanie Presidenta RF Federalnomy sobraniyu ot 15.1.20* [Message from the President to the Federal Assembly from 15.1.20]. Available at: http://kremlin.ru/events/president/news/62582.

Presidential Council. 2019. Speech of Nyuta Federmesser at the Special Meeting of the Russian Human Rights Council on the Observance of Human Rights in Psychoneurological Boarding Homes on June 25th. Available at: http://president-sovet.ru/presscenter/news/read/5612/ (accessed 30/03/2020).

Suddaby, R., Greenwood, R. 2009. Methodological Issues in Researching Institutional Change. In: D.A. Buchanan, A. Bryman (eds.), *The Sage Handbook of Organizational Research Methods*. London: Sage Publications: 177–195.

Tyapkina, T. 2015. *Sirotstvo v SSSR: prichiny i obshchee sostoyanie problemy* [Orphanhood in the USSR: Causes and General State of the Problem]. *Evrazijskij Soyuz Uchenyh* [Eurasian Union of Scientists] 4–11 (13).

Williamson, J., Greenberg, A. 2010. *Families, Not Orphanages*. New York: Better Care Network.

3   The 'last-minute children'

Where did they come from, where will they go? Media portrayals of children deprived of parental care, 2006–2018

Elena Iarskaia-Smirnova, Olga Kosova, and Rostislav Kononenko

Introduction

In an article in the Russian newspaper *Rossiiskaya gazeta*, Nastya, a foster mother to several kids, is presented as the type of person who cannot stand to see suffering. Instead, following her heart, she moves to help children abandoned to the mercy of fate (Nesterova 2007). In the article, Nastya uses the term 'last-minute children' (*goryashchie deti*), which is taken from the expression for last-minute travel deals (*goryashchaya putyovka*). With this, she means these children appear suddenly in her life and are taken into her family due to their extremely desperate life situation (Nesterova 2007). In addition to the sense of sudden acquisition that also occurs with the last-minute travel deals, the literal meaning of '*goryashchie deti*' is 'burning kids', a very emotional and illuminative metaphor of pain and commitment, risk and sacrifice. It is associated with cases of child abuse and neglect, birth families being torn apart, foster parents making decisions to take the children into their families, processes of adaptation, and various conflicts and challenges faced by children and parents.

The preceding example is illustrative of media coverage of policies towards children deprived of parental care. The long-established Soviet tradition in these cases was for the state to care for these children in institutions. As noted in Chapter 1 of this volume, the process of deinstitutionalising care for children deprived of parents began to gather pace after, in his Address to the Federal Assembly of 2006, Russian President Vladimir Putin instructed the Government, together with the regions, to create a mechanism that would 'reduce the number of children in institutions', and strengthen financial support for foster families (Presidential Address 2006). Noting the increased number of foreign adoptions, he offered a somewhat negative assessment of the trend: 'the foreigners coming to our country, it seems to me, adopt far more children than people in our own country' (ibid). Thus, there is a clear contradistinction between 'us' and 'them' and a clear emphasis on 'our own people' as the preferred group. It can be said that the focus on foreign adoption provides a certain dramatic and emotional punch to the issue of adoption. In this light, foreign adoptions are presented as a negative way of solving the problem. In this chapter, we will consider how the print media reacted to this presidential message, what changes occurred to the image of those most involved in the deinstitutionalisation process, and how journalists framed articles on the key priorities and challenges in social policy.[1] We argue that media coverage of childcare policies legitimates the 'right' and 'wrong' agents and practices in the well-being of children deprived of parental care. By doing so, the media construct a social problem and thereby attempt to achieve control through the promotion of an 'us vs. them' discourse in Russian public discussions.

Terminology and theoretical approaches

The process of deinstitutionalising care for children deprived of their birth parents is systemic in nature and is progressing within a rapidly changing legal field. This process affects the rights and interests of not only children who have lost parental care but also their blood relatives and the new foster parents. In addition, a number of other bodies are involved in this, including social welfare agencies, child protection services (*organy opeki*), educational organisations, local government, health care institutions, law enforcement agencies, charitable foundations, and interested private citizens. The difficulties and controversies inherent to this deinstitutionalisation process are reflected in Russian sociopolitical discourse. The press does not limit its role to educating or emphasising the importance of these issues to the public. By placing these issues on the political agenda, supplying stories about children and families with expert commentaries, the media play an important role in determining what the state and society consider normal and what is, conversely, rejected as abnormal.

Texts, as Norman Fairclough argued, are part of social action: 'language is widely perceived as transparent, so that the social and ideological "work" that language does in producing, reproducing or transforming social structures, relations and identities is routinely "overlooked"' (Fairclough 1995: 203–209). Texts can provide evidence of social structures, processes, and relationships. A structured reading of newspaper articles can accurately capture the nature of social change; critical analysis of representations reveals how social control and dominance are achieved via the medium of media texts (Fairclough 1995).

In this study, we analysed the various ways Russian print media presents the deinstitutionalisation of child welfare. To do this, we focused on one state-owned newspaper and one private tabloid. The main objective in this media analysis was to uncover how the basic concepts of deinstitutionalisation were defined within a certain time period. What values are articulated by journalists in these articles, and how do they outline the boundaries of norms and deviations? How has the discourse of deinstitutionalisation developed over time and how do representations differ between broadsheets and tabloids? Using methods of quantitative and qualitative content analysis, we identified the key themes in the representation of children, families, professionals, and the state and also identified a number of discourses changing and evolving from 2006 to 2018 in the two newspapers. By articulating who is right and who is wrong, the media demarcates symbolic boundaries of social relations.

The method and design of the research

We chose to study two Russian print media sources, '*Rossiyskaya Gazeta*' (RG) and '*Komsomolskaya Pravda*' (KP), for three main reasons: (1) both have a high national circulation and distribution levels and issue daily editions; (2) both cover a wide range of social issues; and (3) as one is publicly owned and the other is private, so we could compare discourses in each media context. RG is the daily official publication of Russian Government. It covers sociopolitical issues, publishes federal laws with editorial comments, and specialises in news and analytical reviews. KP is a privately owned tabloid that offers readers news stories on politics, sports, economics, society, and science. When developing our research design, we assumed that, due to differing editorial policies in the two papers, not only the frequency, volume, and the news topic of articles would differ, but also the differences in style would emerge. Differences in how the deinstitutionalisation of child welfare was represented in these two newspapers allowed us to come to certain conclusions about the varying strategies deployed to construct this social problem in public discourse. However, as we will show, both newspapers play an outstanding role in shaping and rooting the discourses of right and wrong, 'us and them', while using various approaches in channelling the official viewpoint and shaping the public opinion. By determining what the state and society consider normal and what is to avoid or reject, the media shape the individual choices and promote and legitimate public agenda.

We analysed editions of RG and KP from 2006, the year of President Putin's Address to the Federal Assembly, up to 2018. In examining the large number of articles selected for analysis, a programme called *Medialogy* was used, which was an effective way of searching texts of the selected publications over a given time period according to certain keywords (Medialogia 2019). All publications on child welfare published in RG and KP over this time were selected for analysis. The final sample amounted to 218 articles: 90 in RG and 128 in KP. During the quantitative content analysis stage, we developed a coding sheet that recorded the output and authorship of articles, the news topic, how children were represented, whether birth or foster families were mentioned and what role they were assigned, and the presence or absence of references to the activities of child protection services and other authorities. The frequency and percentage distribution for each code were calculated and a comparative analysis of the publications was carried out. During the qualitative content analysis stage, we conducted open and axial coding of the full texts of selected analytical articles. In addition, the codes were systematised and thematic clusters were identified. The total number of articles for qualitative content analysis was 56, including 49 in RG and 7 in KP.

The development of the deinstitutionalisation discourse in print media: publication statistics and news topics

Over the past 13 years, materials on the issues of deinstitutionalisation appeared fairly evenly in RG, while there was a peak period (2010–2013) in KP where a number of articles were published drawing attention to these issues. It is worth noting that 2013 was the peak in the number of articles in both newspapers: 34 in KP and 13 in RG (Figure 3.1).

Shifts in editorial interest towards care for children who are deprived of parents can be explained by the general context of Russian sociopolitical life presented in other chapters of this book. As RG is a newspaper whose essential function is to showcase new developments in state policy, it is not surprising its articles have a great deal of material on new directions and implementations in government programmes.

Among the materials we examined in KP, 84% were related to stories on individual cases of children, deprived of parental care, who were still in state institutions looking for a new family. As a media partner in the social project *detskii vopros* (The Question of Children), which was established by *Radio Rossii* and ran until 2016, KP published profiles of child from institutions in different Russian regions and articles on the visits of prospective foster parents to children's homes covered within the framework of a charity event entitled 'The Train of Hope' (*Poezd nadezhdy*). In addition to covering *detskii vopros*, KP articles also focused on higher profile cases, such as stories about large foster families or charity events. The official state discourse was also present, particularly in sharing the results of workshops or the press conferences of state officials, changes in legislation, and in discussions on the deinstitutionalisation of care for children being brought up in various forms of children's homes.

Unsurprisingly for a tabloid, KP articles are more emotionally coloured, and often urge some call to action. Frequently written in the first person, these articles try to draw the reader into the topic. Despite using stereotypes on the birth

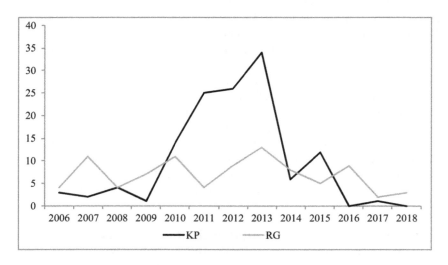

Figure 3.1 Publications on deinstitutionalisation issues in RG and KP according to year and frequency from 2006 to 2018.

families of children who were placed in the institutions, these articles also attempt to elicit a response from the reader and draw public attention to the issue of children deprived of parental care. In addition, KP published a series of special reports that gave a voice to children and adolescents in state institutions, something that made the discourse livelier and more dynamic. KP articles are, however, often full of jargon, stereotyped conclusions, and a range of assertions that are rarely backed by statistics or expert opinion.

In contrast to KP, in RG articles, the tendency is to use a high-profile case as the launchpad for a broader discussion of the issue, leading to general conclusions and recommended possible solutions, such as guidelines for state policy and desirable legislative changes. Although RG does have some emotionally loaded articles with catchy titles to rival a tabloid, in general, an official style is usually employed, and the opinions of experts, officials, and foster parents are often showcased. The sensationalist descriptions applied to certain cases and the simplified interpretation of broader issues observable in these newspapers appear to perform a key function: the media enters the arena of child protection politics, becoming even more influential than professionals in this field. In the literature, this phenomenon is described as 'legislation by tabloid' (Goddard, Saunders 2001).

Media representation of children deprived of parental care

The vast majority of KP articles concerned the fate of one (65%) or two (12%) children at a time. In comparison, 86% of the RG articles considered children deprived of parental care in general, rather than focusing on concrete cases or life stories. With regard to the gender of the children, journalists more often made mention of boys (37% of the total number of articles, 53% in KP in comparison to 14% in RG) than girls, or simply did not mention the gender of the children (37%). According to Veronica Oslon (cited in Zakharova 2014), an expert in child protection policy, boys more often end up without parental care than girls. Furthermore, girls are more often taken in by foster families, due to the popular gender stereotype that girls are more obedient and show more caring behaviour. Thus, the newspapers replicate these statistics and at the same time, reproduce these beliefs.

Another important dimension of the child's image is her/his age. If in 2009 younger children were more often showcased in the business card section, where the children are advertised for potential foster/adopting parents, later teenagers took their place, as the age of children featured in the paper generally increased over the period studied. In addition, the topic of sibling adoption was given more attention, encouraging potential foster parents to adopt sisters and brother together from one institution.

On the whole, articles in both RG and KP were far less likely to mention older children, such as those aged 15–18 years, with only 4% of the total number of analysed articles covering this age group. This minimal attention to children deprived of parental care on the edge of adulthood can be explained by two background factors: (1) a preference to avoid discussing the difficult fate awaiting this group who are the least likely to find a foster family due to their older age; and (2) the fact that changes to child welfare in recent years have not focused on helping this age group. As a result, this oldest group of children ended up being largely forgotten and left outside the media discourse.

A fifth of the total number of our data set focused on child health problems; RG carried more of these articles (28%) than KP (15%). In presenting the health care issues of children, we identified three main themes in reports: (1) the occurrence of severe congenital or acquired diseases in infancy that cause disability and the abandonment of the child by the birth family; (2) chronic diseases resulting from a lack of proper care; and (3) the illegal and unethical procedures of the managers and doctors at institution facilities, such as forcible treatment or giving children an inaccurate diagnosis of their condition and subsequently incorrectly designating them as disabled. The coverage of health problems in these newspapers highlighted the special vulnerability of these children and the need for additional attention to their plight and increased public intervention. During quantitative content analysis, we identified three main discourses on children deprived of parental care in RG and KP articles: pity, social responsibility, and danger (Figure 3.2).

In KP, the discourse of pity is most dominant; 86% of KP articles reproduce the image of a lonely child, forced to fight for the love and attention of adults, thrown into a difficult life situation at a very tender age, and desperately in need of parental warmth and protection. The main discourse in RG was the social responsibility on the role of state and society towards such children; 71% of their articles point to the need to change the lives of children given the socially dangerous situation in which they find themselves. The third discourse, that of danger, presents children

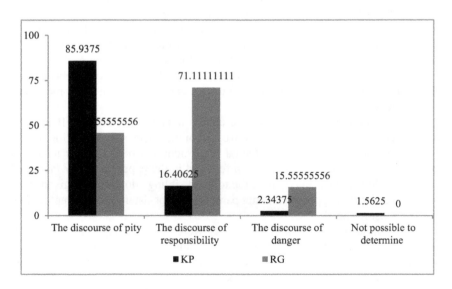

Figure 3.2 Types of discourse in RG and KP (%).

deprived of parental care as potentially dangerous social elements (RG 16%; KP 2%). This discourse typically focuses on criminal offences committed by them, or emphasises the aggressive and dangerous elements of their behaviour, which appear to go unpunished. Here children are presented as a threat to public law and order. If we consider how these discourses have evolved over time, a clear shift from the discourse of danger to the discourse of responsibility is observable in RG. In contrast, the discourse of pity remained consistent in KP across this period.

The policy of deinstitutionalisation: the role of the state in caring for children

The role of state authorities and officials in the life of children is often elaborated in RG, while the vast majority (84%) of KP materials did not pick up this discussion (Figure 3.3). As one of the immediate tasks of RG editorial office is to publicise state policy, it is no surprise that most of the RG articles are framed through the prism of evaluating state initiatives and the activities of officials. Negative representations of state officials as too bureaucratically minded and indifferent to the issues of childcare were also rare (RG: 9%; KP: 4%), as were cases when the state was shown to actually hinder the process of placing the child into foster families or adoption. In the majority of the analysed articles, state policy was taken at face value; it is represented as child-centred and officials are seen to protect the interests of children and ensuring their well-being (RG: 71%; KP: 9%).

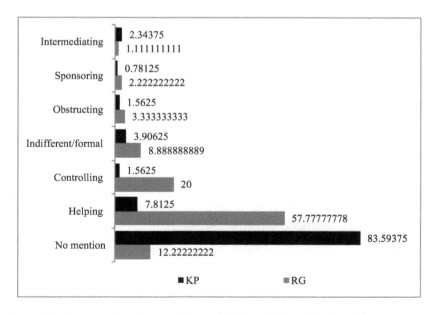

Figure 3.3 Representation of the state's role in RG and KP publications (%).

The overwhelming majority of KP materials reproduced the argument in favour of a transition to raising children in foster families, which is seen to be better given the apparent inability of state institutions to achieve a fuller socialisation of children. RG articles present deinstitutionalisation in a broader way, focusing on issues such as (1) the forms and mechanisms behind the placement of children in foster families; (2) changes to upbringing in institutions, such as the creation of new-style institutions; and (3) the need to help families in situations of high social risk in order to keep them together.

In comparison to the RG, KP's treatment of the need to raise children in families was explained on different grounds. Namely, that the traditional configuration of the family was the best place for providing the thing such children and young adults need most – love. RG articles tended to focus on economic reasoning: keeping children in institutions was more expensive in budgetary terms than providing substantial material support to foster and birth families. In the latter case, preventing family dysfunction and preserving family units was claimed to reduce the number of children requiring institutional or foster family placement.

The dynamics of editorial interest in the issue of deinstitutionalisation of children is linked to changes in the general sociopolitical discourse in the country. This can involve discussions of high-profile cases, such as that of Dima Yakovlev (see Chapter 1 by Kulmala et al.), or coverage of systemic problems, such as how institution staff struggle to cope with teenagers (see Chapter 4 by Kulmala et al.). It can also include how sensible current state spending on children's institutions is, analysis of new legislative initiatives, and reviews of how new strategies are being implemented, such as the closing of institutions and the encouragement of new forms of foster family care. RG discourse responds more subtly to the changing political context and, while carefully capturing virtually every change, the overall dominant and consistent discourse is that of social responsibility for children deprived of parental care. The discourse of deinstitutionalisation in KP is more heterogeneous, developing in two directions: firstly, the 'business card' format, which is designed to elicit reader sympathy for children (the discourse of pity); secondly, a situational discourse responding to high-profile stories that discuss public responsibility for child welfare and raised the fear that their upbringing was being left unattended.

Thematic clusters in newspapers

This section examines the results of our qualitative content analysis and considers the thematic changes that have occurred in the presentation of deinstitutionalisation of care for children deprived of parents in the Russian media. Based on this qualitative analysis, we identified the following thematic clusters: (1) reasons for children to go into the institutions or foster/adopting families; (2) the various justification motifs of policy towards children deprived of parental care; and (3) increase of scepticism towards foster families. As we shall see, in these clusters, the 'we-they' discourse is constructed along several sociopolitical divides.

By shaping these discourses, the mass media influence public opinion and legitimate political decisions in area of child welfare and family policy.

The reasons children leave their birth families

Such articles drew attention to the fact that many children with living parents are sleeping rough in Russia's streets and institutions. A 2013 RG article contains an interesting quote from Russia's then Children's Rights Commissioner Pavel Astakhov[2] on the causes of this phenomenon:

> firstly, social orphans are the product of antisocial families . . . . Secondly, they [social orphans] are a product of a family who fell into a difficult, life crisis situation. . . . The third source is the failure of many fathers and mothers in providing an upbringing, the loss of the traditions. . . or even just parental indifference. The fourth [source] is psychological and material unpreparedness for motherhood . . . of those who abandon their child.
>
> (Bryntseva 2013)

One journalist pinpointed three causes that, 'according to one study' (source not cited), explain abandonment in maternity hospitals: (i) the personal characteristics of the mother; (ii) the social situation of the mother; (iii) the presence or absence of expanded family support and the financial situation of the mother (Karandyuk, Zashirinskaya 2013). In these explanations, the role of structural factors such as poverty and unemployment are noted. On the other hand, these causes are individualised in separate cases and such 'privatisation' of social problems leads to the stigmatisation of the families in question while deeper systemic failures in the family and childhood support system remain unacknowledged.

One symptomatic case was the treatment of a large-scale sociological study conducted by the Institute of Sociology. This study was presented in one article in RG that discussed the causes of maternal abandonment of children in terms of intrafamily limitations (Dobrynina 2012). As reported in the RG article, the researchers of this project, which was based on more than 200 qualitative interviews with foster parents, argued: 'the roots must be sought a generation deeper. More than half of people deprived of lacked any conception of what a normal, full-fledged and friendly family should be; they had no role models in their childhood' (ibid).

In several articles, journalists construct categories of children in institutions: those with serious disabilities; those with criminal pasts. These categories of children are seen as very unlikely to be adopted. Apparently, there is a great need for special professionally trained foster parents who can take such children, but this need is not acknowledged in press. Instead, according to Astakhov, institutions will always be needed because 'there are children who can only live in institution facilities, such as severely disabled people who need special medical care or juvenile delinquents' (Bryntseva 2013; see Chapter 4 by Kulmala et al. of this volume). Such children are deemed to be suitable for family life on a selective basis. This concept of selective deinstitutionalisation resembles a sieve with holes through which children fall and do not end up in families. In fact, this brings us to another theme, the inevitability of institutional care, basically due to under-professionalisation in the area of foster family or adoption practices, lack of supporting agents and specialists qualified to provide assistance.

A number of articles present juvenile delinquents from institutions as unsuitable for family or even normal adult life. Here the focus is on children who pose a risk to others. A 2010 KP article described one institution, located in a 'village forgotten by God', with practices similar to prison life. The children steal, manipulate, and intimidate adults; they work for both criminal gangs and the authorities:

> [I]f it can be said that a child from a prosperous family who steals money from dad to buy some sweets can grow up and become wiser, then these guys are stuck on a bad road. They have already chosen it. Or, rather, it was chosen for them.
>
> (Tokareva 2010)

Thus, the author writes about the stigma of institutions and the children that no one needs, and society is in a hurry to get rid of them by sending them to some kind of correctional facility. Incompetent specialists are presented as only working in institutions due to a hopeless sense of no other alternatives. The focus of this chapter is not foster families or post-institutional adaptation; instead it examines the actors who are influential in the fate of the children such as the institution director, social educators, state investigators, as well as criminal gang leaders. The article actually reads as a sad diagnosis of the reproduction of social structure and the downward social mobility children sent to such places suffer.

The studied newspapers rarely mention the issues of family placement for children with severe disabilities, chronic illnesses, or difficult behaviour. This might be because there are only a few such foster families in Russia which possess the necessary skills, knowledge, and experience of adopting these children. Thus, the only solution, according to these media sources, is to keep such children in institutions permanently, something also discussed in the next chapter of this volume.

The various justification motifs of policy towards children deprived of parental care

A second group of articles focuses on the benefits of foster families over institutional forms. In these articles, several arguments explaining the emergence of foster families were noticeable: economic, administrative, and cultural. Arguments based on an economic rationale are quite simple and convincing: 'As practice has shown, this is beneficial for everyone. Parents, get a kind of employment opportunity, children are brought up in a family, and the region saves a lot by investing less money' (Vyazov 2006). Transferring children to a foster family is three times cheaper than keeping them in institutions (Filimonova 2008). However, in order to bring these calculations to life, not only material resources are needed, but also effective administration, a normally functioning executive branch, and also the personal will of the leadership. Family placement policy is organised at the regional level, and due to this fact, journalists noticed the issue of regional inequality, contrasting the 'relatively prosperous and well-fed capital' with other Russian regions (Danilova 2006).

Themes of criticism and competition are not uncommon in representing regional experience of policy administration. Family actors in the regions are most often the governor, sometimes the church and NGOs. When poorly performing regions are mentioned in these articles, this can be interpreted as an attack on the local authorities and result in bad PR for the regional officials involved. Strong regions are those who can be seen as pioneers in a process towards family replacements who have actively taken a course in this right direction. Their great experience, capacity for managing processes, and the courage to take on new, complex and unique tasks are praised. Interestingly, the economic condition of the region is not a determining factor. Thus, the discourse of economic efficiency spills over and flows into the discourse on the managerial abilities of the regional authorities, and it is also complemented by motives of political loyalty as well as the governor's commitment to the goals formulated by the country's political leader Vladimir Putin.

Here we find another reason why metaphor of 'last-minute children' is a good characterisation of how deinstitutionalisation has started out in Russia: when regional leaders are suddenly given a new task and had to achieve quick results, they are forced to keep up the pace in order not to lag behind or stand accused of not understanding or taking seriously the directives set by the ruling party and the president. The priorities of this period were to increase institution closures and transfer more children to Russian families. By accelerating this work in ways similar to the last-minute deals of the tourist industry, by the end of the period in question, 'good results' were achieved. After this progress along the road of deinstitutionalisation was made, the phenomenon of 'last-minute children' started to fade away and, in parallel, new measures emerged placing barriers around adoption processes.

The topic of children deprived of parental care is a policy and a political field in which agents of varying forms with differing resources compete with each other. Discussions on the problems of children in institutional care can open up an opportunity to criticise the opposition, which, for example, opposed the 'Dima Yakovlev law'. This is one way to justify the stances of the ruling party United Russia:

Unfortunately, as we expected, opposition leaders simply used children as an excuse to attack the regime. All their pity for orphans (siroty) and the terrible concern that they showed during their demonstrations immediately disappeared when new topics came up. Have you heard anything about the assistance to children without parental care provided by Kasyanov, Nemtsov, Gudkov, Akhedzhakova or other organizers of the march against the Dima Yakovlev law? Have they shown their support for institutions and foster families? At the same time, United Russia, which they hate so much, formed a working group that over the course of these two years addressed specific problems.

(Isaev 2014)

In many RG materials, normative judgements such as these are presented in the form of quotes from authorities figures such as regional officials. To give one example, the governor of Samara region, Konstantin Titov, who was behind the creation of Russia's first foster care institute, provided his own positive PR for those currently in power: 'our experience proves that children from foster families adapt back into society without serious problems. . . . In other words, our investment in care is paying off on a very large scale' (Vyazov 2006).

Children in foster care are shown to be objects of concern for the state, care specialists, and foster parents. They are also presented as the victims of negligent birth parents or sexually perverted guardians. Along with these discourses of paternalism and victimisation, there is also less frequently observed discourse of subjectivity, responsibility, and independence. As a rule, in these cases, the topic is adopted teenage children who, in the course of growing up and becoming independent, show character, perseverance, and determination while retaining close emotional and physical ties with their foster family (Shepeleva 2011).

A final theme in justifying the benefits of foster families refers to cultural characteristics. A series of articles outline the advantages or features of Russian culture. These are complemented by articles on the good and bad things about life overseas. Journalists not only explain the formal meaning of the foster family to the readers, but also try to position the institution of foster family in the context of Russia's traditions, mentality, and culture, which is seen to be better than what can be found in the West. One special feature of the 'Russian mentality' highlighted in the newspapers is the idea that with Russian foster families, bonds become almost as close as that of original birth families. To take one quote,

experts say, nine out of ten foster families [in Russia] are no different from ordinary ones. In European countries where the institution of a foster family is being developed, such as in England, this kind of development is viewed negatively and equated with malfunction . . . but in Russia things are different.

(Vyazov 2006)

On the other hand, activists and civil society leaders criticise Russian culture for its selfishness and indifference towards such issues. One philanthropist, well known for her assistance to the children who are homeless and placed in the institutions, Elizaveta Glinka (known as Dr. Lisa) penned an article in RG on the decline in morals and the rise of indifference in Russian society to the fate of children (Glinka 2011). With the help of her blog and other media, she manages to attract public attention to the problems of those under her care, breaking typical patterns in attitudes towards such 'children of nobody'.

Given the multi-ethnic composition as well as economic and urban–rural differences of the Russian Federation, it comes as no surprise to find family values and attitudes towards institutional care for children vary strongly from region to region. Picking up on such differences, one journalist noted that many families in the North Caucasus have a large number of children despite their very modest economic situations. The journalist claims in this region that 'there is traditionally a special relationship between children and families, and there were practically no orphanages' (Kulikov 2010). In other words, children in the institutions are a rarity because relatives are always on hand to look after such children. At the same time, the local culture may support an increase of children left behind in the Caucasus: 'If an unmarried Caucasian woman gives birth to a child, this is perceived as a disgrace to a family and results in serious social obstructions, especially in rural areas' (Larina 2007). However, as the number of children in institutional care increased in Chechnya due to armed conflicts and terrorist attacks, new shelters and rehabilitation centres were opened. The picture of the 'traditional Caucasus' presented in the media allows us to reconstruct a contradictory field of relationships between women and children, family and children deprived of parental care. Different ideologies compete for dominance in this question. At the heart of these contradictions is the tension between tradition and modernisation, familiar and new ways of solving social problems, all of which occurs alongside the painful legacies of recent military conflicts and the measures implemented by the current regimes of these republics.

In contrast to the North Caucasus, it would appear that 'Russian culture' is not quite as traditional. On the other hand, Russian culture is not quite as modern as 'the standards of the West'. Liberal values in particular are often subjected to criticism on the pages of the Russian press. In these articles, Russian culture is seen to have nothing against corporal punishment of children, although it does oppose gender equality. One RG article covered parliamentary hearings on a national action plan for children (Novikov 2012). The meeting was addressed by the Deputy Secretary General of the Council of Europe, Maud de Boer-Buquicchio, who gave a speech on the campaign to prevent corporal punishment in Europe in 2008 and the 'One in Five' programme to combat sexual violence. These speeches elicited a cold response in Russia: the then Children's Rights Commissioner Pavel Astakhov noted that Europe was legalising adoption for same-sex couples, but that those behind the 'One in Five' initiative were driven by politically correct motives and run by 'asexual green creatures'.[3] He continued: 'We have our own heroes such as Ivan Tsarevich or Ivan the Fool' and opposed the idea that Russia would cravenly copy the strategies in these new European models (Novikov 2012). Although the topic of forbidding corporal punishment was not mentioned in the article, what can be seen is a symbolic division between 'our' and 'their' cultures in childcare issues.

Another concept and value system presented as 'alien' was juvenile justice. In a 2010 RG article, narratives on child welfare were dramatised by a focus on 'improper' sexual education, with a particular concept of foster care being demonised, that of *patronat* families:

> One of the most important premises of juvenile care is the sexual education of children. Here the concept of sex is being replaced by that of gender. A whitepaper along these lines on gender equality has been registered in our State Duma. The proposed legislation forbids criticism of those with a non-traditional sexual orientation and promotes freedom in sexual choice. In fact, it is proposed to remove references to 'boy' and 'girl' as such imposed gender (polovaya) self-identification is considered harmful.
>
> (Kozlova 2013)

In conclusion, the journalist applied the adjective 'juvenile' to these measures on gender equality, *patronat* families,[4] and public control of children in institutional care. The policy of replacing families with *patronat* families is declared to be alien to Russian traditions and culture (Kozlova 2013). From the point of view of the experts quoted in the article, the European concept of 'juvenile justice' represents the family as the main enemy of children and elevates the rights of children to a higher plain than the rights of other citizens (Kozlova 2013). The then Children's Rights Commissioner Astakhov noted the inapplicability of many European methods for solving problems of the modern family and children deprived of their birth parents' care in a Russian context. This is explained with reference to the way such measures profoundly contradict Russia's 'historical, cultural, national traditions in the rearing and upbringing of children' (Borisenko 2013).

A series of articles can be grouped into 'Foreign Adoption' cluster, which largely focus on the negative characteristics of parents from outside of Russia. Such articles can be found in both RG and KP. The Public Prosecutor's Office of Russia conducted special inspections; corruption in the field of child protection services was detected in many regions. Moreover, informal payments were required not only from foreign adoptive parents but also from Russian citizens. Being in the state's care was compared to a 'circle of hell' (RG: Kulikov 2010). The culprits were exposed and punished, and those foreign foster parents involved were shown the door: 'Our state told the French: Halt! It is time for us to check whether this is all above board' (KP: Ryabtsev 2007). Nevertheless, journalists at that time sympathised with children who 'as a result of the prosecutor's office campaign lost all hope of becoming happy' speak out in terms of children's rights and from the point of view of children: 'The state did not understand that orphans are not goods that can be confiscated at the border, or thrown into the warehouse until the end of investigations. Orphans cannot wait. For them, each year is an eternity' (ibid).

The drama in the stories has grown starker over time, with violence and murder becoming hot news topics. In an article published shortly after the adoption of the so-called Dima Yakovlev law, criticism of foreign adoption revolved mainly around homophobic arguments. The subheading of the article reads: 'French gays will never receive Russian orphans' (Bryntseva, Yakovleva 2013). Inappropriate foreign foster parents were again identified in 2014 in the governmental decree; these included not only same-sex couples but also unmarried citizens in states where gay marriage is legally permitted (Barshev 2014). Thus, such countries are marked with a negative connotation, underlining the point that relations with such countries is deeply problematic.

In stories on foreign adoptions, images of 'foreign countries' are clearly constructed. Media portraits of states, both positive and negative, can influence public opinion about international relations, as well as contribute to the formation of national identity. Foreign adoption is a central topic in deinstitutionalisation of child welfare. Journalists have used this particular thematic field as a way to argue what constitutes 'correct' upbringing strategies, political decisions, as well as 'correct' citizens and politician behaviour. The search for 'who is to blame' begins with foreign adoptive parents, and then shifts towards domestic actors in the field of adoption and juvenile justice.

In the material we studied, journalists raised questions about regional inequality and the effectiveness of regional officials. They suggested that poverty and unemployment were among the systemic causes of 'social orphanhood'. But in considering this problem, intersectionality is important[5]: while foster families are more affluent, birth families are usually poorer; helping the more successful and affluent is always easier than assisting the poor and neglected. So far, the inequality between birth and foster families is not considered as an issue.

Foster families: scepticism and an increase in monitoring

At the beginning of the period we analysed, a question rose in the newspapers: how to find parents for a child; how to fit 'potential parents' with 'left-behind children?' (Nesterova 2007). Here a clear tendency towards the glorification of foster families can be noticed. Consider such stories as the heroic tractor driver and teacher foster parents who brought up ten foster children, or the eight children adopted by a locksmith and a teacher (Vladimirov 2007). These stories are always strongly personalised and include the names of the heroes.

At the same time, criticism towards foster families is noticeable in our selection. In 2006, one KP article, which covered Health Minister Mikhail Zurabov's proposal to distribute children without parental care among foster families, showed a fair amount of scepticism and even cynicism towards the policy decisions made and imposed 'from above'. By personifying a political decision and trivialising a complex process, the journalist in question transforms the issue under discussion into nothing more than an incident, or the strange initiative of Minister Zurabov. A central reason for such scepticism is a lack of faith in the potential and good will of ordinary citizens: 'Are there really so many foster families in our country who are materially and psychologically prepared to adopt such children?' (Danilova 2006). Along with stigmatising the children coming from institutions, the journalist also implicitly raises the problem of the kind of special training needed for foster parents.

Later, in the 2010s, more and more articles appeared on the actual return statistics of children from foster families. The reasons for such returns in these articles include the non-disclosure to foster or future adopting parents of vital information on the child that then come to light (Egorov 2015), the inaction of the foster care authorities, and low trust towards them on the part of foster families (Lebedeva 2018). Indeed, foster parents must know the key details in the adopted child's case history in order to decide if they are to be able to provide the necessary assistance. However, far less attention is paid to the deficiencies of state system of professional support for foster families. Moreover, there appears to be no expectation of any real support: 'people do not trust the adoption and the child protection services as they are concerned they may take the child back off them, and so are afraid to contact them for help' (ibid).

While the discourse around foster parents is shifting, economic support for foster families has become more controversial over time. While in the beginning, the matter of economic support for such families was presented as a necessary measure, through the years, the foster family is increasingly facing stigmatisation: when it is discussed in the context of its professionalisation and paid work, relationships between foster parent and child are often pictured in contractual terms rather than those of human feelings and warmth. As one journalist put it, 'there are public apprehensions that the children would be taken under guardianship not because of love to them, but for remuneration' (Gritsyuk 2014). By 2018, these arguments had only become sharper. At a discussion in the Russian Civic Chamber, the opinion was voiced that the state should stop encouraging potential foster parents with cash incentives: 'There should be no paid guardianship. If you want to adopt children from orphanages, please do but bring them up as you would a blood relative' (Krivyakina 2018).

A number of RG publications in 2010s covered the issues of 'foster family' and the 'child protection services' in terms of criminal activities. One child protection services official was convicted for the death of a child killed by his foster parents when the official had ignored the warnings of the local kindergarten. News coverage of child abuse in the news raises public awareness and helps people understand the importance of such situations and prevent future tragedies (Saint-Jacques et al. 2011). Meanwhile, in covering stories on children dying at the hands of fosters parents, journalists do not mention the problem of corporal punishment. The issue of corporal punishment enters the focus of public attention from time to time, being a matter of conflict of interests of proponents and opponents of child-centred approach (see Iarskaia-Smirnova, Romanov 2015).

In one 2017 RG publication, the term 'punitive child protection services' (*karatel'naya opeka*) was used: this refers to the growing number of cases where foster children were being taken back out of foster families in the southern regions, which were previously referred to as strongholds of the traditional strong family (Lebedeva, Yakovleva 2017). The words 'worn-out jeans' and 'half-empty refrigerator' have become memes' (Lebedeva, Yakovleva 2017).

Recently, the theme of foster family oversight has only intensified further. In August 2018, the Ministry of Education introduced a bill to limit the number of children in foster and adoptive families to no more than three. Another limitation was that each foster family can only adopt a maximum of one child per year (Lebedeva 2018). On the other hand, the bill does not address the quality of the work done by support services and child protection to foster families. KP articles take a typically emotional tone: 'We will tighten it up – I mean really tighten it up – the selection of these so-called parents' is how one KP journalist conveys the words of the Minister of Education (Konyukhova 2018). Indeed, in this short piece, the verb 'tighten up' is repeated four times. The same article also notes the Minister's rejection of the idea that people who are HIV positive should be allowed to adopt children.

Another journalist gives quote from a ministry spokesperson: 'We do not transfer orphans to families for them to die there!' (Krivyakina 2018). Meanwhile, another monitoring mechanism – the psychological testing of family members – is said to be introduced. There are, however, no proven methods for determining whether a person can become a good foster parent (ibid).

By the end of the period under review in this chapter, articles appeared that show how issue of foster family oversight has entered the public arena, where the various state and non-state actors battle it out. On the whole, KP and RG articles are silent with regard to inadequate support resources for foster families. Instead, the focus is on the need for oversight of foster families, the search for those to blame, and ways they can be punished. The increasingly serious problem of children returning from foster or adopting families back to institutional care may largely be explained due to the lack of supporting agents and helping professionals in the first place.

The changing representations in these media sources moved from generally positive coverage to more critical content, something that reflects opinions in the state elite but does not refer to public opinion (Levada centre 2017). Although many new aspects of child welfare have become part of media reports, controversial and challenging topics are not examined by journalists in such a way as to present both sides. Instead, complex issues are reduced into simplified, unambiguous interpretations.

Images of children in care differed in the two newspapers. While RG presents a generalised image of children placed into an institution or foster care or adoption, which requires care and management from the side of the state, KP articles offered a more personalised picture of children's life apart from their birth families. These contained more details and personal experiences, but tended to focus more on boys than girls, while adolescents over 15 years of age were practically excluded from the KP discourse. Birth parents who give their children up for adoption were often presented as infantile or socially dysfunctional people disinterested in raising their children and whose effect on children is largely detrimental. After the child is removed from the birth family, almost all communication ceases, and parents are excluded from the picture.

Overall, KP articles offered a more positive treatment of the role foster parents play in the fate of children: foster families are presented as loving, responsible, and prosperous, as well as ready to show patience and bring about positive changes in the life of the child. RG representations of foster parents are more mixed: alongside positive examples, we also found stories of foster parents returning children to state care institutions, as well as cases of abuse or foster parents whose main interest in adoption was material gain. Given RG's designated role in the transmission of official state policy, it is no surprise they often present the issue of childcare as a matter of state responsibility. Quotes from the president, various ministers, the Children's Rights Commissioner, and scientists, all come together to give the impression the problem is being handled by experts. This has the effect of somewhat blurring the issue and pushing it out to the margins; if the problem is being managed by 'experts', then it can be presented to the reader as not so urgent. Meanwhile, the results of public opinion surveys, the views of foster parents, and the children themselves are rarely heard. In comparison, KP has more personal stories with an emphasis on feelings, although, all the same, there are still references to the strong hand of the state administration.

Conclusion

The deinstitutionalisation of child welfare in the Russian Federation is not yet complete and the full transition to exclusively family forms of childcare has not yet been possible. Therefore, while the discourse on children deprived of parental care has become less intense than in the West, it is still present in the Russian case. This chapter has considered the print media coverage of the issues of children in foster care or adoption and shown how social control and dominance are conducted via media texts. The issue of children in care moves the intimate field of close family relations into the public domain, where the state plays the main role, thereby making the problem social and public: a clear case of 'legislation by tabloid' (Franklin, Lavery 1989: 26).

One key finding of this study is that the development of a 'we-they' discourse in the Russian public reflection of childcare policies is represented in motives of foreign adoption and the highlighting of 'right' and 'wrong' agents and practices in the well-being of children. The cultural values behind childhood protection are legitimised and reproduced by the mass media, shaping ideological concepts behind a decent upbringing, as well as demarcating the symbolic boundaries of the nation. In the case of the latter, references to specific foreign countries are revealing, as well as the interrelationship between new foster care policies and the ideological hostility to the 'alien' concept of juvenile justice. Hostility is also directed towards *patronat* parents in Russia, then to the concept of juvenile justice, and, finally, to those who have adopted a large number of children. Discussions of controversial points and contradictions tend towards the clash between conservative and liberal discourses. The language deployed in this debate may be influencing how the public perceives the rights of children in care, both as part of the national political agenda and, in a more negative manner, as an alien phenomenon that is handled with a slightly condescending tone, occasional sarcasm, and a sense that it is all a kind of perversion.

A second clear point emerging from this study is that many children are on the margins; as the metaphor of 'last-minute' children, raised in one article, shows that they are only adopted unexpectedly and, in many cases, not at all. With time changes came to the statistics and the number of children in institutions dramatically fell by the end of the 2010s. Children with serious disabilities or illnesses, as well as older children, however, still struggle to find families.

A third vital point is that, while children find themselves in a situation where the responsibility for their upbringing and well-being is shared between many agents, there are still many blind spots: places where responsibility is either absent or is replaced by an abuse of power. Some themes are missing or very rarely mentioned in the studied press: professionalisation of care that relates to children's rights, the supporting role of psychologists, social workers, etc. This lack of such topics as professional help might mean that the issues of foster care and adoption are shared between the families and the bureaucrats. In spite of the involvement of social welfare agencies and child protection services (*organy opeki*), the field itself is not sufficiently professionalised. Practice of evaluating and improving care programmes is deserving of more attention and should be studied in future research. Regardless of the emotional tone behind their presentation, children are generally treated as an object than a subject of social relations, victims of circumstances, the decisions of their birth parents, or the deficiencies of state upbringing.

Finally, while there are differences in approaches to the topic in terms of genres, the level of emotional expression, and analytic boldness, in general these two newspapers rather complement each other: one being official organ of the state and another translating more popular voice, both use various ways to translate official view on deinstitutionalisation.

The metaphor of 'last-minute' children brings with it the sense of feverish rush, a 'last chance', as well as unexpected luck. But there is also the chance of failure and trauma, the sense of great risk. Thus, the topic of adoption and 'social orphanhood' is highly dramatised in Russia today. Given the childcare policies reforms currently ongoing in the Russian Federation, it remains to be seen how this policy and children's probability of finding families to live in will develop further.

Notes

1 This research was conducted with the support of the Russian Science Foundation grant No. 18–18–00321.
2 Pavel Astakhov was Children's Rights Commissioner from 2009 to 2016. He was removed from his post in 2016 after a scandal emerging from visiting children who had survived a huge storm on a Karelian lake, where he asked 'Well, well children, how was your little swim'? As a number of other children had died in the storm, the question provoked a scandal.
3 The green creature he refers to is Kiko, an animated character and a symbol of an EC campaign on the issue of sexual violence against children. Available at: www.coe.int/t/dg3/children/1in5/kiko_en.asp
4 *Patronatnaya sem'ya* (patronat family) is a form of paid guardianship. For more details, see Chapter 1.

5 Intersectionality is an important emphasis in child welfare policy focusing on heteronor-
   mative values and on what is the best interest of a particular child (e.g. Nourie, Harris
   2018). Here we draw an attention towards the various differences between the birth and
   foster families that should be taken into account while developing support policies.

References

In this volume

> Chapter 4: Kulmala, Shpakovskaya and Chernova
> Chapter 9: Chernova and Shpakovaskaya
> Chapter 11: Kulmala, Jäppinen, Tarasenko and Pivovarova

Barshev, V. 2014. *Bezdetnye. Sirot ne otdadut v odnopolye sem'i* [Childless: Orphans Will
   Not Be Given to the Same-Sex Families]. RG, 14/02/2014.
Borisenko, A. 2013. *Vladimir Grammatikov: Khorosho vse delat' vmeste* [Vladimir Gram-
   matikov: It Is Good to Do Everything Together]. KP, 22/11/2013.
Bryntseva, G. 2013. *Detyam pora domoi* [It's Time for Kids to Go Home]. RG, 08/02/2013.
   6:00.
Bryntseva, G., Yakovleva, E. 2013. *Rancho neispravimykh* [Ranch for the Incorrigible].
   RG, 05/02/2013.
Danilova, S. 2006. *Tcherez 5 let v Rossii ne budet detdomov?* [In Five Years, There Won't
   Be Orphanages in Russia?]. KP, 16/12/2006.
Dobrynina, E. 2012. *Dotchki-materi* [Daughters-Mothers]. RG, 28/03/2012.
Egorov, I. 2015. *Genprokuror vnyos predstavlenie ministru obrazovaniya iz-za sirot* [Attor-
   ney General Submits to Minister of Education a Note Due to Orphans]. RG, 11/02/2015.
Fairclough, N. 1995. *Critical Discourse Analysis*. London: Longman.
Filimonova, T. 2008. *Zhalkie krokhi* [Miserable Crumbs]. RG, 20/05/2008.
Franklin, B., Lavery, G. 1989. Legislation by Tabloid? *Community Care* 23 (3): 26–29.
Glinka, E. 2011. *Kto ne proplyvaet* [Who Does Not Swim by]. RG, 18/07/2011.
Goddard, C., Saunders, B.J. 2001. Child Abuse and the Media, National Child Protec-
   tion. *Clearinghouse Issues* (14). Available at: https://aifs.gov.au/cfca/publications/child-
   abuse-and-media.
Gritsyuk, M. 2014. *Lyubov za den'gi* [Love for Money]. RG, 14/11/2014.
Iarskaia-Smirnova, E.R., Romanov, P.V. 2015. Social Work in Russia: Between the Global
   and the Local. In: G. Palattiyil, D. Sidhva, M. Chakrabarti (eds.), *Social Work in a
   Global Context: Issues and Challenges*. New York: Routledge: 207–223.
Isaev, A. 2014. *Zakon Dimy Yakovleva. Dva goda* [The Dima Yakovlev Law: Two Years
   on]. RG, 26/11/2014.
Karandyuk, K., Zashirinskaya, O. 2013. *Svezhaya golova* [A Fresh Head]. RG, 03/12/2013.
Konyukhova, K. 2018. *Minprosveshcheniya uzhestochaet trebovaniya k priemnym rodite-
   lyam* [Ministry of Education Tightens Requirements for Foster Parents]. KP, 16/08/2018.
Kozlova, N. 2013, *Sem'yu stavyat v ugol* [The Family Is Punished]. RG, 12/02/2013.
Krivyakina, E. 2018. *Novyi antisirotskii zakon: tchinovniki i obshchestvenniki sporyat,
   nado li uzhestochat' trebovaniya k priemnym sem'yam* [New Anti-Orphan Law: Offi-
   cials and Social Activists Argue Whether It Is Necessary to Tighten Requirements for
   Foster Families]. KP, 31/08/2018.
Kulikov, V. 2010. *Semia i volya* [Family and Will]. RG, 27/12/2010.
Larina, A. 2007. *Siroty kavkazskie* [Caucasus Orphans]. RG, 18/05/2007.

Lebedeva, N. 2018. *Olga Vasilieva: Ya protiv ogranicheniya usynovlyaevmukh detei do tryokh* [I Am Against Restricting Adopted Children to Three]. RG, 20/08/2018.

Lebedeva, N., Yakovleva, E. 2017. *Otobrannoe stchast'e* [Taken away Happiness]. RG, 14/02/2017.

Levada Centre. 2017. *Deti-siroty* [Children Deprived of Parental Care]. Available at: www.levada.ru/2017/03/30/deti-siroty/ (accessed 14/02/2020).

Medialogia. 2019. Available at: www.mlg.ru/ (accessed 19/05/2019).

Nesterova, O. 2007. *Vo sne oni zovut mamu* [In a Dream They Call Mom]. RG, 25/12/2007.

Nourie, A.E., Harris, V.W. 2018. An Intersectional Feminist Perspective on LGBTQ Youth in Foster Care: Implications for Service Providers. *World Journal of Education* 8 (4): 177–187.

Novikov, K. 2012. *Zashchita po planu* [Planned Protection]. RG, 30/03/2012.

Presidential Address. 2006. *Poslanie Presidenta RF Federalnomy sobraniyu of 10.05.2006* [Presidential Address to the Federal Assembly of 10.05.06]. Available at: www.consultant.ru/document/cons_doc_LAW_60109/.

Ryabtsev, A. 2007. *Sirot prodavali, kak pupsov v magazine* [Orphans Were Sold Like Baby Dolls in a Store]. KP, 13/04/2007.

Saint-Jacques, M.-C., Villeneuve, P., Turcotte, D., Drapeau, S., Ivers, H. 2011. The Role of Media in Reporting Child Abuse. *Journal of Social Service Research*: 1–13. Available at: www.researchgate.net/publication/254376357_The_Role_of_Media_in_Reporting_Child_Abuse.

Shepeleva, A. 2011. *Optimisticheskaia demogrpafia* [Optimistic Demography]. RG, 25/01/2011.

Tokareva, D. 2010. *V detdomakh kriminal'nye avtoritety rastyat sebe smenu* [In the Orphanages Criminal Bosses Are Growing Their Shift]. KP, 23/03/2010. Avalaible at: https://www.vrn.kp.ru/daily/24462.4/623034/.

Vladimirov, D. 2007. *Den'gi ne ekonomit'* [Don't Be Tight with Money]. RG, 16/05/2007.

Vyazov, A. 2006. *Sotsial'nyi zakaz na rebenka* [Social Order on a Child]. RG, 06/04/2006.

Zakharova, S. 2014. *Veronica Oslon: U malchikov potrebnost'v materinskoi lyubvi bolshe tchem u devotchek* [Veronica Oslon: Boys Need Mother's Love More Than Girls]. *Tomskie novosti*, October 10 Available at: http://tomsk-novosti.ru/veronika-oslon-u-malchikov-potrebnost-v-materinskoj-lyubvi-bolshe-chem-u-devochek/ (accessed 30/03/2020).

Part III
Transforming institutions

4 The ideal (re)organisation of care

Child welfare reform as a battlefield over resources and recognition

Meri Kulmala, Larisa Shpakovskaya, and Zhanna Chernova

Introduction

Current child welfare reforms in Russia aim at changing the ideal of care for children deprived of parental care. This shift takes us from the previously dominant ideal of looking after children in large, state-run residential institutions to the clearly set priority of care taking place in families and, when this is not possible, institutional care being provided in the new form of small, home-like residential units. This ideational shift obviously requires wide reorganisation of institutional designs. Moreover, the transforming institutions are assigned with new tasks, including support services for birth, foster and foster families, as well as young adults leaving care. Reform is an ongoing process that opens up a wholly new space with new opportunities within which old and new actors compete for old and new – material and symbolic – resources. As one of the top priorities of the Russian government (Kulmala et al. 2017), there is much at stake: in our understanding, thus, the reform serves as a battleground over the reorganisation of the care system with consequent redivision of labour and redistribution of resources among the different actors. Even if the new ideal of care in families is a commonly accepted principle by most of the actors in different spheres, there are different opinions about how the system should be ideally reorganised.

In this chapter, we examine the question of how Russian child welfare experts and professionals from various societal sectors – public (state), third (NGOs), and private (foster parents) – perceive the ideal organisation of the new system according to new principles. We therefore focus on the perceptions of the ideal implementation of the reform from these three different, as we soon argue, perspectives. Even if the priority of family care is widely shared, each of three stakeholders located in these different societal sectors have a different view of the ideal organisation, which corresponds with their existing resources and perceived opportunities to gain new resources in the future. It should be noted that these differently located actors obviously have both coinciding and competing interests. For our exploration, we apply a neo-institutionalist theoretical framework, more precisely, the theory of social learning (Hall 1993) and strategic interaction approach (Jasper 2004, 2015).

Social learning and strategic interaction theory as a lens to the implementation of the new policy

We conceptualise the child welfare reform as a paradigmatic policy shift in Russian child welfare policy (Kulmala et al. 2017). Policy paradigms are defined as broad overarching ideas about means and aims of policy, whereas paradigmatic policy shifts are fundamental revisions of thinking about those aims and means within a particular policy field (Khmelnitskaya 2015: 16). Usually, the policy cycle is divided into several stages, from the development of ideas to their full implementation and evaluation: (1) the formation of the political agenda, including recognition of the problem and choice of problem areas; (2) policy formulation; (3) decision-making; (4) adaptation; (5) implementation; and (6) evaluation (Werner, Wegrich 2007). Instead of focusing on the early stages of the Russian child welfare reform, which we have analysed in our earlier works (e.g. Bindman et al. 2019; Kulmala et al. 2017; An, Kulmala 2020), the focus of our attention is on the adaptation of new ideas at the level of practitioners: how the new policies can be implemented.

We focus on the perceptions of street-level experts with regard to how new policies can best be brought into practice. In other words, we are interested in the ideals of care and in views of their ideal implementation: how these practitioners would ideally arrange the new ideal of care at the level of care practices. Following Monique Kremer (2006), we use the concept of ideals (of care) in order to emphasise that child welfare (policy) is not only about economics or institutions, but is also a moral discussion of what is supposed to constitute good care. Our focus on the ideal organisation brings together the perceptions on ideals of good care for a child and consequently on institutional design in which a child is well cared for. As Victoria Schmidt (2014: 13) put it, child welfare policy has the elements of both ideas and institutions: ideas refer to 'what-is-to-be-done' and argumentations in favour of different approaches, whereas institutions are organisational approaches to solve the concrete tasks.

A drastic change to the priority of family,[1] compared to the previous priority of residential care, can be conceptualised as a revolutionary mode of paradigmatic change (Khmelnitskaya 2015: 28). As typical to such mode, the change was impacted by external crisis (Bindman et al. 2019), a new paradigm was available and was supported by a diverse set of actors (An, Kulmala 2020). Implementation is still an ongoing process: the new policy is currently being implemented throughout the country at a considerable scale and speed. According to Marina Khmelnitskaya (2015: 26–28), in the Russian context of the hybrid political regime, the model of social learning at the stage of policy implementation includes two additional stages: the introduction of the new policy into practice and its approval by street-level actors.

According to the social learning theory (Hall 1993), principles and contents of specific policies change through the transformations of the policy paradigms. A change in the policy paradigm initiates the process of change of policy instruments and settings (Khmelnitskaya 2015: 16). Even when new ideas get adopted, there is still room for manoeuvre as to what concrete form(s) the final product will take. In other words, even if the overall goal of the reform is commonly shared, the final form is still contested. We examine the perceptions of the actors who are involved as the potential care providers (i.e. state-based, public family centres, NGOs, and foster parents) in the new system, concerning the particular instruments and settings of the policy implementation. Our research questions concerning the views of street-level practitioners, located in different societal sectors, are as follows: Who should take care of children deprived of parental care? Where they should be taken care of if not in families? Where should the resources for this come from?

To analyse expert positions on the implementation of deinstitutionalisation, we use the strategic interaction approach developed by James Jasper (2004, 2015), which suggests distinguishing between (policy) arenas and their players. According to the author, the arena is a 'field of struggle defined by the relations between players, some with dominant and others subordinate but all trying to improve their positions' (Jasper 2015: 17–18). The arenas are structured by a set of rules and resources. Some rules are written (such as new laws in our case), some are moral (as cultural understandings and wisdom of good care). Each player in the arena has resources and capabilities (e.g. skills and technologies) that determine the possible repertoires of his/her actions. As Jasper (2015: 12) put it, 'like positions on a field of battle, positions in an arena allow players to do certain things'.

Concerning the question of resources, Jasper relies on the Bordieuan metaphor of capital which can be divided into symbolic capital and material one (ibid). In the current Russian system, the state (federal and regional budgets) is the main provider of funding: this concerns not only the public centres but also various benefits for children in alternative care and foster parents (see Kulmala et al. forthcoming). State funding is a key source for NGOs through the various grant competitions and outsourcing instruments of social service provision (Bogdanova et al. 2018). There are also charity foundations and individual donors that provide funding – especially for NGOs but also for state institutions and individuals, who can acquire funding through private sources. The existing infrastructure – buildings and paid staff, for instance – can be viewed as material capital, while symbolic capital includes reputation, knowledge, and experience, all of matter for those trying to obtain a recognised position in the field. The players in the arena (in the 'battlefield' of the reform) play, as already noted, to 'improve their positions' (Jasper 2015: 17), which allows them to accumulate symbolic and material capital, which in turn strengthens their position.

The Jasperian analytic scheme was originally developed for the analysis of social movements. Yet, as the author himself puts it (ibid: 12), it can be useful for the study of 'any aspects of social interaction among individuals or organizations or collectives, where there are clashing wills' and where actors engage in a strategic game. As a whole, the Jasperian framework can be considered as a research programme with many aspects that could be investigated (Jasper 2004) that are impossible to cover all at once. Drawing from this wide set of analytical tools, we conceptualise the child welfare reform itself as an arena to play which is structured by (old and new) rules and (old and new) resources. We focus in our analysis on the key players whom we have identified for this analytical purpose and who engage in the arena with their own goals and capabilities, including forms of capital. From their position, each player defends their understanding of the ideal implementation of the overall goal, i.e. good care of a child. As Jasper (2015: 18) wrote, 'some positions, like the high ground on the battlefield, are more advantageous than others'. The achievement of their goals would bring a stronger position in the sphere (Jasper 2015: 17–18; see also 'power of nomination' by Bourdieu 1993), which obviously comes with more capital – both material and symbolic.

In our analysis of the key players in the arena, we explore their key goals, as well as the discursive and implementation strategies used to achieve these goals. Discursive strategies are the articulated justifications for their existence and roles (why exactly we can best meet interests of a certain child?), while the implementation strategies refer to their action plan, i.e. to their narrations of the concrete actions needed to implement their goals (what exactly we do to meet the best interest of a child?).

Data and analysis

We analyse the opinions of experts, including street-level care providers at the different sectors: representatives of public centres and NGOs and foster parents. These interviews are a part of a larger data sets compiled between 2015 and 2019 in two different research projects.[2] The interview data consist of 196 interviews with various actors in nine different regions of Russia (Karelia, Leningrad Region, Moscow City, Moscow Region, Murmansk Region, Nizhniy Novgorod Region, Pskov Region, Samara Region, and St. Petersburg city: officials, decision-makers, and independent experts (17), child welfare NGOs (43), child welfare professionals (29), foster parents (65), and young care leavers (42). In addition, we conducted six focus group discussions: five focus groups with foster parents with altogether 54 participants in four different regions (Krasnodarski district, Leningrad region, Moscow region, and Pskov region) and one focus group with three young care leavers in the Russian Arctic. In this data, we rely mainly on interviews with child welfare professionals of the state sector, child welfare NGOs, and foster parents.

Meri Kulmala was also invited to participate in an all-Russian meeting of children's homes (in Moscow in September 2018) with the attendance of child welfare officials and professionals from all Russian regions. Numerous observations and conversations in this event with representatives all over Russia have been crucial in creating a more comprehensive understanding of the development of the reform throughout the country. Zhanna Chernova and Larisa Shpakovskaya have been involved in monitoring and evaluation work of the reform together with Russian NGOs and other experts. Thus, our communication with practitioners has been ongoing through these years.

Alongside the aforementioned interview and observation data, we have arranged five different research-practice seminars with mainly Russian child welfare street-level practitioners during which we engaged in close dialogue with practitioners and conducted participant observation. In one of these seminars, targeted to Russian street-level practitioners and foster parents, we ran a role game in which the participants randomly took the positions of the different actors in the sphere. These materials are seen by us to be valuable because they allow us to construct the ideal-typical, sometimes rather polarised perspectives of actors located in different sectors. All the empirical data for this chapter was collected in 2016–2019.

When analysing the transcripts of the interviews, focus groups, and certain sections of the mentioned research-practice seminars, we coded out the necessary conditions for good care and ideas about the roles and tasks of the different actors in the provision of good care. Because these are narrated views of the respondents, we focus on analysing their vision on the ideal organisation of the system in the making instead of the real practices.

Based on our analysis, we have distinguished three key players as main care providers: (1) state institutions, including, most of all, administrators and professionals of the state-based public family centres, but also state officials at different levels of the Russian government; (2) NGOs; and (3) foster parents. In our investigation we have tried to understand their goals, capabilities, and capitals to invest in the game to gain a strong(er) position. We are aware that three different players with three different views is reductionist given that none of the players is a monolith; instead there is more heterogeneity in each of the groups than our analysis would suggest. Furthermore, these categories might overlap (Jasper 2015: 11). For example, in a state institution, people open an NGO to gain extra resources to perform better; foster parents form parental associations to advocate their interests; or an employee of an institution takes foster children as often happens. Yet, for the sake of our analysis, we had to focus on the dominant views in each group. To some extent, we paid less attention to some variations in views within the group. The advantage of this, however, is that we were able to construct the dominant discourses.

Arena: the Russian child welfare system in the making

In this chapter, we understand the ongoing child welfare reform as an arena, a field of struggle in which the involved players all try to improve their positions (Jasper 2015: 17–18). As usual, this arena is structured by a set of resources. As one of the top governmental priorities (Kulmala et al. 2017), there is obviously much at stake and new resources available as the reform redistributes the existing resources and changes the previous division of labour. Different actors with coinciding and conflicting interests participate in this battle over the concrete forms of implementation of the new policy in which they would have maximally beneficial position of their own which comes with more capital.

The arena is structured also by rules. These can come in written form, such as new legislative norms concerning alternative care, introduced in Chapter 1 of this volume, which have set the new rules of the game, and are now being implemented. Under the current top-down led political regime, there is a strong pressure at the lower levers to make changes to happen. But how?

With regard to the moral rule, our analysis shows that the paradigm change in Russian child welfare reaches from official declarations to the attitudes of practitioners. All interviewed expert-practitioners, including state professionals, NGO representatives, and foster parents, seemed to agree upon two things, which make common meaning space of the arena. Firstly, there is the common view that it is in the best interests of a child to grow up in a family environment. However, there are a number of issues to debate and disagree within this agreed stance on the primacy of the family. For instance, what kinds of families are most suitable? What are the limits of their competence and who can care for whom? Can, for instance, an ordinary foster parent take care of a child with special needs or do we need a 'professional foster parent' or a specialised institution for that? When can the state – or an NGO – intervene in the lives of (birth or foster) families? What is support and what is control? What is professionalism? Who has the most up-to-date knowledge?

The second point experts tend to agree on is that care institutions need fundamental reform. There is a shared understanding that the previous ideal of collective care in Soviet-type institutions is outdated. Yet, there is no unanimous understanding of whether institutions are needed in the long run or, if needed, what size or form they should take, or who should manage and work in them. Many things have moved in accordance with new principles of reform. Yet, none of these developments have been unambiguous, as all chapters of this volume show. As Biryukova and Makarentseva show in this volume, the number of children deprived of parental care has been on a steady decline. We also see dramatic change in terms of the location of placements: fewer and fewer children live in residential care and more in foster families. This has meant that many institutions have been closed down, as Tarasenko shows in her chapter. What is evident too is that despite the overall goals, residential institutions are still here to stay. This is especially the case for certain categories of children, as is shown by Biryukova and Makarentseva and Jäppinen and Kulmala in their chapters, and as we discuss in more detail in the following sections. All in all, even if the goals and rules of the reform have been set, their practical implementation is still contested.

Three distinctly positioned key players: public centres, NGOs, and foster families

Even if the overall ideas of the reform are shared, analysing interviews with the practitioners in the field, we identified three quite different views on how to ideally implement the new policy and, thus, reorganise the system. These views interestingly – yet perhaps not surprisingly – followed the lines of the societal sectors (public, third, and private sectors), which is why we distinguish three key differently located players in our analysis: public centres (i.e. former residential institutions) with traditionally dominant positions (Khlinovskaya Rockhill 2010), child welfare NGOs with significant input to the formulation of new policies

(Bindman et al. 2019), and foster families, a newcomer as a key political player in the arena (Chernova, Kulmala 2018). Each of these types of players has their own ideas about the well-being of a child and how to achieve it: they have their own interests – which might coincide or compete with the interest of the other players – and their own constellation of capital with which to play to gain more resources. These resources might be unevenly distributed between players, who, importantly, possess certain resources that allow a certain repertoire of actions (Jasper 2015). In our analysis of action that follows, we distinguish discursive and implementation strategies: the former refers to the justifications of their role by each player, while the latter refers to their concrete actions.

Player 1: state-run public centres struggling to maintain their dominant position

Traditionally, in the Russian child welfare system, the state has had the dominant position in all terms. In the previous, Soviet-type model, characterised by collective care by state professionals in residential institutions (Khlinovskaya Rockhill 2010), the omnipotent state had it all: expertise, finances, and infrastructure (buildings and personnel). The current reforms, following the new ideal of care in families, question both the ideal of care and institutional design.

The position of the federal state is to minimise costs but at the same time guarantee the best care possible to ensure a good upbringing for healthy citizens. Institutional care is the most expensive option and, according to global DI ideology, results in poor outcomes in terms of social adaptation of children, which has a high price as well. This position of the federal state was well illustrated by one participant who played the role of the 'state' in one of our role-play research-practice seminars:

> Accordingly, the state wants to minimize its spending for this area [children's homes]. This is a publicly financed sphere, it is costly, it is unprofitable, so the less we spend on it, the better. . . . [T]he goal is for as few children as possible to remain on the budget. . . . Another task still is, when these children graduate, for statistics to show that these children have become full-fledged members of society, and it is very important for us that these children nevertheless become, well, conscientious, taxpayers, blah blah and all the rest. That's why we understand that the system of children's homes that currently exists . . . this method doesn't work, so we came up with a beautiful name . . . 'deinstitutionalization'.

Such position, obviously, means less resources: both in symbolic terms due to a shift in the ideal of care and in material terms due to institutional closures. This is a less solid solution from the viewpoint of the regional governments, as seen in one dialogue of participants:

PARTICIPANT 1: Well, to maintain the system, I mean in the form of children's homes, this costs a lot of money: buildings, structures.

PARTICIPANT 2: I understand that for the federal government this is not a good option (*ne vygodno*). For the regional government, perhaps.

For the regional governments, the closures obviously mean that many people in old-style, institutions traditionally were also responsible for education and medical services, and they would lose their jobs. From the perspective of the regional economy possibly, growing unemployment is nothing but beneficial. This clearly leads to a tension, as articulated in an interview with a former professional in a residential institution currently working in an NGO:

> On the one hand, the system wants the children to grow up and live in normal conditions. On the other hand, there is an opposite response. . . . There are two arguments in the system: we place children in families. The second argument says no because that would mean closing institutions.

She continued describing a meeting with a director of one institution while working on an NGO-based project when she proposed collaboration with the institution in question:

> and the first thing he said me was 'Well, you understand that we have our own selfish interests?' I said: 'What do you mean?' 'We will not give you these children [to be placed] in families'. Because my opening phrase was: 'this project is for family placements and mentoring [of children]'. He said: 'We simply won't give the children to families. Our existence depends on them.' He said this openly.

Later in this volume, this tension is in more depth analysed by Jäppinen and Kulmala, but it is relevant also for our analysis as we wish to understand those discursive strategies through which the state institutions justify their existence in the new environment. As shown in the following section, instead of an economic issue, these justifications are however articulated as an issue of competence.

Justifications (discursive strategy)

Public centres are now assigned with new tasks – including work with birth, foster, and adoptive families as well as care leavers and temporary replacements of children under their care. Yet, representatives of the state institutions make it clear that not all children can live in a family, which is why these centres are still needed for residential care. New functions require less justification, while the necessity of residential care, under attack with the reforms, is another story. The representatives of the public centres repeatedly name the same categories of 'difficult children', including children with disabilities and health issues, sibling groups, and teenagers. According to this view, such children cannot be placed in families because they do not have the necessary resources to ensure their wellbeing, while state institutions and their staff have the experience, knowledge, and sufficient facilities to provide care for such difficult children. The following quote from an interview with a regional-level state official illustrates a typical argument used to justify the need for state-based boarding schools in the case of 'difficult teenagers':

> Children [teenagers] are difficult because they understand that they have been separated from their families. This category is difficult and to say that it will ever go away, they will always be. Nobody will take them to family, not even close relatives will take them because they are difficult.

The position of the state towards placing children with severe disabilities in institutional care was clearly articulated in the conversation that we had in the aforementioned research seminar:

P1: And what about [a child] with severe disability? Where [to place] when getting a 23-year-old?

P2: It is understandable that with severe disability, despite the state [centre] we cannot [place them] anywhere. In addition, according to the law in many regions for [families taking] children with disabilities, a lot of money is paid. . . . It is not beneficial (vygodno)[3] for the state to give them [to families]. Plus, it is very complicated. Very difficult to monitor. It is trouble. These children will, unfortunately, stay in institutions.

P2: They will stay in the state system.

As the quotation illustrates, residential care in state institutions was seen less expensive than in families in the case of disabled children. In addition, the state-run institutions are seen having what takes in terms of expertise to work with 'difficult children': the capacity and knowledge to work with children with psychological and behavioural issues (caused often by separation from birth families). They also have the medical competence when it comes to disabilities and severe health issues. In this bio-medical discourse, state-sector professionals are seen as experienced and equipped with the needed knowledge and material resources to guarantee proper and balanced nutrition, necessary medical treatment, and cleanliness and hygiene in residential care. Pride in professional capacity was demonstrated in an interview with the director of a correctional boarding school (*shkola-internat*):

> Two of our institutions remained purely correctional, the demand for them is huge, the specialists work great, they really provide worthwhile help to the children, and at the end we see children who not only go to secondary schools after the preschool, we even see those children from the boarding schools [for] the mentally retarded successfully socializing . . ., this shows the high professionalism of the staff who work in these institutions.

Besides justifying the state's ability to take care of 'difficult categories of children', the representatives of state institutions justify the need of their services by new requirements to give help to birth families, by which they often assume temporary placement of children from the poorest and most neglectful families. Concerning this obligation to engage in preventive work with birth families, Jäppinen and Kulmala in this volume critically evaluate temporary institutional placements of children to allow their parents to solve their problem as the primary means and proof of state institutions engaging in preventive work such as supporting birth families.

The justification of the needs of institutional care can be discursively built around their ability to take anyone without other options, especially in emergency situations, something that was spelled out in the research-practice seminars:

> the children's home takes [if necessary] six hard-to-raise siblings, with drug addiction, with delinquent behaviour. It takes them in one day. A family is identified [as dangerous for children], the commission makes the decision to place [the children] in children's home number 123. . . . The obligation of the children's home is, if six children were found in a basement – any children's home takes them immediately.

If the justification for long- and short-term institutional care required some rather defensive argumentation, new functions concerning the work with foster parents and care leavers provide rather explicit legitimation of the existence of institutions. These functions were widely taken as a 'one's gotta do what one's gotta do' attitude, something seen in an interview excerpt with the director of a family centre: *'Today the law simply says to us that until the age of 23 we need to feed, water and sustain them [children in state care].'* In order to guarantee their traditionally advantageous position to at minimum keep their existing material resources at the same level as they used to be, public centres justify their existence – especially when it comes to residential care – through a biomedical discourse that draws from their long experience in the sphere.

Action plan (implementation strategy)

As a result of the reasoning of their existence, the state institutions have corresponding action strategies. Because the image of the state care institutions as good carers is clearly losing its strength, these institutions have to change. What should they do to be able to compete in the field?

The key action strategy of the state institutions in adapting to the new rules is to transform themselves into family-like units through renovations of their buildings. If long-term residential care is still needed, as is short-term care for sure, it cannot be provided anymore in the old style. Premises should be reorganised into apartment-style types, which is impossible in the existing buildings, which were designed for large and segregated groups. The issue of reconstructing old Soviet standardised buildings was commonplace in our interviews with state officials and professionals. Many of them described the physical changes in the organisation of lives of children, sometimes also as a catalyst for more meaningful changes, as one director explained to us:

[New] Conditions are created in the children's home, family-type groups, where children are of different ages, eight people in one group. We put a washing machine in these groups, we have a 'head of the washing machine' who knows what to do. Waffle makers, toasters. Various holidays are celebrated, tea parties held, as in the family. We have one child responsible for one [issue], another for does something else. And when there are fewer children in group, teachers have the opportunity to pay special attention to each [child].

Yet, many are still stuck in old buildings as renovating them is costly and there are not enough funds for all. It seems that in the affluent regions, such as the city of Moscow, Moscow region, and Tyumen, for instance, far more progress has been made with renovation than in other regions. This is a problem in terms of money, but also from the point of view of contradicting laws and requirements that hinder the implementation of new reform principles, which is a point also discussed by Jäppinen and Kulmala in this volume.

Buildings are renovated not only to apartment-type living standards but also to other (new) purposes of supporting birth and foster families, such as facilities for consultation and training. In addition, the new function of aftercare services for care leavers brings new kinds of requirements for physical spaces, which is described by the director of a former correctional institution:

We have created a department for aftercare services. We have a room on the ground floor, a 'social hostel' for the care leavers. After all, if boys and girls who are without an apartment, have no money for food, no work, no school, to go anywhere, [they will] steal or live in some dump. And we have very nice rooms, equipped, cosy. . . . I wrote a letter to the ministry, to make a separate entrance to it from the street.

In addition to the question of the buildings, new family centres try to innovate with new forms of care that they can provide inside the state structure: one form that is widely discussed is the practice in which a caregiver-adult provides care at home but is simultaneously a state employee. The second strategy of the state institutions is to keep people in their existing jobs while they make the transition of (re)training for new functions, as one professional narrated:

She [the director] said, I will do everything, I will do my best to keep the whole team. We will not let anyone from the staff go, we will be reorganising, there will be a social hostel, we will provide other services, maybe someone will have to retrain, take a training course, but I will definitely keep the entire contingent – and people calmed down immediately.

(Re)training is also about overcoming the bad image associated with state-based care. Many institutions actively engage in training programmes to improve the qualifications of their professionals so as to meet the new standards of care. Yet, this is something that many still struggle with, as one director of a family centre confirmed:

> In carrying out the reforms, unfortunately, things did not work out so well and we could not fully prepare our staff. Again, we did not have enough time. Maybe not enough, well, opportunities. There was no chance to train the staff. Nevertheless, this means that there is lots of work to be done.

It seems that state institutions are often forced to acknowledge that to overcome problems related to financial and resource deficiencies or to deal with new qualitative changes in the ideal of care, they must open their doors to NGOs. NGOs can, with their experience and expertise, provide extra hands and capacities through providing volunteers, training personnel, and many kinds of material assistance for children, as will be discussed in more detail in the following.

Yet, state policy towards NGOs in Russia is dualist in nature: certain activities are heavily controlled and restricted, while, for instance, the work of the NGOs oriented to social welfare, including child welfare, is usually welcomed (Bogdanova et al. 2018). In such an environment, the state holds the power over how to define how (un)useful someone is. Thus, NGOs remain highly dependent on state (dis)approval. The discourse of 'smart NGOs', applied by a state official in the following quote, has proven to be rather prevalent in our data:

> Any intervention in children's homes is a big problem, most volunteers don't think about it, there is such a thing as reactive mental disorders, which occurs in children when a huge number of unknown people are inside walking around you. Especially if we are talking about small children who might think that these people [non-professional volunteers] have come to take them. But they come, smile and that's all. We are against that. . . . . Therefore, our motto is 'smart help to children' [in care].

As we show soon, collaborating with the state has its price for NGOs, who need to navigate and play according to the rules set by the state (see also Bogdanova et al. 2018). In addition to the already described action strategies, one of the action strategies of the state institutions is to engage in faking their performance, among others, by manipulating the numbers, as argued by Jäppinen and Kulmala in this volume.

To maintain their existing position and capital, the public state centres make efforts to adapt to the new rules and environment. Their advantageous position in terms of existing material resources (e.g. infrastructure) allows a quite wide repertoire of actions to achieve the goal of maintenance.

The current position of the public centres

It is important to note that representatives of state institutions do not oppose the new ideal of family(-like) care. They argue, however, that institutions are needed for 'difficult' and 'status-less' children, which gives justification to their existence (see also Jäppinen & Kulmala, in this volume). This, and their active engagement with their new tasks, allows them to demand more material resources, which are clearly diminishing in comparison to their old dominant position. Yet, they are still strong in terms of their material capital: they have the infrastructure and professionals – both of which require a serious improvement of their public image. Most institutions have proceeded with the renovations of their buildings and the retraining of their staff according to the new ideals. Yet, their biggest problem is that institutional care has lost its value; in other words, much of their symbolic capital is gone. All in all, their position is still strong, yet much more ambiguous and vulnerable than it used to be.

Player 2: expert NGOs seeking a more stable material basis

NGOs are a relatively new actor in the Russian social policymaking. Child welfare NGOs yet had a significant role in setting the agenda for the reform (Bindman et al. 2019), and they seek for a role in implementation as well. The new environment that emerged in the 2000s, when new state policies on cross-sectoral collaboration, social partnership, and socially oriented NGOs were devised, opened up a window for Russian NGOs to bring their expertise to social policy making (cf. Bogdanova et al. 2018). In the case of this reform, child welfare NGOs were among those with the most expertise to contribute, which was a result of their connections with both the international child rights community and street-level practitioners in Russia.

As we have argued (An, Kulmala 2020; Bindman et al. 2019), the federal government had the political will to reform the system, but it did not quite know how to achieve this, and, therefore, came to rely on NGOs, a point explained by one Moscow-based NGO leader who illustrated how the state recognised their professional capacities:

> Conferences were held, first at the regional level, then at the interregional . . . . We were getting close to the federal level, yes. We created expert advice for them. We said: 'this is a problem, it can be solved in this way, this experience already exists.'

As argued by Bindman et al. (2019), although final decisions were made by the federal government, NGOs played an important role in the process of changing the political paradigm, including concretely writing the content of the reform (also An, Kulmala 2020; Kulmala et al. 2017). Thus, they were recognised as legitimate experts. Yet, without stable funding and infrastructure, they are actively involved in the struggle for more material and symbolic resources, offering their own way of understanding the best care and seeing themselves as their best suppliers of this knowledge to everyone, including the state and families.

Justifications (discursive strategy)

NGOs are the bearers of the new ideal of care; thus, their key resource is new knowledge based on the international child rights norms and best practices in the global deinstitutionalisation trends. Yet, as the representatives of the studied NGOs argue, this knowledge needs to be translated into the Russian reality (cf. An, Kulmala 2020), something that depends on their ability to 'innovate', as one Moscow-based NGO leader argued:

> None of the Western [approach to work with children without parental care] would work here in practice. If you start transporting it here, so to speak, [you must] translate it into Russian and applying it. Therefore, everything we do is based on Russian experience. And what was created here, or adapted, or in some way arose here . . . . By the way, here are non-profit organizations, then, there in the 90's, we were the first innovators.

Among the NGOs themselves, one can witness a widely spread discourse on NGOs' supremacy as the best experts who have the most recent and advanced knowledge as the ability to flexible and innovative action, as well as the following quote from an NGO expert:

> As a rule, non-profit organisations are more advanced in [carrying out] preventive work and [the development of foster] family placement, supporting families in difficult situations. Over the last few years, they have had wider access to research results, training, and knowledge. They have had more freedom to implement their projects and develop their activities, they were less regulated, so now their experience can serve as a catalyst for constructive changes in institutions; non-profit organisations can share their experience and train specialists. . . . Authoritative experts have emerged in the field of child psychology and the protection of childhood, who were able to convincingly show and prove to decision-makers among the authorities the importance for the child of living in a family, and not in institutions.

As the NGOs argue, they have the most updated knowledge to understand the well-being of children and the best organisation of care. Whereas the views of the state professionals on best care practices are often rooted in the traditions of Soviet pedagogy and medicine, a new ideological component of the attachment theory attachment is seen in the accounts of the NGOs:

> We started from the very beginning with the goal of filling the gap that exists in Russia in the training and retraining of specialists in this field. Nobody teaches them [with up to date knowledge] anywhere, neither in universities, nor in additional courses, nowhere. . . . Our main work takes place in the regions, that is, we go to the regions and train specialists there, we try to cram into our short courses all that is probably studied for years in European universities: communication with service users, professional ethics, theories of attachment, prevention of burnout, all that constitutes, in fact, curricular in social work in the West, but which is not present at all in Russian programs.

As seen in the preceding quotation, the development of professional social work is also on the agenda. With such new knowledge, the NGOs see themselves as needed by every actor in the field: they are in the best position to assist the state, families, and children. Such an attitude is well illustrated, for instance, in the title of a training programme of the NGO 'AllTrain' which targets everyone working with issues of childhood. Naming the programme as such can be viewed as a discursive strategic action to show its necessity to all possible agents involved in child welfare.

Yet, as was also referred to in the accounts of the state professionals, the NGOs themselves engage in a discursive game concerning the 'smart' and 'non-smart' NGOs. They thus agree with the rules of the game set and controlled by the state. This obviously happens as a part of the struggle for the domestic financial resources provided by the Russian state, which are nowadays available from many sources for socially beneficial activities of NGOs (see Tarasenko 2018). Partly, however, it is an action strategy to survive in the game to which we turn next.

In order to strengthen their position, NGOs claim they must be wherever that children may need them. With their symbolic capital, they are in advantageous position and claim to have up-to-date knowledge that builds on their expertise on both international and domestic best practices. Yet, as we will see in the following section, they often struggle to improve their material resources.

Action plan (implementation strategy)

The strongest resource of the NGOs is symbolic: advanced knowledge concerning care. As one expert put it: '[they operate] in the field of knowledge.' 'Psychologists, pedagogues, physicians, all form NGOs and implement their [ideas].' At that level 'a fusion of professionals' emerges. Yet, even if the expert position of NGOs is widely recognised, they suffer from an unstable material base due to the fact that much of their finances are state-controlled and project-based.

As their biggest shortage lies in material resources, which are mainly in the hands of the state, one major NGO strategy is to collaborate with the state. As Bindman et al. (2019) documented, they engage in this collaboration by playing the 'rules of the game': avoiding open confrontation with their state counterparts, as explained by one NGO leader:

> Of course, they [NGOs] are part of a civil society, they have the right to make demands to the authorities. But now we have such a political situation, where just go ahead and make demands, you will end up a political refugee. Well, well . . . (laughs). If you want changes, don't make demands.

Instead of the more controversial and internationally oriented child rights–based discourse, such NGOs tend to conform to the well-fitting and less-confrontational discourse about (Russian) the family code (cf. Johnson et al. 2016; also An,

Kulmala 2020). The current political regime tends to shut down critical voices and be hostile to foreign influence (Bogdanova et al. 2018; An, Kulmala 2020). This is pointed out as follows:

R: We play there among another different organizations. I just wanted to say that, it's our niche, not a niche, but a feature, a principle that has always been implemented, historically, that the foundation has always been oriented towards cooperation, constructive dialog with the authorities, at all levels, and there were enough reasonable people, who knew how to build it, in this regard.

I: Do you in a different way than the human-rights work style?

R: Well, you could say that, yes, [different from] the human rights defender style, which is noisy and demanding.

One concrete occasion when the right tones are particularly needed is when social NGOs apply to state-run funding mechanisms. In order to acquire such funding, NGOs and public organisations sometimes come together to form hybrid organisations in which the pubic, state-based organisation has the infrastructure, while the NGO provides expertise on the issue of child welfare itself and project management. More often, however, NGOs are encouraged to come into state care as independent actors to provide assistance and support – for both the children and personnel – through different kinds of projects and training for both children and staff. One of the key strategies of NGOs is to complement state services by improving the quality of care.

NGOs also supplement state provision of care by providing services of their own through grants from different foundations: for instance, many of the children's villages providing foster care operate under such principle (Chernova, Kulmala 2018). Or they might contract with the state, which often happens with provision of the mandatory training for the foster parents to be, for example, as one NGO leader explains:

Plus, we have at our institute a large school of foster parents, probably one of the largest in Moscow. We have ten groups per year. There are resource groups for foster parents, there are consultations for foster parents. . . . Parents-graduates of our SFP (school for foster parents) and not only our SFP, who are in the period of adaptation during the first or second year of a child's life in their family. There is a resource group for them where they meet, the programme is built around the prevention of emotional burnout among parents. It lasts for six months, and this is a closed group.

NGOs also intervene when the state fails in its obligations, as one NGO leader points out:

I: I wanted to ask whether you know someone who works with care leavers?

R: Basically, NGOs do this, because the whole system of aftercare started during the so-called 'optimization reforms'. In the first place, social care case workers were supposed to take responsibility for 15–25 care leavers but, at some point, they were told the happy news that there will be around 75–120 [for each case worker]. With this number of people, one cannot remember the name of each person – never mind maintain a relationship or understand the situation they are in. That's why NGOs mainly [do this].

As shown also in the chapter by Jäppinen and Kulmala in this volume, it was often repeated that no one is specifically charged to work with the birth families, even if the state implies that this is a crucial task of the current reforms. Here, once again, NGOs step in to fill the gap.

Even if all the NGOs in this study provide many kinds of support and services for all groups that are involved in the field, only few of them are listed in the state register of social service providers (Bogdanova et al. 2018; Tarasenko 2018). This fact enables them to take over state obligations while receiving monetary compensation from the state. One of the NGO leaders, whose organisation is in the register, spoke about the prices offered for NGO services. She had clearly picked up the most expensive ones, while most of NGOs struggle to be included on the list due to their strict requirements. This shows how NGOs are in better position when it comes to the symbolic resource of having the knowledge and skills to navigate within the arena and rules of the game set by the state.

In addition, NGOs perform a wide repertoire of actions, ranging from complementing and supplementing the state provision to filling the gaps left by the official system. Their biggest advantage is their innovativeness and flexibility in adapting quickly to constant changes in the arena. Due to the current environment, they avoid open confrontation to maintain their position as a well-recognised player.

The current position of NGOs

The strongest capital of NGOs is symbolic: their advanced knowledge concerning techniques and expertise on how to provide care. On the other hand, their position is unstable as they lack material capital and remain dependent on the state. They justify their position in the field by presenting themselves as experts with the most up-to-date internationally valid knowledge and practical experience of work with children at the grassroots level. They emphasise their ability to flexibly and innovatively meet the best interests of children wherever they are. They can serve everyone from children to birth and foster parents and help the state with their reforms. NGOs must maintain good relations with state bodies because most of their activity is dependent on acquiring state funding. They have to play according to the rules of the game in which different NGOs are unevenly positioned. Thus, in the end, the NGOs are in strong position with the fact that their expertise is very much needed; yet, this capital can be utilised – and transformed into material capital – only under the conditions set by the state.

Player 3: foster parents struggling for autonomy

Foster parenting is no new phenomenon in Russian society, although, in the course of reforms, foster parents have obviously entered the arena as a new political player with strong symbolic capital. This position is strengthened by the strong consensus over the family being the best place for a child to be brought up. Moreover, despite official goals concerning preventive work, so far the reforms have focused on changes to alternative care (Jäppinen, Kulmala in this volume; Kulmala et al. forthcoming). As a result, fostering is moved to the front of the arena. In this situation, foster families are symbolically in an advantageous position: they are the only player who has what it takes to provide family-like care. From the point of view of foster parents, it is family and family environment that offer good care for children, because it is only parents, engaged in daily care and affective relationship with a child, who can be aware of children's real needs. In the Russian context, where fostering, as discussed in many chapters of this volume, is most often seen as permanent and almost equivalent to adoption, foster parents are seen to be the only agent with the most appreciated capacity – the ability to love. Thus, in the current situation, foster families are much needed and their role is highly appreciated. Yet, in their own view, they are not paid enough nor recognised as legitimate experts; neither by the state nor by the NGOs, both of which want to intervene into family life. Thus, in the game, foster families are searching for more material resources, more expert recognition, and, most of all, more autonomy.

Justifications (discursive strategy)

In the arena, parental love becomes a specific area of competence for foster parents that other agents do not have, not even in family-like units, as is well illustrated in a quotation from a foster parent:

> What is the point of what we do? Anyway, in children's homes, so-called small foster groups were created. . . . Here the main thing is professionalism, not parental love for children. These groups are professionals who provide care at home; they [professionals providing care at their home] can be called home workers, if we speak bluntly. Or home-based care groups. That's it.

Or, as another parent concluded in an interview about love and foster parenting: 'first you love, then you think about whether there is money or no money, status or no status.' Nevertheless, there seems to be a commonly accepted position among foster parents that their compensation from the state is far from sufficient. At the same time, they have an image problem in Russian society (Iarskaia-Smirnova et al. 2015; Chernova and Shpakovskaya in this volume) – the sense they exploit children's agony for their own economic benefit, as one foster mom commented:

> Some people have said, 'this is not normal'. Some said: 'You won't start loving these children. Why do you take them? Because of money!' I said: 'Because

of money, those pennies? What kind money is that?' Back then it was 200 Roubles per child. What kind money is that? It was not enough even for food.

As others have argued (Chernova, Kulmala 2018), the contradiction between money and love is one of the major issues that foster parents have to struggle with: they are the only player with the ability to love but, there is the inconvenient point that giving this love requires material resources. In contrast to the state's stance, the goal of foster parents is to eliminate all forms of institutional care, regardless of the size of the institution or care group or the age and health of the children in question. Despite their advantageous position in terms of symbolic capital (parental love), in addition to the shortage of material capital, foster parents also lack recognition of their competence from the other players in the arena.

Action plan (implementation strategy)

To pursue their interests in their search for more capital to strengthen their position in the game, foster parents try to navigate their way through a system of support and services, trying to benefit and simultaneously strengthen their autonomy. One strategy used by foster parents is to treat fostering as an adoption-like family forming. Instead of adopting a child, they foster one in order to have certain state benefits which would be lost in the adoption. This is done for the sake of the child and their rights, as one foster mother explained concerning the right to receive an apartment of their own from the state:

> We have the term 'hidden adoption'. In principle, we as parents adopt our children and children do understand that and they feel that they are parental, family children. We do not [officially] go to adoption because then we cannot fully fulfil the rights of a child [for benefits], that is first of all about housing.

For such a stance, as further illustrated in the following quotation, any reference to fostering as work is unacceptable:

> And if we look at the question from the viewpoint that professional foster families are better than any children's home, yes, I do agree. But let's take out the word 'family'. If it is a professional group in which children are cared in family-like circumstances, then this is better than children's home but let's not call it family. . . . So, if it is a family, it is a family. If it is work under the contract, then it is work under the contract.

Some foster parents – especially in the particular circumstances of the children's villages in which several foster families live together and provide foster care (Chernova, Kulmala 2018) – consider themselves to be working as 'professional' care providers instead of parenting. Yet, in most of cases, fostering is seen as requiring experience, professionalism, and love. Therefore, it can be labelled as 'professional love', as one foster dad concluded in an interview:

> For sure it is not work but support for individual children around you. . . . But things should be more transparent. One would like this experience to be more systemized and this knowledge to be distributed among people. Yet again, what it is? Love – yes. Perhaps, some kind of professional [love].

Whether it is a healthy child or a child with health issues, a small child, or a teenager, foster families see themselves as experienced and competent love/care providers. An essential part of this competence is the result of specific training for foster parents which is acquired with the help of other players, such as public family centres or NGOs. As one mother explained, training plays a crucial role in becoming a competent foster parent:

> Of course, I would say it is not easy. One must not wear any rose-coloured glasses. Especially now when more and more unhealthy children, with severe health issues, are offered [to families]. I understand that one needs to be ready for everything and that is very important to go through foster parent training to be prepared. It is also a good result [of training] if one says 'no' [to fostering].

While foster parents accept some monetary benefits and other support from the state, they prefer to see themselves as autonomous agents who should be supported but not controlled. Support should be provided only upon request of a family, as parents know best the needs of their family. Foster parents wish to be surrounded by community-based services and would prefer to select whatever provider of these services they see as best. In this way, foster families can be seen as consumers who have the freedom to choose which service and what provider they prefer, be it NGOs or public providers. Other than support requested by foster families, everything else is considered to be interference into family life, as is well illustrated in the excerpt from a focus group discussion:

P1: If a foster family doesn't want help, please don't help. Please do the minimum, do not interfere. Everyone likes to interfere.
P2: Thank god, our opeka [child protection services] is normal, they have friendly people who basically help without interfering. Overall, something terrible is going on in this sphere all over the country. Of course, there are old-school people, old-type teachers in schools and kindergartens – I have seen it.

The state is often seen as a controlling body, instead of having any useful support functions (except money), as the following focus group conversation clearly shows:

P1: It [the state] only has control functions, it does not practice its support function. I didn't see support happening yet.

P2: So, do you understand, the state gives a child [to a family] and says: 'Good-
bye. We will come to make a control visit. You can flop around as you want.'
We are very lucky here since we are many and we support each other, we help
and know where to go and whom to approach. We have built a community
here.

As said by Participant 2, support from peers is much appreciated. Foster parents
actively form parental associations and consider peer online/offline networks as a
helpful resource. Such more or less informal associations, unlike the state control,
inspire confidence, on the one hand, because they see the problems of foster parents 'from within'. On the other hand, informal associations are a form of mutual
assistance as opposed to external control. Parental associations and peer groups
also work as a way to build a more collectively legitimised expert position on fostering, which, in turn, can strengthen not only the authority of the foster parents as
self-made experienced experts but also provide much wanted autonomy.

Foster parents do not need to justify their supremacy as the best environment,
especially in cases of single and healthy children. On the other hand, foster parents need to constantly involve many strategies to give proof of their competence
as autonomous players. They lack many other resources that the other players
have; in addition to shortages of stable material resources, they are also not recognised as a legitimate expert by the other players who, therefore, tend to intervene
in foster family affairs. Foster parents see themselves as the only player capable of
providing good care for children. Despite this, they need some assistance, instead
of control and interference, from the other players.

The current position of foster families

Parents as political actors in the arena possess a unique resource – the ability to
give parental love and provide a 'true' family environment – which they claim
makes them the best at meeting any child's needs. As the only player who has
what it takes to provide loving care (the essence of the reforms), they enter battle
with very strong symbolic capital to gain more material capital (subsidies and
other kinds of support). Their collective mobilisation can be seen as an attempt
to legitimise their competence and improve their position through gaining more
symbolic capital. Yet, even with this strong symbolic capital, their position is
subordinate to the other two players upon whose material assistance and moral
support they remain highly dependent. Yet, foster parents wish to choose independently when and by whom they are assisted. All in all, their position cannot be
underestimated as, in contrast to the other players, they possess the most important symbolic capital.

Three different approaches in implementing the new policy

Childcare reforms build on the widely accepted idea of the family being the best
locus for children to grow up. Still, there is room to manoeuvre as to how the
alternative care system is, in practice, reorganised. The reforms have changed the

rules of game by providing legal space for actions and resources to new actors, such as NGOs and foster families. NGOs and foster parents, mainly with symbolic capital, have entered the field as serious care providers capable of challenging and competing with state-run public services. Even while new principles in the ideal of care are commonly shared by these actors, the division of labour between them is still contested.

In this study, we mapped newly opened spaces of competitions for redistributed resources and defined how deinstitutionalisation reforms have changed positions. We conceptualised the reforms as an arena and identified three key players which all search for maximally beneficial positions for accessing symbolic and material capital. State institutions seek to maintain their traditionally dominant position, which is now diminishing in new conditions where institutional care has lost much of its prestige. According to state institutions, this is not the case everywhere: after all, not all children can be removed from institutions and placed in families. NGOs challenge the dominance of the state as owners of advanced expert knowledge and claim they are in a position to provide better quality care. Everyone, including the state, foster or birth families, or children themselves, needs NGOs. Only foster families in turn have what it takes: they can provide a genuine family environment and give parental love to any child. What they lack is sufficient monetary compensation. They are also suspected of incompetence and exploiting benefits. As a result, it is argued that foster parents need to be closely monitored by the state and NGOs, a point that limits their autonomy. In this game, each player, pointing to their own areas of competence, struggles for more material and symbolic resources that are being redistributed in the course of the reform.

Thus, each of the players in the arena have their own view how to implement the paradigm change in Russian child welfare policy based on three different approaches to the organisation of the alternative care services policy: statist, neo-liberal, and community-based ones. The position of the state comes close to what is usually labelled as statist paternalism (cf. Rivkin-Fish 2017). Even if it were not the only provider of care, the state would keep a tight grasp on the other providers. The state controls which NGOs are let in and might arbitrarily interfere in family life. The position of NGOs in turn somewhat resembles a neo-liberally oriented mixed model of service provision in which expertise and services are on sale. In the absence of commercial providers of care, it is NGOs which benefit from the wider trend of outsourcing and contracting social services. With significant mistrust from families to state bodies, NGOs could also benefit from freedom of choice concerning the services (upon request) that foster families advocate for. The view of foster parents becomes close to what is usually labelled as community-based child welfare system (Waldfoger 1998).

It is actually the community-based approach with its focus on preventive and support services that could be considered as optimal in terms of the new ideals and goals of the current reforms. Yet, the current environment of heavy state control over other agents hinders the implementation of the community-based model. The Russian version of the mixed model resembles a quasi-liberal model because the rules of the game are set by the state. In sum, due to many path dependences, the current (child) welfare model in Russia still continues many paternalist practices despite the official goals that are initially far from paternalist.

The current reforms have redistributed the labour between the state, third sector, and family. Despite the fact that the activity of other players is controlled by the state in a highly paternalistic manner, these two other players hold significant capital and have the capacity to play a greater role in the care provision. NGOs, in particular, have the capability to develop new innovations to change the instruments used for (birth and foster) families and children deprived of parental care.

Notes

1 Family as a priority issue concerns not only child welfare. Since 2005, a strong family-centred ideology started to characterise policy programmes and a new conservative protection of the family became a key task for the Russian government. President Vladimir Putin's 2006 annual address set Russian family and family policy as the major priority through which the demographic crisis was to be tackled. Aiming at increasing the birth rate, numerous pronatalist measures were introduced. Finally, in the 2010s, the increasing attention towards Russian families also encompassed children deprived of parental care. (Kulmala et al. 2017). The most recent presidential address in January 2020 again highlighted the family values and concerned decreasing birth rate introducing new measures to encourage Russian women to give more births.
2 One was led by Meri Kulmala on 'A Child's Right to a Family: Deinstitutionalization of Child Welfare in Putin's Russia', funded by the Academy of Finland, University of Helsinki and Kone Foundation; the other focused on youth well-being in the Arctic 'Live, Work or Leave? Youth – wellbeing and the viability of (post) extractive Arctic industrial cities in Finland and Russia (2018–2020)', funded by the Academy of Finland and Russian Academy of Science.
3 The word *vygodno* is used often by state officials and does not translate directly into English but combines adjectives such as 'advantageous' 'profitable', 'beneficial', 'economically viable', and 'profitable'.

References

In this volume:

> Chapter 2: Biryukova, Makarentseva
> Chapter 5: Tarasenko
> Chapter 6: Jäppinen, Kulmala
> Chapter 7: Chernova, Shpakovskaya

An, S., Kulmala, M. 2020. Global Deinstitutionalisation Policy in Post-Soviet Space: A Comparison of Child-Welfare Reforms in Russia and Kazakhstan. *Global Social Policy*, OnlineFirst (May 19, 2020): 1–24.
Bindman, E., Kulmala, M., Bogdanova, E. 2019. NGOs and the Policy-Making Process in Russia: The Case of Child Welfare Reform. *Governance: An International Journal of Policy, Administration, and Institutions* 32 (2): 207–222.
Bogdanova, E., Cook, L., Kulmala, M. 2018. The Carrot or the Stick? Constraints and Opportunities of Russia's CSO Policy. *Europe-Asia Studies* 70 (4): 501–513.
Bourdieu, P. 1993. *The Field of Cultural Production: Essays on Art and Literature*. Cambridge: Polity Press.

Chernova, Z., Kulmala, M. 2018. *'Po slozhnosti – eto rabota, po sostayaniyu dushi – sem'ya': professionalizatciya priemnogo roditel'stva v sovremennoi Rossii* ['In Terms of Difficulty It's a Job, But the Heart Tells Me It Is My Family': The Professionalisation of Foster Parenting in Modern Russia]. *Zhurnal sotciologii i sotcial'noi antropologii* [Journal of Sociology and Social Anthropology] 21 (3): 46–70.

Hall, P.A. 1993. Policy Paradigms, Social Learning, and the State: The Case of Economic Policymaking in Britain. *Comparative Politics* 25 (3): 275–296.

Iarskaia-Smirnova, E., Prisiazhniuk, D., Verbilovich, O. 2015. *Priemnaya sem'ya v Rossii: Publichnyi diskurs i mneniya kliuchevykh aktorov* [Foster Families in Russia: Public Discourse and the Opinion of Key Actors]. *Zhurnal sotciologii i sotcial'noi antropologii* [Journal of Sociology and Social Anthropology] 18 (4): 157–173.

Jasper, J. 2004. A Strategic Approach to Collective Action: Looking for Agency in Social-Movement Choices. *Mobilization: An International Quarterly* 9 (1): 1–16.

Jasper, J. 2015. *Players and Arenas: The Interactive Dynamic of Protest*. Amsterdam: Amsterdam University Press.

Johnson, J., Kulmala, M., Jäppinen, M. 2016. Street-level Practice of Russia's Social Policymaking in Saint Petersburg: Federalism, Informal Politics, and Domestic Violence. Journal of Social Policy 45 (2): 287–304.

Khlinovskaya Rockhill, E. 2010. *Lost to the State: Family Discontinuity, Social Orphanhood and Residential Care in the Russian Far East*. New York: Berghahn Books.

Khmelnitskaya, M. 2015. *The Policy-Making Process and Social Learning in Russia: The Case of Housing Policy*. London: Palgrave Macmillan.

Kremer, M. 2006. The Politics of Ideals of Care: Danish and Flemish Child Care Policy Compared. *Social Politics: International Studies in Gender, State and Society* 13 (2): 261–285.

Kulmala, M., Jäppinen, M., Chernova, Z. Forthcoming. Reforming Russia's Child Protection System: From Institutional to Family Care. In: J.D. Berrick, N. Gilbert, M. Skivenes (eds.), *Oxford International Handbook of Child Protection Systems*. Oxford: Oxford University Press.

Kulmala, M., Rasell, M., Chernova, Z. 2017. Overhauling Russia's Child Welfare System: Institutional and Ideational Factors behind the Paradigm Shift. *The Journal of Social Policy Studies* 15 (3): 353–366.

Rivkin-Fish, M. 2017. Legacies of 1917 in Contemporary Russian Public Health: Addiction, HIV, and Abortion. *American Journal of Public Health* 107 (11): 1731–1735.

Schmidt, V. 2014. *'Obrechennye na turlulennost': idei i instituty zaschity detei na postsoveestkom prostranstve* ['Destined to Turbulence': Ideas and Institutions of Child Protection in Post-Socialist Space]. In: V. Schmidt, E. Iarskaia-Smirnova, Z. Chernova (eds.), *Politka semi'i i detstva* [Politics of Family and Childhood in Post-Socialism], Moskva: Variant.

Tarasenko, A. 2018. *Regional'nye osobennosti reformy sirotskikh uchrezhdenii v Rossii* [Regional Particularities of Orphan Institutional Reform]. *Zhurnal sotsiologii i sotsial'noi antropologii* [Journal of Sociology and Social Anthropology] 21 (3): 115–139.

Waldfoger, J. 1998. *Future of Child Protection: How to Break the Cycle of Abuse and Neglect*. Cambridge: Harvard University Press.

Werner, J., Wegrich, K. 2007. Theories of the Policy Cycle. In: F. Fischer, G. Miller, G. Sidney (eds.), *Handbook of Public Policy Analysis: Theory, Politics, Methods*. Boca Raton, FL: CRC Press: 43–61.

5 Institutional variety rather than the end of residential care

Regional responses to deinstitutionalisation reforms in Russia

Anna Tarasenko

Introduction

The chapter traces responses to deinstitutionalisation reforms in the Russian regions seeking to explain them. Regional differences are taken as an empirical puzzle to examine how typical these responses are and what socioeconomic contexts account for them. As with many other social policy reforms (such as the monetisation reform or the introduction of the Unified State Exam), deinstitutionalisation is a highly centralised policy change initiated by the federal government, which is responsible for setting key principles. Being in charge of the implementation of the imposed policy, regional authorities experience pressure caused by many factors, including limitation of available resources and infrastructure, state capacity, and path dependency. Placed in various local contexts, regional heads also experience political enforcement of delivering regional statistics to demonstrate the results of the DI reform. In particular, a percentage of children deprived of parental care was used among other 12 criteria to evaluate the effectiveness of governors' performance in January 2013 (Presidential Decree 2012). Even if this criterion was removed from the evaluation of governors' performance five years later in November 2017 (Presidential Decree 2017), the political importance of this reform was emphasised by the federal authorities, and consequent policy measures were undertaken at the regional level. The federal pressure of federal governance and a variety of socioeconomic contexts within which DI reform takes place explain the need for studying regional responses to the reform.

The logic of the chapter evolves as follows. Firstly, I discuss two meanings of deinstitutionalisation, distinguishing between the expert approach and the neo-institutional theoretical perspective. Formulating my key theoretical assumptions, relevant for the examination of the institutional variety of alternative care, I then consider the methodological implications of my empirical analysis. Secondly, I scrutinise broader public sector shifts and their underlying principles. Thirdly, I examine institutional changes in care for those birth families at risk of losing their parental rights and for children deprived of parents across the country considering public providers of three sectors: health care, education, and social protection. Finally, I provide an empirical analysis of regional differences in terms of institutional responses to the reforms and examine the socioeconomic context that produces compliance or resistance to the reform.

Deinstitutionalisation: expert and theoretical perspectives

It is plausible to make a distinction between expert interpretation of deinstitutionalisation and theoretical, i.e. neo-institutional, perspective. Deinstitutionalisation of residential care is promoted by professional communities and policy experts. The reforms aim to relocate residents living in institutional care to community-based housing with family-like placement, accompanied by the development of services that support participation in the community. This understanding of DI is elaborated to humanise the treatment of persons with disabilities and with mental illness, the elderly, and children deprived of parental care as well as criminal offenders, and, more recently, the homeless. This expert interpretation of the DI is taken from the Špidla report. This report was delivered by the experts of the European Commission in 2009 and targeted the topic of transition from institutional to community-based care for the aforementioned unprivileged categories of people (Report of the Ad Hoc 2009). In this report, institutions for children without parental care are identified

> as (often large) residential settings that are not built around the needs of the child nor close to a family situation, and display the characteristics typical of institutional culture (depersonalisation, rigidity of routine, block treatment, social distance, dependence, lack of accountability, etc.).
>
> (European Expert Group 2019)

The phenomenon of deinstitutionalisation is thus understood as more complex than just the closure of institutions (organisations providing residential care). In particular, it entails two processes: firstly, restructuring public segregated institutionalised care into a family-like environment; and secondly, the development of a variety of services (such as community-based services), including rehabilitation and assistance with employment for birth parents; as well as training for foster families and support for children in aftercare. In this sense, deinstitutionalisation implies that institutions (organisations) are to be replaced by family-like forms of care enabling children without parental care to obtain access to the same social environment and opportunities other children possess. Within the Russian expert community, deinstitutionalisation is slightly different. In particular, deinstitutionalisation is considered to be an analytical term meaning the reduction of the residential care provided by public organisations (also an equivalent to an institution), with the emphasis and development of the foster family system and support services for birth families to prevent parents losing their parental rights (ASI 2005: 4; Introduction of this volume).

Taking a neo-institutionalist theoretical perspective, I make a distinction between 'institution' and 'organisation', in contrast to the analytical approach described previously. In particular, I follow the definition whereby

> organisations and institutions exist in a state of mutual reinforcement where, on the one hand, organisations inculcate and reflectively manifest norms,

values and meanings drawn from the institutions that surround and support them; and, on the other hand, institutions are reproduced through the actions of organisations.

(Suddaby, Greenwood 2009: 177)

Considering institutions as rules and norms according to which organisations perform, deinstitutionalisation thus aims to change and replace previously existing institutions with new ones. New ideals of care formulated by authorities, expert community, or non-profit organisations are translated into practice through new institutional design, i.e. a set of new institutions (see also the Introduction). Therefore, from the neo-institutionalist perspective, deinstitutionalisation reforms are not simply about the elimination of organisations (residential institutions in analytical terms) but the replacement of institutional rules according to which organisations operate. To sum up, the neo-institutionalist perspective takes a more expansive view, suggesting that DI imposes new institutions and authorised actors are expected to react, either adapting new institutional rules or resisting them.

Taking regional responses to the reform as an empirical example, this chapter focuses on changes in three institutional norms. Firstly, changes to which ministries are in charge of alternative care for children from educational to social protection are scrutinised. This transition implies that public organisations that previously belonged to the educational system are expected to start operating in accordance with the rules and official regulations of the system of social protection. As a result, the reorientation of the activity of public providers from delivering residential care and education to providing support services for families, children, temporary placement, and prevention and training of foster parents was expected to be developed. From the neo-institutional perspective, this component of the new institutional design is responsible for shifting the policy emphasis from residential care to other forms of alternative care and prevention. Being implemented, the transition could signal about regional openness to the DI reform. Secondly, the downsizing of the public sector responsible for alternative care is examined. The introduced institutional norm is rooted in austerity policies and justified through a new public management ideology: cost effectiveness and targeting. This ideology emerged as part of administrative reforms and found many followers in the national government during the economic crisis that began in 2014. This institutional norm was introduced in many social policy areas, including health care, education, and care for children deprived of parental care. In practice, this means shrinking opportunities for service provision in comparison with previous policy of social provision. Thirdly, the outsourcing of services to non-profit organisations is expected to diversify providers and reduce the monopoly of public sector organisations, and in a way contribute to the development of the community-based services. These three components of the new institutional design are studied to identify how different regions respond. Compliance and resistance are expected to be found as the main responses to these components of the new institutional design.

This chapter borrows two key assumptions from the neo-institutionalist approach. Firstly, it admits the resisting and durable nature of institutions which contribute to inertia and resistance to any change, especially such large-scale and paradigmatic reform as deinstitutionalisation. In other words, I assume that institutions are difficult to change (Introduction of this collective volume). Following this assumption, I seek to identify regional responses which demonstrate compliance with the new institutional design or resistance to it. Secondly, the external context creates stimuli for actors (welfare bureaucracies, public managers of social providers) to either implement the reform or resist it, creating various types of rules to shape one of the reactions. As we know from studies of other policy areas, compliance with multiple, sometimes contradicting laws, is strictly monitored by regulatory authorities in Russia, contributing to the development of the phenomenon of excessive regulation or redundancy in control. Both private and public providers suffer from excessive attention from monitoring by law enforcement agencies (Guba 2017; Matveev 2015). Taking this into consideration, I assume that regional responses to the reforms are carefully chosen as a result of compromise between the local environment and pressure to comply with imposed institutional design. Taking into consideration the socioeconomic context, regional well-being, as well as percentage of children placed in foster care, I seek to explain regional differences in responses to the reform, meaning compliance and resistance.

The socioeconomic environment is taken as the key context to examine whether such a structural and unchangeable characteristic as societal well-being in a given region effects the response to the imposed institutional change. It is a well-known fact that the majority of children placed in residential facilities in Russia do have parents, but their socioeconomic or health conditions do not allow them to care properly for children (Sirotstvo 2011). The problem definitely has social roots, i.e. poverty, and related to it, alcoholism and drug abuse. Many Russian and foreign experts and practitioners admit this and consider alcohol and drug abuse to be the key explanation for the increasing role of residential care (Courtney et al. 2009; Bouché, Volden 2011: 436). Relying on these studies and bearing in mind the rigid nature of institutions, I expect that poor socioeconomic conditions produce resistance to the reform securing the dominant role of residential facilities in childcare. For this reason, such characteristics as the percentage of alcohol and drug abuse as well as regional gross product (RGP) are utilised to test this assumption.

The methodological background of the empirical analysis

Empirically the chapter draws on both qualitative and quantitative data. Regional data is taken from all three executive departments (educational, health care, and social protection) which are in charge of care for children deprived of parental care. Many experts agree that there are no up-to-date official statistics available showing the actual number of public residential organisations for alternative care and/or non-state organisations, let alone regional statistics and differences in them (Biryukova, Sinyavskaya 2017: 374). The collected data combines unique numbers of public entities in 70 Russian regions under sub-national ministries (departments) of social protection in 2017. This data is not available as aggregated figures provided by the national Ministry of Social Development or the Russian Statistical Service and I collected them from the websites of the regional governments. Data from the Ministries of Education and Health Care is available on the official website of the Federal Statistical Service per 2016 year as the latest. The year 2016–2017 was selected to study institutional changes after reform because of the limitations of available data from all the executive departments. In addition, the most up-to-date figures on socioeconomic conditions (in particular, regional gross product per capita) as well as other indicators such as alcohol and drug abuse in Russian regions were only available per 2017.

Regional statistics are limited and not available for all Russian regions across all three public sectors (educational, health care, and social protection). In addition, the number of Russian sub-national units has increased from 83 regions in 2005 to 85 regions in 2017. Due to these reasons, statistics for educational organisations comprised 83 Russian sub-national, and for health care, data for 68 regions is available for 2005, 2009, 2011, 2017, and 2019 years. For social protection, figures from 70 regions were collected per 2017 year, and per 2005, 2009, 2011 and 2019, data for 83 regions has been scrutinised. Gathered statistical data is limited in a way that one cannot measure the size of public organisations or the number of children placed there. Conclusions are made relying on an analysis of the affiliation of public childcare providers and their dynamic in numbers which reflect the regional response (either compliance or resistance) to the two out of three aspects of the DI reform in the focus of this chapter.

Any quantitative analysis inevitably sacrifices details and some information in favour of the description of large trends, and this logic dominates in the first part of the empirical analysis based on statistics. To partly compensate for this limitation, qualitative data from interviews and open sources in the Internet was used. In particular, data derived from interviews was utilised to demonstrate the evaluation of various aspects of deinstitutionalisation reform by managers of residential facilities, regional ombudsmen for children, non-profits (non-profit organisations), and experts. In particular, this data was introduced to reveal strategies used by public managers to restructure and downsize the public sector.

New institutional designs for childcare introduced by three social policy shifts

The Russian child welfare system is influenced by three major reforms. Firstly, the Governmental Decree #481 (2014) *'On the Performance of Organizations for Children-orphans and Children Deprived of Parents, and on Placement of Children in These Organizations'* (Governmental Decree 2014), which implies that residential care is to be gradually diminished and replaced with small units of family-like temporary placement of children deprived of parents (no more than eight children in one group) and the development of care in foster families. Secondly, public residential care organisations (which previously belonged to the educational and health care system) were put under the responsibility of the Ministry of Labour and Social Protection, which answers for social service delivery within Russian social policy. This policy shift placed care organisations under the 442 Federal Law on *'On the Basis of Social Provision for Citizens in the Russian Federation'*, which came into force in January 2015 (Federal Law 2013). Comprising such neo-liberal features as needs-testing, individualisation of social risks, and outsourcing of services to non-state providers, this legislation targets underprivileged families at risk. In other words, the neo-liberal principle was introduced for the policy of prevention for one of the most vulnerable social groups as an instrument of keeping families together and assisting parents in need. In addition, public organisations and non-state organisations are expected to compete among each other to provide social services. As a result, the segregated institutionalised care that previously dominated is aimed to be partly substituted by non-state forms of welfare provision that can be based on either/or in combination of professionals (experts), social centres' assistance, various types of non-profits (parents' initiatives, religious and professional associations). Thirdly, the reform of the public sphere itself (so-called administrative reforms or public sector reforms) reconsiders the previous ideal of the state being responsible for social provision and replaces this with a neo-liberal service provision discourse and new public management practice. With the 'optimisation' of the public sector, more effective forms of social provision and organisation are to replace the less effective and redundant (Dmitriev, Yurtaev 2010). In practice, this translates into economisation (austerity) and reduction of access to these services for citizens in remote areas. The reform also implies opportunities for state-dependent, public organisations (for example, children's homes) become more open to clients and representatives of non-profit organisations who are invited as members of the supervisory board (*popechitelskii sovet*) and can even engage in for-profit activity (see the case of Permskii Krai later in this chapter). According to the NGO-based (non-governmental-based) experts and practitioners, this openness to the public is a very important aspect of the reform. It is well-known that various types of residential care organisations, such as *internats* (boarding schools), used to be immune to any impact from society, including NGOs, charities, citizens' initiatives, and volunteers (Klepikova 2019). Therefore, the introduced principle of transparency could contribute to the development of community services as well as the outsourcing of social services to non-profit organisations.

Before the reforms, care for children without families was dominated by the principle of permanent placement in residential facilities, i.e. children's homes which were a part of the educational system. Returning children to their birth families and/or their adoption were rather rare cases. The reforms introduced the principle of temporary placement as the key solution which should be arranged through various public providers of social support and protection (centres of support for children without parental care, families, and women; centres of rehabilitation for underaged children, etc.) and support services for birth parents and foster parents, especially those in 'socially dangerous situations' who require rehabilitation or the assistance of psychologists and social workers.

Preventive work with families at risk of losing parental rights lies in the sphere of responsibility of the national Ministry of Labour and Social Protection and the equivalent regional executive authorities.[1] All in all, the executive welfare bodies responsible for this policy sphere belong to the social protection system of the Russian Federation. Federal Law 442 stipulates that parents have the right to apply for public services in order to improve their living conditions and living situation (psychological consultations, prevention or rehabilitation from alcohol and drug abuse) in order to fulfil their parental obligations. Though the idea is to reach those families and parents who are in need of state support, it implies that only those of them who already faced difficulties will have a chance to prove (which is required) that they have a real need for assistance. This leads to a situation where it is only those families and parents who are already in trouble can actually turn to the state for support. The principle of means-testing is therefore prioritised over the preventive actions for families and parents aimed to protect them from facing troubles which could potentially harm their own lives and the well-being of their children.

According to Article 3 of the Governmental Decree #481, public entities for children without parental care operate in the form of 'educational and medical organisations as well as those that deliver social services'. At the same time, the key responsibility is shifted from the educational executive department to social protection and development for two main reasons. Firstly, the reform puts an emphasis on the temporary placement of children 'under supervision' and on primary work with birth families in order to reintegrate a child with the extended family in cases where it is not dangerous for them. The priority of securing the customary social environment for a child is prescribed by Article 17 of the Governmental Decree #481 which stipulates a child should continue education in the school they attended while being temporary placed in alternative care. The Ministry of Social Development, being in charge of children's homes for disabled, rehabilitation centres, and centres of support for underaged children and families at risk, is set to become the central body in child welfare. Secondly, the principle of inclusion for all children, including those with disabilities, into the general educational system implies the reduction of residential facilities that used to belong to the Ministry of Education. From the content of the reform, this means that social protection organisations stick to the principle of inclusion to keep children in ordinary kindergartens and schools. When being implemented, this principle contributes to the deinstitutionalisation of care and socialisation of children who live in residential facilities. Technically it is implemented through giving the social service branch of the welfare bureaucracy the leading role in this sphere of child welfare. One leading expert, Elena Al'shanskaya, stated that the reform aims at

> overcoming cross sectoral disconnection and the closure of the [child welfare] system . . . for example, Moscow has completed this process . . . and all public organisations are under the same governmental department . . . so that public providers could accept children of different age and health condition.
>
> (Vogazeta 2019)

The empirical analysis aims to examine the introduction of these new principles of childcare.

The transition of care under social protection and the downsizing of the public sector: national and regional dynamics

The move of public organisations from the educational system to social development and protection is demonstrated by the number of public organisations aligned with the corresponding executive body. Available data on various types of public facilities under the health care, education, and social protection demonstrates a steady decline of the number of organisations in general (see Table 5.1).

The reduction in the number of all types of public organisations during the last 14 years across the country is obvious and dramatic. Yet, it is necessary to take a look at the regional level to see whether one can see resistance to this general tendency. The analysis of all types of public organisations (education, health care, and social provision) in 70 regions in 2011 and 2017 demonstrates that 87% of regions (61 regions) downsized social provision for children, but 10% (7 regions) even increased the sector, while 3% of the regions (2 regions) showed no changes (see Figure 5.1). Though, a dominant strategy on downsizing is obvious, not all regions follow the national dynamic of optimising and cutting budget costs for social provision.

The reduction of organisations in some regions is so massive that cuts reached 80% of all public organisations in 2017 compared with 2011, considering educational, health care, and social protection spheres. Medical organisations (such as children's homes for 0–3 year olds) have been reduced in all Russian regions analysed, apart from the single case of Smolenskaya oblast' where one health care organisation for children has been established in addition to those that previously

Table 5.1 The number of public organisations for alternative care under the education, social protection, and health care systems

	2005	2009	2011	2017	2019 (Al'shanskaya 2019)
Children's homes (educational system) in 83 Russian regions (Fedstat 2005, 2009, 2011, 2017)	1,561	1,408	1,265	787	459
Social service provision organisations (social service system) in 83 Russian regions (Fedstat 2005a, 2009a, 2011a, 2017a)	2,353	2,090	1,732	1 223[2]	695
Children's homes for 0–3 year olds (health care system) in 68 Russian regions (Fedstat 2005b, 2009b, 2011b)	254	243	185	161 (Fedstat 2016)	148
Total	**4,168**	**3,741**	**3,182**	**2,171**	**1,302**

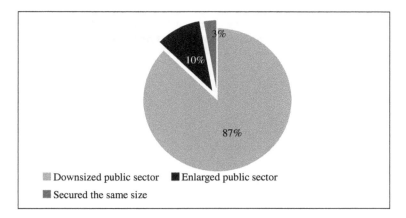

Figure 5.1 The dynamic of all types of public organisations (education, health care, and social protection) providing alternative care for children deprived of parents in 70 regions in 2017 compared with 2011 (percentage of regions)

existed. The social protection public organisations were cut in 44 regions (63% out of 70 analysed regions) and enlarged in 16 regions (23% out of 70 analysed regions) while 10 regions (14% out of 70 analysed regions) secured the same size for the same period of time. In comparison with all the three policy spheres, the social protection seems to be downsized less extensively than education and health care. This data demonstrates a preliminary reform outcome which is in line with the idea to make an emphasis on social protection as the key public sphere in charge of childcare.

Comparing the figures of all types of educational residential public organisations in 83 Russian regions in 2011 and 2017, the tendency towards reduction is evident (see Figure 5.2). All types of educational residential organisations have been cut by more than 40% from 2011 to 2017. This drastic reduction of educational organisations, in particular, such as 'children's homes-schools' (*detskie doma-shkoly*) in Russia from 92 organisations in 2004 to 42 in 2011 and 15 organisations in 2017, clearly demonstrates the reduction of 'all-inclusive' facilities for children deprived of parental care. It seems that even the concern expressed by experts and professionals about difficulties placing children with mental and physical disabilities into foster families (see more in the chapter by Biryukova, Kosova in this volume) does not prevent reducing boarding schools (*shkola-internat*) by 47% and special (correctional) boarding schools (*korrektsionnyi detskii dom*) by 43% within a studied six-year period. This might be about supporting the implementation of the principle of inclusion, according to which children in alternative care must attend local schools to secure the customary social environment for a child, as prescribed by Article 17 of the Governmental Decree #481.

Though the reduction looks impressive, it is instructive to bear in mind that only 12 regions (14% out of all 83 regions) got rid of all residential educational

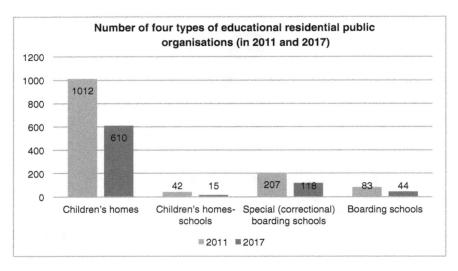

Figure 5.2 Number of four types of educational residential public organisations in 83 Russian regions in 2011 and 2017.

facilities completely in the year 2017 compared with 2011. There are only several regions, including Moscow city and Permskii krai, where the responsibilities of alternative care were transferred from the sphere of education to social protection. As a result, one can find no educational public organisations taking care for children deprived of parental care there. The case of Moscow is easy to comprehend because the reform itself was initiated and pushed by Moscow-based NGOs and other experts (Bindman et al. 2019). Permskii krai is also one of the forerunners when it comes to restructuring governance in accordance with neo-liberal principles. In these two regions, the restructuring has definitely been completed and all educational organisations were either restructured (through the reorganisation or merging) or shut down.

There is a set of regional cases where the total reduction of the educational residential organisations happened, but the change was not drastic due to the specific of the local context. Southern ethnic republics have traditionally relied less on public care and more on family, relatives, and other community ties (see Table 5.2), and therefore it was not a big challenge to cut the existing residential facilities under the sphere of education in Ingushetia, Chechnya, and Kalmykia by 2017. This specific regional context entails a relatively small percentage of children deprived of parental care (per child population) and the limited accessibility of public care measured as the number of children's care organisations per 100,000 children. To compare with the average situation in Russia, the median for the percentage of children deprived of parental care per child population calculated in 2016 is 1.9% and for the number of public organisations per 100,000 children in 2017 is 1.8%.

Table 5.2 Characteristics of the Republics of the North Caucasus

No.	Region	Percentage of children deprived of parental care per child population (2016)	The number of public organisations for children per 100,000 children in a region (2017)	Regional gross product per capita (RUB, 2016)
1	Karachaevo-Cherkesskaya Respublika	1%	0.9	143,790
2	Kabardino-Balkarskaya Respublika	0.7%	0.9	145,555
3	Respublika Ingushetiya	0.7%	–	116,008
4	Respublika Dagestan	0.6%	–	186,370
5	Respublika Severnaya Osetia	1%	1.6	181,040
6	Chechenskaya Respublika	0.6%	–	116,120
7	Respublika Kalmykia	0.7%	1.1	201,406

The aforementioned cases are exceptional, because in the majority of regions, the tendency is to keep educational residential facilities (at least one of the four existing types: children's homes, children's homes-schools, special (correctional) boarding schools, and boarding schools). The specific features of the North Caucasus have already been described by experts and scholars (Sirotstvo 2011; Nuzhna Pomoshch 2018). In particular, these regions are known for a low percentage of children deprived of parental care registered. The current analysis demonstrates the persistence of this regional pattern in the post-reform period. The regional pattern in this case embraces several Russian regions with similar characteristics reproduced in time.

Relying on qualitative data, I have identified three ways in which educational organisations are reformed: closure, reorganisation, and merging. Firstly, the closure of educational residential facilities entails firing all the personnel and giving up facilities, which can be demonstrated by the example of Murmanskaya oblast' where two children's homes were closed (in the cities of Monchegorsk and Apatity) in 2018. Sometimes the closure of the residential facility has meant giving up even newly renovated facilities. As the head of the child protection services (*opeka*) in North-western Russia said:

A year ago, the repair of the entire building of the children's home was completed. . . . [T]he facility is huge, and conditions are ideal. . . . [T]here are individual rooms for children, banya and showers . . . but the children's home was shut down and nobody wants this building now.

This case demonstrates how closures are implemented even when this is economically inefficient and implies budget losses. Yet, as the preceding analysis demonstrates, regions rarely shut down all their educational residential organisations. For example, despite the closure of children's homes in Murmanskaya oblast', there were still five functioning in 2017.

The reorganisation and merging of public organisations pursue the general goal of 'optimisation', yet the second one, merging, allows the restructuring and securing of at least some resources (staff, facilities, etc.). Reorganisation implies that former educational residential organisations are transferred under social protection keeping the title or changing it. For example, in Voronezhskaya oblast', two former educational organisations, i.e. children's homes ('*Mirovskii detskii dom*' and '*Detskii dom goroda Voronezha*'), were moved to the responsibility of the regional department of social protection in 2015–2016 even without a change in their titles. The same situation has been found in Kurganskaya oblast' where six children's homes that had been operating under the system of education since the 1990s were transferred to the Head Department on Social Protection of Kurganskaya oblast', which would mean the substitution of residential facilities with temporary placement and supporting services. Yet, all these organisations secured their status as residential facilities.[3] Altogether nine different types of educational residential facilities (including children's homes, boarding schools, and correctional schools) have previously operated in Kurganskaya oblast' since the beginning of 2000s, so there is a slight reduction in the size of the sector.

A slightly different example of reorganisation is the case of the Novodvinskii *detskii dom-internat* in Arkhangelskaya oblast', which had huge facilities for holding up to 600 children in the Soviet period. This public organisation reduced its activity and only 33 children were reported to have been living in 2012–2013.[4] There is also the example of the former 'Children's home No. 4' in the Tomsk region, which was established in 1961 as a boarding school and has been registered as a 'Centre for assistance to children deprived of parents' since 2015. Judging by official information on its website (as with many other similar organisations), its premises were renovated and transformed into a family-like environment. This organisation has restructured its performance and diversified services, offering in addition to temporary placement of children such services as training for foster parents, assistance for parents and children, rehabilitation and day care for children whose families face difficulties. As Jäppinen and Kulmala discuss in this volume, such former residential organisations tend to restructure their care services in accordance with the new requirements while still keeping long-term residential care. This kind of restructuring is heavily criticised by regional experts for formal compliance without much change in the quality of activity, as the report of the ombudsman for children, Irkutskaya oblast', demonstrates (Ombudsman 2016).

Another way of restructuring educational residential facilities is by merging of children's homes with other public organisations, such as centres of support or a rehabilitation centre for parents, women, or underaged children. Merging implies securing personnel or partly cutting it. As a rule, former public residential facilities are transformed into centres which provide social support for families with new tasks of facilitation of family placement, including work with birth and foster families and continuing to provide residential care but now on a temporary, short-term basis. The available statistical data is limited in that one cannot measure the size of public organisations, but the general consideration is that some changes contribute to the enlargement of public organisations while other do not. As one of the directors of a current centre of support for children and families (a former residential facility which now provides temporary placement) in Karelia said: 'In Karelia in fact a lot of public providers were merged . . . so making these organisations larger . . . because of that saving of budget funding was achieved.'

One of the results of such unification is that public providers find themselves according to contradictory legislation. As she continued:

> Our centre of assistance for children deprived of parental care was united with the former children's home . . . and now we're operating in compliance with the 442 Governmental Decree as well as 120 Federal Law on a system of preventive measures against unsupervised children and law violations and 442 Federal Law on a system of social provision . . . and there are some contradictory rules of these three regulations.

The fact that educational residential organisations (children's homes) still operate means that the transition of the child's care to the Ministry of Labour and Social Protection had not been accomplished by 2017. This conclusion lies in the logic of one of the neo-institutionalist assumptions adopted for this analysis which holds that the public sector would resist the reduction of their responsibility and the shrinking of their facilities and staff. My analysis of the Ulyanovskaya oblast' (Tarasenko 2018) demonstrates how resistance to the reorganisation of the public residential facilities was initiated by the sub-national Ministry of Health Care, Family and Social Welfare. This regional executive body initiated a law according to which no reorganisation of a public provider under education or health care is possible without preliminary negotiations with representatives of workers and managers of these organisations arranged through various consultative bodies. It is safe to say that the adopted regional law proved to be an effective instrument of resistance because seven out of ten children's homes operating in 2004 were still functioning in 2018 (Fedstat 2019).

There are several regions that employ a resistance strategy by maintaining the existing structure and size of the public sector entirely or with slight reduction. For example, Kaliningradskaya oblast' only reduced the public sector by 11% (three educational organisations) in 2017 compared with 2011. In Kurganskaya oblast', the reduction was equal to 13% (two social protection and one health care organisation) in 2017 compared with 2011. The most minimal reduction can be found in Cheliabinskaya oblast' where the reduction accounted for 4% (three educational and two health care organisations) and in Primorskii krai with a 6.5% cut (three educational organisations). In Saint Petersburg (2 health care and 21 educational organisations were closed, while 16 social protection entities were created) as well as in Smolenskaya oblast' (2 social protection and 1 educational organisation diminished), the reduction equalled 8%. Two regional cases, Magadanskaya oblast' and Kabardino-Balkarskaya Respublika, demonstrate no reduction in 2017 compared with the year 2011.

It is worth mentioning three regional cases where the number of educational organisations for children increased. In Astrakhanskaya oblast', the number of children's homes has been increased from 4 in 2011 to 14 in 2017; in Belgorods-kaya oblast', free new special (correctional) boarding schools were established in 2017 while none were operating in 2011; and in Kabardino-Balkarskaya Respub-lika, one more children's home was established in 2017 in addition to the one already functioning in 2011. Considering the number of these regional cases and the slight increase in numbers of alternative care public organisations, one can say that they definitely do not interfere with the country dynamics and rather support the general trend on downsizing.

Downsizing in the light of regional socioeconomic contexts

There are two regional patterns identified with the first set of the majority of regions which complied with the downsizing and a small number of them resist-ing this tendency. Seventeen regions where the reduction of the public sector reached more than 53% were identified (see Table 5.3). It is worth noticing that all these regions belong to North-West, Central, and Southern parts of Russia, except for Altaiskii krai, Tyumenskaya oblast', and Respublika Khakasia.

The main assumption for those regions where the public sector was reduced by more than 50% would be that children are placed in foster families and con-sequently the need for public facilities diminishes. The percentage of children deprived of parental care placed in foster families in these regions demonstrates that this is the case for the majority of these regions (see first 11 regions listed in the Table 5.3) where this indicator is higher than average (the median is 87%). Six out of these 11 regions are wealthy, taking into consideration that the median for the regional gross product per capita in 2016 was 344,487 roubles (4,900 euros) and three regions are comparatively wealthy demonstrating slightly less gross regional product (GRP) per capita than in average Russian region (Respub-lika Khakasia, Respublika Bashkortostan, Omskaya oblast'). Only two regions (Respublika Adygeia and Altaiskii krai) demonstrated much lower level of socio-economic wealth. In another six regions where the amount of public sector facili-ties was drastically cut (the last six listed in the Table 5.3), the number of children placed in foster families was smaller than average in Russia and the level of socio-economic wealth is much less in four of them compared with the median (exclud-ing Murmanskaya oblast' and Tul'skaya oblast'). Though this data is not enough to determine influential factors, these observations suggest the importance of socioeconomic wealth and big share of children placed in foster families for mas-sive reduction of all types of public organisations for children, including educa-tional residential facilities as well as health care and social protection entities.

Interestingly, those regions which increased their public sector or kept the same size in 2017 compared to 2011 are territorially situated in Siberia and the Russian Far East, including Tomskaya oblast', Respublika Buryatia, Respublika Altai, Astrakhanskaya oblast', and Amurskaya oblast'. There are only three exceptions to this pattern: Belgorodskaya oblast', Ulyanovskaya oblast', and Kabardino-Balkarskaya Respublika. These examples demonstrate the pattern of the regions in the Far East being more reluctant to follow the general trend on optimisation

Table 5.3 Regions with the highest reduction in percentage of public organisations (education, health care, and social protection) out of 70 regions in 2017 compared to 2011

No.	Region	The percentage of reduced organisations in 2017 compared with 2011	Regional gross product per capita (RUB, 2016)	Percentage of children deprived of parental care placed in foster families (2017)	Percentage of children deprived of parental care per child population (2017)	Alcohol and drug abusers per population in 2016 (median is 1.3%)
1	Moskovskaya oblast'	69%	483,683	92%	1.8%	1.4%
2	Krasnodarskii krai	72%	363,731	97%	1.6%	0.7%
3	Kaluzhskaya oblast'	60%	368,913	91%	2.3%	1.2%
4	Novgorodskaya oblast'	55%	398,141	93%	3.1%	1.9%
5	Tyumenskaya oblast'	59%	1,627,946	95%	1.7%	1%
6	Respublika Khakasia	76%	339,586	96%	3.1%	1.5%
7	Respublika Bashkortostan	68%	330,389	91%	1.5%	1.2%
8	Omskaya oblast'	52%	316,829	92%	1.8%	1.2%
9	Respublika Adygeia	73%	201,918	99%	1.4%	1.8%
10	Altaiskii krai	53%	210,351	88%	2.5%	1.4%
11	Orenburgskaya oblast'	55%	387,570	87%	2.1%	0.9%
12	Murmanskaya oblast'	58%	560,380	86%	1.6%	0.8%
13	Tul'skaya oblast'	74%	344,487	85%	2.7%	1.6%
14	Respublika Marii Yel	66%	234,160	86%	2%	1.6%
15	Pskovskaya oblast'	69%	224,152	83%	2.2%	1.5%
16	Kirovskaya oblast'	60%	224,776	79%	1.8%	1.4%
17	Respublika Mordovia	70%	245,215	84%	1.5%	1.2%

of the public sector (see Table 5.4). In addition, there are relatively many children deprived of parental care in these regions, except for Belgorodskaya oblast', and the placement of children in foster families is smaller than in the average region (87%), except for Respublika Buryatia and Tomskaya oblast'. So, in these regions, the enlargement of the public sector can be at least partly explained by the fact that the citizens of these regions rarely adopt or take children deprived of parental care in foster care, compared with other regions. Because society is reluctant to take over childcare, the public sector does it instead.

There are two regions which kept the same size of the public sector, though differing in terms of socioeconomic wealth: Kabardino-Balkarskaya Respublika, with a regional gross product per capita equalling 153,711 roubles in 2016; and Magadanskaya oblast', where this indicator was as high as 1 006,588 roubles. For Kabardino-Balkarskaya Respublika, however, the problem of children deprived of parental care is not too vital because their percentage out of the entire child population is less than average in Russia – 0.7% of children were registered in 2016 and 88% of them are placed in foster families. Also in Magadanskaya oblast', 0.7% of children deprived of parental care out of the entire child population were registered in 2016, and 88% of them are placed in foster families. The case of Magadanskaya oblast' is often considered by experts to be an example of path dependence related to the penitentiary system inherited from Gulag (Nuzhna Pomoshch 2018). Interestingly, even political pressure from the federal centre described in the introduction of this chapter and dominated austerity principle in social policy did not make much difference to the situation. In terms of the neo-institutional explanation, this means that socioeconomic factors and path dependence seem to be more influential than political considerations and rational choice made by regional

Table 5.4 Regions with the largest increase in percentage of public organisations out of 70 Russian regions in 2017 compared to 2011

No.	Region	The percentage of reduced organisations in 2017 compared with 2011	Regional gross product per capita (RUB, 2016)	Percentage of children deprived of parental care placed in foster families (2016)	Percentage of children deprived of parental care per child population (2016)
1.	Respublika Altai	–40%	640,623	86%	2.3%
2.	Respublika Buryatia	–24%	202,628	90%	2.4%
3.	Astrakhanskaya oblast'	–15%	332,447	85%	2.4%
4.	Amurskaya oblast'	–10%	357,829	81%	2.8%
5.	Belgorodskaya oblast'	–4%	470,874	86%	0.8%
6.	Ulyanovskaya oblast'	–4%	261,500	86%	3.3%
7.	Tomskaya oblast'	–3%	451,824	89%	2.3%

decision-makers. However, it should be noted that the influence of these factors is limited to the realm of the described cases of mainly Far East regions.

Outsourcing care for children and birth families: non-state providers

The monopoly of public providers in social protection in Russia is a long-existing practice inherited from Soviet times. Yet, several policy steps were made to diversify social service provision, inviting non-state providers to assist the elderly, people with disabilities, the homeless, and children deprived of parental care, including the 442-FZ (Federal Law 2013) which has introduced outsourcing (Tarasenko 2018). There are 87 non-state organisations that have been registered as official providers of social services for children and families, which equals to 16% out of all non-state providers working for all categories of clients in 2017. There has been no outsourcing practice identified in half of the studied Russian regions (37 regions out of 70) in the sphere of child's care. Yet, some regions intensively attract non-state providers, including Permskii krai with ten non-state organisations (including limited liability companies), Saint Petersburg where seven non-profits operated, Khabarovskii krai, Stavropol'skii krai, and Novosibirskaya oblast' where in each five non-profits were functioning in 2017. There are several types of services which are outsourced to non-state organisations: alternative care for children, trainings and support for foster parents, supporting services for children in alternative care, and parents in risk of losing parental rights.

Community-based services are mainly delivered by seven children's villages (north-west and central parts of the Russian Federation, SOS villages 2020) which operate in the form of non-profit organisations and rely both on private donations and on state subsidies or grants. Four SOS villages are officially registered as providers of social services and thus receive monetary reimbursements from regional budgets for outsourced services: Orlovskaya oblast', Vologodskaya oblast', Murmanskaya oblast', and Pskovskaya oblast'. SOS villages in Leningradskaya oblast' and Moskovskaya oblast' do not have the status of official providers. Recognised as a rather efficient practice, the experience of SOS villages is still rather limited in Russia (Bogdanova, Bindman 2016). There are examples of something similar to SOS villages run by the charity foundation 'Viktoria' (Viktoria 2020) and other non-profits (Chernova, Kulmala 2018). There is a unique example of the centre of support for children in the form of private-state partnership – the former Kovalevskii children's home which has operated in Kostromskaya oblast' since 1996. The regional authorities and the Russian Orthodox Church are the founding shareholders of this centre. Initially, this children's home operated as a classic public residential facility. Since 1999, however, this organisation has functioned in accordance with the principles of a 'children's village' with multi-child families who live separately (Kovalevskii 2020). Such a partnership is virtually unique, although servants of the Russian Orthodox Church are known for being active in adopting and taking care of children deprived of parental care.

The majority of NGOs registered as providers support women, young pregnant women, and mothers as well as families in troubles. The underlying idea resonates with the aims of the deinstitutionalisation reform as it is promoted by the government and conservative organisations and advocates saving the family, i.e. prioritising children's rights over parental rights. There is only one project that promotes baby-boxes, a safe place where a woman can leave a child voluntarily giving up her parental rights. This project is managed by a charity foundation on social support and protection of children's right and upbringing in a family called 'The Cradle of Hope' (*Kolybel' nadezhdy*) in Permskii krai. This is the only case of a non-state project being supported from the budget which defends rights of a women. As a rule, supporting services for women imply prevention of termination of parental rights. As a head of the Karelian non-profit organisation comments on their activity as providers:

> We have been working with a mother who has alcohol addiction and helped to restore her parental rights. . . . [B]ut we're afraid that in this hopeful situation she will not be allowed to obtain services anymore because the situation has been improved. . . . [B]ut in order to acquire state support a person needs to prove a need for them.

There is another case of a civic foundation '*Voskresenie*' affiliated with Russian Orthodox Church in Kostromskaya oblast' (Voskresenie 2020) that supports imprisoned women and their children aiming to unite families after sentences are served. In a similar way, the activity of four regional branches of the 'Russian Children's Foundation' (*Rossiiskii detskii fond*) aims at providing assistance for children out of parental care and public organisations for social orphans in Russia in Sverdlovskaya oblast', Respublika Severnaya Osetia, Stavropol'skii krai, and Kurganskaya oblast'. Apart from the support of these children, the activities of these kinds of organisations include creating profiles of children with their pictures and characteristics in the 'federal data bank of children deprived of parental care' (*federal'ny bank dannykh o detiakh-sirotakh*) in order to encourage their placement in foster families.

There are three non-state schools for foster parents registered in Murmansk region, Kalinigradskaya oblast', and Sverdlovskaya oblast' registered as non-state providers of services. For example, 'The Centre for the Development of Family Forms of Children's Settlement' in Murmansk region (created in 2005) was officially delegated the right to qualify foster parents. In Novosibirsk region, the civic organisation 'Day of the Stork' (*Den' Aista*) aims at encouraging children's adoption, as well as arranging schools for foster parents. There are several examples of service providers which were founded by foster parents. For example, the case of Khabarovsk regional civic organisation of foster families 'There are no Alien Children' (*Khabarovskaya kraevaya obschestvennaya organizatsia zameschajuschikh semei 'Chuzhikh detei ne byvaet'*), the NGO 'The Centre for the Development of Charity Programmes Land of Mercy' ('*Tsentr razvitiya blagotvoritel'nykh program 'Krai Miloserdia'*') in Krasnodarskii krai, and organisations of parents and foster families 'Warm home' (*Teply dom*) in Leningradskaya oblast' are key examples. These cases demonstrate how the self-help activity of foster families evolved into professional organisations which deliver services.

It is important to mention that Permskii krai also experimented with six social enterprises (limited liability companies) which were registered as official social service providers to assist parents and families who were in the process of losing their parental rights. As the head of a non-profit organisation working with families at risk of losing parental rights in Permskii krai recalls:

> Working in this sphere [care for children deprived of parental care'] for many years in Permskii krai, I can't remember good cases when these private companies really assisted people in need. Relying on this evaluation and the fact that these organisations are not working anymore as official providers, one can admit this experience unsuccessful.

The aforementioned cases demonstrate that the public sector domination in the sphere of social service provision for children deprived of parental care. Yet, there are examples of activity of organisations which operate as official providers of preventive services for families and care for children. And only very unique regional contexts produce experimental practices with state–private partnership or the outsourcing of services to private companies.

Conclusions

The objective of this chapter has been to identify regions which demonstrate various responses to the DI reform with regard to the three components of the new institutional design: the transition of childcare from education and social protection, the downsizing of the public sector, and outsourcing of services to non-state providers. The analysis of the implementation of deinstitutionalisation reform at the regional level in Russia demonstrates crucial changes in the public sector. Yet, as the neo-institutionalist assumptions predicted, there is a space for resistance to such new imposed institutions as the transition of care to the social protection from education and outsourcing of service to non-profits. The logic of downsizing the public sector appeared to trump the deinstitutionalisation reform aimed at substituting massive residential facilities with such alternatives as family-like public facilities, non-profit, or foster families. The data demonstrates that the majority of regions cut off the public sector significantly, but only a few actually diminished all the educational residential organisations. As a result, the actual transfer of care for children to the responsibility of social protection has not yet been reached and the deinstitutionalisation reform appears to be fragmented.

In the light of the neo-institutionalist perspective, the transition from educational to social protection sector was to trigger a policy shift from residential care to family type of alternative care and prevention. This transition was expected to contribute to cross-sectoral cooperation in the public sector of care for children, including health care, educational, and social protection providers.

Yet, the existing obstacles and the invention of new practice by residential organisations prevented this transition. Firstly, regions tend to resist this transfer of responsibility, formally changing titles of public providers but keeping the main responsibility by educational welfare bureaucracy (ministries of education) (from educational to social protection). Secondly, social protection public providers are employed for the purposes of residential care using the possibility of keeping children without status on the basis of parental notifications (as Jäppinen and Kulmala show in this volume).

As the neo-institutionalist theory suggests, the regional context plays a crucial role in determining strategy: resistance or compliance in response to the new institutional design imposed by the federal government. In particular, socioeconomic wealth and the scope of children deprived of parental care and the percentage of those placed in foster families might partly explain resistance or compliance with reform requirements. Such societal conditions which characterise the consumption of drugs and alcohol per population do not seem to contribute to the reform outcomes, but more systematic research is definitely required to reveal influential factors. The analysis of this chapter revealed geographically relevant patterns with a small number of exclusions. In particular, the data suggests that Far East regions are reluctant to follow the general trend on optimisation of public sector, while North-West, Central, and Southern parts of Russia tend to comply with the federal expectations. The data also enabled to show how the region of the North Caucuses differs in terms of the initial conditions and responses to the childcare reform. These cases helped to shed light on cultural and path dependence factors which account for reform outcomes.

Federal legislation introduced rather limited opportunities for outsourcing of services to non-profit organisations or social enterprises with support from regional and local budgets. Yet, half of the Russian regions use this contracting scheme to diversify public providers and erode the monopoly of the state. Such services include alternative care for children, training and support for foster parents, and supporting services for children in alternative care and parents in risk of losing parental rights. Yet, the introduction of outsourcing schemes may inhibit the development of community services. This is because outsourcing implies the delivery of the same services as provided by public organisations. Being a part of the contracting system, non-profit organisations are disincentivised to develop a menu of services which is essential for the evolvement of community services.

All in all, DI reform in Russia was hugely criticised for neglecting preventive care (Introduction of this collective volume). This chapter demonstrated how the social protection public providers being responsible for arranging preventive measures were downsized in the same scope as educational and health care organisations. This trend limits opportunities for families in risk of losing their parental rights to access preventive services. In addition, the contradicting legislature makes public provider managers act very carefully, prioritising an escape from rule-breaking rather than following the interest of their clients. Moreover, the neo-liberal principle on the basis of the preventive care was introduced for the most vulnerable social groups as an instrument of keeping families together and assisting parents in need. From the point of the social policy model, this demonstrates a transition to austerity policy with regard to the neediest.

Notes

1 There are several regional exceptions of different executive authorities in charge, including the Department of Family, Social and Demographic Policy of Brianskaya oblast', the Ministry of Social Development, Custody and Patronage of Irkutskaya oblast', the Department on Issues of Family and Children of Tomskaya oblast', and the Ministry of Health Care, Family and Social Wellbeing of Ulyanovskaya oblast'.
2 Analysis of regional registers of official social service providers in 70 Russian regions in 2017 conducted by myself for the purpose of this chapter.
3 In the register of official providers of social services in Kurganskaya oblast', see: http://rpost.uszn.kurganobl.ru/reestr_last.html?PageSize=30&Sort=&PageNumber=2 (accessed 19 March 2020) all residential facilities are listed: 'Dalmatovskii detskii dom', 'Zhitnikovskii detskii dom', 'Kataiskii detskii dom', 'Kipel'skii detskii dom', 'Kurganskii detskii dom', Vvedenskii detskii dom'.
4 The official website of Novodvinskii detskii dom-internat in Arkhangelskaya oblast': http://novdetdom.ucoz.ru/index/osnovnye_svedenija/0-69

References

In this volume

Chapter 6 by Jäppinen and Kulmala

ASI (Agentstvo Sotsial'noi Informatsii). 2005. *Reforma Sirotskhikh Uchrezhdenii. Deinstitutsializatsia: Za i Protiv* [Reform of Orphan Institutional Care: De-Institutionalisation: For and against]. In: Gribanova, Krjuchkova (eds.), *ASI*. Available at: www.asi.org.ru/wp-content/uploads/2013/06/RefSirotskikh-Uchrezhdenij1.pdf.
Bindman, E., Kulmala, M., Bogdanova, E. 2019. NGOs and the Policy-Making Process in Russia: The Case of Child Welfare Reform. *Governance: An International Journal of Policy, Administration, and Institutions* 32 (2): 207–222.
Biryukova, S., Sinyavskaya, O. 2017. Children Out of Parental Care in Russia: What We Can Learn from Statistics. *Journal of Social Policy Studies* 15 (3): 367–382.
Bogdanova, E., Bindman, E. 2016. NGOs, Policy Entrepreneurship and Child Protection in Russia: Pitfalls and Prospects for Civil Society. *Demokratizatsiya: The Journal of Post-Soviet Democratization* 24 (2): 143–171.
Bouché, V., Volden, C. 2011. Privatization and the Diffusion of Innovations. *The Journal of Politics* 73 (2): 428–442.
Chernova, Z., Kulmala, M. 2018. *'Po slozhnosti – eto rabota, po sostayaniyu dushi – sem'ya': professionalizatciya premenogo roditel'stva v sovremennoi Rossii* [In Terms of Difficulty It's a Job, But the Heart Tells Me It Is My Family]. *Zhurnal sotciologii i sotcial'noi antropologii* [Journal of Sociology and Social Anthropology] 21 (3): 46–70.
Courtney, M., Doley, R., Gilligan, R. 2009. Looking Backward to See Clarity: A Cross-National Perspective on Residential Care. In: M. Courtney, D. Iwaniec (eds.), *Residential Care of Children: Comparative Perspective*. Oxford: Oxford University Press.
Decree #481. 2014. Decree of the Government of the Russian Federation of May 24, 2014 No. 481 'On the Performance of Organizations for Orphaned Children and Children without Parental Care, and on Placement of Children in these Organizations' (*Postanovlenie*

Pravitel'stva Rossijskoj Federacii ot 24 maja 2014 g. N 481 g. Moskva 'O dejatel'nosti organizacij dlja detej-sirot i detej, ostavshihsja bez popechenija roditelej, i ob ustrojstve v nih detej, ostavshihsja bez popechenija roditelej'). Available at: http://static.government.ru/media/files/41d4e0dc986dd6284920.pdf (accessed 30/03/2020).

Dmitriev, M., Yurtaev, A. 2010. Strategia-2010: Itogi Realizatsii 10 Let Spustia [Results of Implementation Ten Years Later]. *Ekonomicheskaya Politika* 3 (107): 114. Available at: http://ecsocman.hse.ru/data/2012/11/28/1251387244/5.pdf.

European Expert Group. 2019. *Terminology: On the Transition from Institutional to Community-Based Care.* Available at: https://deinstitutionalisation.com/terminology/ (accessed 29/11/2019).

Federal Law # 442-FZ. 2013. Federal Law of December 28, 2013 No. 48-FZ 'On the Basis of Social Provision for Citizens in the Russian Federation' (*Federal'nyj zakon ot 28.12.2013 N 442- FZ 'Ob osnovah social'nogo obsluzhivanija grazhdan v Rossijskoj Federacii'*). Available at: www.kremlin.ru/acts/bank/38016 (accessed 30/03/2020).

Fedstat. 2005, 2009, 2011, 2017. The Data from the Federal Statistical Services of Russian Federation for 2005, 2009, 2011 and 2017 Years. Available at the official website: https://fedstat.ru/indicator/37465 (accessed 28/02/2020).

Fedstat. 2005a, 2009a, 2011a, 2017a. The Data from the Federal Statistical Services of Russian Federation for 2005, 2009, 2011 and 2017 Years. Available at: https://fedstat.ru/indicator/41610 (accessed 28/02/2020).

Fedstat. 2005b, 2009b, 2011b. The Data from the Federal Statistical Services of Russian Federation for 2005, 2009 and 2011 Years. Available at: https://fedstat.ru/indicator/41672 (accessed 28/02/2020).

Fedstat. 2016. The Data from the Federal Statistical Services of Russian Federation for 2005, 2009 and 2011 Years. Available at: https://fedstat.ru/indicator/41672 (accessed 28/02/2020).

Fedstat. 2019. Integrated Intergovernmental Information-Statistical System (Data of the Ministry of Education on the Number of Children's Homes in Russian Regions in 2004–2017). Available at: https://fedstat.ru/indicator/37468 (accessed 28/11/2019).

Guba, K. 2017. *Kak Rabotaet Rosobrnadzor. Analiz Otkrytykh Dannykh* [How Rosobrnadzor Operates: An Analysis of Open-Source Materials]. *Vedomosti*, October 11. Available at: www.vedomosti.ru/opinion/articles/2017/10/12/737515-rosobrnadzor-analiz-dannih (accessed 30/03/20).

Klepikova, A. 2019. Residential Care Institutions for People with Disabilities in Russia: Questioning Totality. *The Journal of Social Policy Studies* 13 (3): 453–464.

Kovalevskii, 2020. *The Official Website of the Kovalevskii Center of Support for Children.* Available at: http://kovalevo.org/about/about.html (accessed 28/02/2020).

Matveev, I. 2015. *Gibridnaya Liberalizatsia: Gosudarstvo, Legitimnost' i Neoliberalism v Putinskoi Rossii* [Hybrid Liberalisation: The State, Legitimacy and Neo-Liberalism in Putin's Russia]. *Rossiiskaya Politia* 4 (79): 25–47.

Nuzhna Pomoshch. 2018. Orphanage in Russian Regions. Report Produced by the Research Office of the Charity Foundation 'Help Required', Moscow. Available at: https://takiedela.ru/wp-content/uploads/2018/12/NP_Sirotstvo_v_regionakh_RF_2017.pdf?_ga=2.1747 26434.1451582718.1582046338-1861792563.1582046338 (accessed 28/02/2020).

Ombudsman. 2016. Special Report of the Child's Ombudsman in Irkutskaya Oblast' on 'The Right of a Child to a Family'. Available at: http://docs.cntd.ru/document/441628460 (accessed 19/02/2020).

Presidential Decree #548. 2017. Presidential Decree of November 14, 2017 No. 548 'On Assessing the Effectiveness of the Executive Bodies of the Constituent Entities of the

Russian Federation' (*Ukaz Prezidenta Rossijskoj Federacii ot 14.11.2017 g. No. 548 'Ob ocenke jeffektivnosti dejatel'nosti organov ispolnitel'noj vlasti sub"ektov Rossijskoj Federacii'*). Available at: http://kremlin.ru/acts/bank/42465 (accessed 30/03/2020).

Presidential Decree #1199. 2012. Presidential Decree of August 21, 2012 No. 1199 'On Assessing the Effectiveness of the Executive Bodies of the Constituent Entities of the Russian Federation' (*Ukaz Prezidenta Rossijskoj Federacii ot 21.08.2012 g. No. 1199 'Ob ocenke jeffektivnosti dejatel'nosti organov ispolnitel'noj vlasti sub"ektov Rossijskoj Federacii'*). Available at: http://kremlin.ru/acts/bank/35958 (accessed 30/03/2020).

Report of the Ad Hoc. 2009. Report of the Ad Hoc Expert Group on the Transition from Institutional to Community-Based Care. European Commission. Directorate-General for Employment, Social Affairs and Equal Opportunities. Available at: https://deinsti tutionalisationdotcom.files.wordpress.com/2017/11/report-fo-the-ad-hoc_2009.pdf. (accessed 29/11/2019).

Sirotstvo. 2011. Sirotstvo v Rossii: Problemy i Puti Ikh Reshenia. Moskva. Available at: www.psychologos.ru/images/ZCKti9UQHD_1431501427.pdf (accessed 18/02/2020).

SOS villages. 2020. *The Official Website of SOS Villages in Russia*. Available at: https://sos-dd.ru/where/ (accessed 30/03/2020).

Suddaby, R., Greenwood, R. 2009. Methodological Issues in Researching Institutional Change. In: D.A. Buchanan, A. Bryman (eds.), *The Sage Handbook of Organizational Research Methods*. London: Sage Publications: 177–195.

Tarasenko, A. 2018. Russian Non-Profit Organisations in Service Delivery: Neoliberal and Statist Social Policy Principles Intertwined. *Europe-Asia Studies* 70 (4): 514–530.

Viktoria. 2020. *The Official Website of the Foundation 'Viktoria'*. Available at: https://vic toriacf.ru/detskaya-derevnya/chto-takoe-detskie-derevni/ (accessed 28/02/2020).

Vogazeta. 2019. *Sistema uchrezhdenii dlia detei-sirot beznadezhno ustarela, ee reforma neizbezhna*. Interview with Elena Al'shanskaya published on 24 of June 2019. Available at: https://vogazeta.ru/articles/2019/6/24/children/8159-cistema_uchrezhdeniy_dlya_ detey_sirot_beznadezhno_ustarela_ee_reforma_neizbezhna. (accessed 18/03/2020).

Voskresenie. 2020. *The Official Website of the Organisation 'Voskresenie'*. Available at: http://voskreseniye.ru/. (accessed 18/03/2020).

6 'One has to stop chasing numbers!'

The unintended consequences of Russian child welfare reforms

Maija Jäppinen and Meri Kulmala[1]

Introduction

Russia is undergoing a paradigm shift in its child welfare policy, which is fundamentally changing the ideal of care from collective and institutional to family-based care (Kulmala et al. 2017). The new ideal of prioritising families has multiple elements. The primary goal at the level of ideas is prevention, which seems to be understood broadly in the reform. Ideally, a child in need of protection would stay in their birth family, supported by community-based services, which would function to prevent the child ending up in alternative care outside their home. Another option would be the temporary placement of a child in a family-like environment while social services worked with the parent(s) and child in order to facilitate a return to the birth family. As we have shown (Kulmala et al. forthcoming), offering parents temporary institutional placements for their children as a means of support is a common practice in Russia (Khlinovskaya Rockhill 2010). The next option, if it is not possible for the child to stay in the birth family, is their placement in either a guardianship or foster family or domestic adoption. At the level of ideas and goals, long-term residential placements are seen as the last possible resort. Old residential institutions are to be closed or restructured into family support centres with the possibility of the aforementioned temporary placements. Thus, the reform aims at improving the flaws that the Russian system has been criticised for: its inability to support families at risk and consequently its orientation towards alternative care in large residential care institutions (Kulmala et al. forthcoming).

This ideational shift is supposed to lead to fundamental changes in institutional design (Mätzke, Ostner 2010). All in all, the reforms have already led to certain concrete changes: a large number of residential institutions have been shut down and/or transformed into family-type units; there has been a clear shift from residential care to care in foster families; and some baby steps towards new preventive work practices are underway (more in Kulmala et al. forthcoming). As Biryukova and Makarentseva (in this volume) show, the overall number of children deprived of parental care has been not drastically but steadily decreasing from 2005 onwards, being a little less than 600,000 in 2017. Terminations of parental rights still dominate the field, but the limitation of parental rights is, however, increasingly used as a 'lighter' option: the share of children whose parents' parental rights were limited instead of being terminated has grown fourfold in comparison to 2002. The overall number of children's homes has declined by almost half during the 2010s. In other words, much has happened, yet partly on paper and with unintended, even paradoxical results.

In this chapter, we examine these paradoxes and their unintended consequences, which we argue result from the fact that the evaluation mechanisms for the intended qualitative changes in care clearly promote quantitative measuring. We do not argue that quantitative measurement would not be needed, but that there should be other kinds of follow-ups as well. As we show in this chapter, in certain kinds of environments, such as Russia, looking merely at the numbers becomes the leading principle of the evaluation of the outcomes. In Russia's current political system, the prioritisation of the reform by the highest level of government is creating strong pressure for regional governments who, lacking the necessary resources and infrastructure, attempt to implement the new policy. Such pressure encourages the regional authorities and street-level officials to fake their performance by manipulating the numbers (Paneyakh 2014).

In this chapter, we argue that a few frequently referred to numeric indicators are predominantly used to evaluate the outcomes and implementation of the reform, which in fact hinders the realisation of the qualitative goals of the reform. These indicators are (1) a decrease in the overall number of children deprived of parental care and not placed in guardianship or foster families[2]; (2) an increase in the number of children placed in foster families, which automatically decreases the number of children in the databank; and (3) a decrease in the number of residential institutions after closures. These three ways of measurement intertwine with the three key goals of the reform: (1) developing community-based preventive measures and supporting families at risk; (2) developing foster care; and (3) dismantling residential care in large institutions. These two three-point lists of quantitative measurement and qualitative goals form the basis of our empirical puzzle.

Our empirical analysis is based on qualitative interviews with the child protection officials and other practitioners and experts in 2015–2018 in North-West Russia and Moscow. Our investigation is structured by the exploration of three empirical cases, which we have named 'Status-less children', 'Children in catalogues', and 'Conflicting criteria'. We have chosen these cases from a large body of qualitative data based on our evaluation that they are the most illustrative for those key problems, which we have identified and want to analyse in this study. These cases are selected to shed light on the tensions and contradictions, which typically lead to playing with the numbers to hit the targets set for the performance evaluation (Paneyakh 2014). After an analysis of the empirical cases, we explain the key reasons for the identified unintended outcomes. As a result, we argue that the quantitative measurement of the studied institutional change has led to severe unintended consequences, which hamper the achievement of the intended qualitative changes in care for children deprived of parental care.

Our exploration of the unintended consequences of the reform stems from neo-institutionalist inquiries of institutional change. In our understanding, the directions of institutional change are shaped by certain organisational principles, which can be conceptualised as institutional logics (Novkunskaya 2020: 51). In our discussion of different institutional logics, we draw from the regulatory logics by Eliot Freidson (2001), who distinguished three different logics of regulation of professional practice. A more global, neo-liberal tendency to transform any action and particularly evaluating its performance into numeric indicators – which we see now in Russian child welfare (as in health care, Litvina et al. 2020; Novkunskaya 2020) – is characteristic of the managerial logic of regulation. As Litvina et al. (2020) found in the sphere of health care, the professional logic with an emphasis on professionals' autonomous decision-making becomes frequently challenged by marketisation and managerialism. Yet, the sphere of social services, including child welfare, is less commercialised than health care. Our findings, however, clearly support their argument that, in the Russian context, besides marketisation and managerialism, governmental paternalism systematically restricts professional autonomy (Litvina et al. 2020: 5). As we argue, much of the combination of managerialism and paternalism is path dependent in its nature and creates institutional traps, i.e. inefficient yet persisting norms and practices inherited from the old system. In our understanding, these traps are 'lock-in situations' in which new ideas clash with the old practices and institutional logics, which in turn blocks the change sought from above.

In the next sections, we first discuss the current environment of top-down pressure to reform the system and then move on to our methodology and neo-institutionalist concepts. After this, we demonstrate these tensions through an examination of three cases. After this, we discuss the unintended consequences and reasons behind them and what should be done to overcome the pitfalls and flaws of the reform.

Reforming child welfare in conditions of top-down political pressure

As argued in the introduction of this book, the reforms have served as one of the top priorities of the Russian government in the sphere of social policy in the 2010s. In the current non-democratic, top-down political regime (Gel'man, Starodubtsev 2016), what is important for lower level leaders is to show good results in terms of the aforementioned numeric indicators. The most obvious example of such 'performance evaluation' (Paneyakh 2014) is measuring the efficiency of the regional governor in terms of the number of children placed in foster families. As noted in the introduction of this book, this practice was used in 2013–2017, and presumably contributed to placing children into foster families.

Pressure, however, is not always explicit enough to be reduced to one single indicator. In fact, pressure is more about the prevalent managerial logic of regulation in the Russian model of governance. According to this logic, it is the manager, the central government, or the ministry in charge of the reform that orders a given service (Novkunskaya 2020: 37). We have witnessed the efforts of the central government to create an atmosphere within which the regions are ranked according to their performance, while discontent is expressed to those who lag behind. For example, at the 'All-Russian Meeting of the Directors of Children Homes' held in Moscow in September 2017, in the closing plenary a representative of the Ministry of Education listed those regions which had not adequately reported the process of completing their obligations. He directly appealed to the representatives of those regions to pass this information to their regional leaders and warned that a letter from Moscow would follow in next day.[3]

Sometimes it is simply impossible to show good performance concerning all the numbers simultaneously, because a good showing in one indicator does not necessarily look good from the perspective of another. This tension is well-articulated in the following quotation from an active campaigner for the reform and member of the Coordination Council for the implementation of the reform:

> Last year or the year before it, the deputy prime minister [of the federal government] said that we should cut the databank [of children without parental care] by 30 per cent. . . . We were monitoring the regions, how many children are placed in families. Oh, you have made so many family placements, well done. You are in first place [in the ranking of regions]. Separately they looked at how many children we have registered [to the database] and how many parents have been terminated of their rights. They said: 'Oh, how many, oh, you are doing very well.' Prevention is working, we are registering fewer than before. But these are two interrelated processes. . . . You let something flow into one tube and out from another, be it a bathtub or a swimming pool. We construct a pool for each region every year. We flow those, who have been registered, into one tube, and those, who have been placed into the family forms of care out from another tube. Inflow and outflow happen all the time, and the height of the water in the pool shows how many children we have in the databank. . . . Those who terminate more parental rights also place more in families. One can ask, who should we applaud? Those who are responsible for the family placements? Or those who are responsible for the social policy? This process goes on all the time. And we have made it the indicator of deinstitutionalisation.

So, as illustrated in the preceding quotation, it appears that if one wants to show good numbers in family placements, it is beneficial to have children entering the system and then being placed in a family. This means that officials responsible for family placements have done their job, but what about those who are responsible for social policy more generally and social support for families at risk particularly? The same tension was expressed by another interviewed NGO representative:

> Keeping a child in their family is the priority anyhow. That is the basis. And this tendency, you see, this decreasing the number of children deprived of parental care, also makes the decreasing number of children who are raised in [foster] families. So, there is an imbalance.

This 'imbalance' grows from the inability of the system to focus on preventive work and the consequent lack of relevant indicators to measure the effectiveness of this work. Paradoxically, terminating fewer parental rights would result in bad performance with family placements. Moreover, the smaller number of terminations is not necessarily evidence of effective preventive work. Under pressure, local officials might become more circumspect with this particular number and avoid terminating parental rights even in severe cases, in order to 'hit the number' (Paneyakh 2014).

As the first quotation well shows, the federal government sets the concrete numeric goals. The regional government is responsible for implementing the change, as with more generally many other spheres of social policy (Kainu et al. 2017). In the current non-democratic, top-down led political environment, such incentives obviously create pressure on the lower level officials, and this might encourage them to fake their performance by manipulating and 'massaging' numbers (Paneyakh 2014). There is a practice of qualitatively monitoring the reform by independent experts in the regions, too, but this seems to have a less important role in measuring the outcomes of the reform. According to our data, monitoring visits are considered merely check-ups instead of an opportunity to develop best practices. Importantly, concentrating too much on the numeric indicators also directs the prevailing daily practices, which might result in several unintended consequences as we soon show.

Methods and conceptual framework

Our analysis builds on extensive data sets compiled between 2015 and 2019 as a part of the interdisciplinary research project led by Kulmala on 'A Child's Right to a Family: Deinstitutionalisation of Child Welfare in Putin's Russia'.[4] In addition to analysing relevant policy and legislative documents and media sources, this project has involved 200 interviews with representatives from federal-level, regional, and local non-governmental organisations; regional officials; directors of residential institutions for children; foster parents; and young adults leaving care in several regions of Russia (An, Kulmala 2020). The empirical data used in this chapter consists mainly of 18 expert interviews with street-level bureaucrats, NGO actors and policymakers, conducted in two regions of North-West Russia and in Moscow. Additionally, we rely on ethnographic data from the all-Russian Meeting of Directors of Children's Homes mentioned previously and other child welfare official events that representatives from Russia's regions attended.

The starting point of the analysis was to track the unintended consequences of the reforms. We constructed three cases through which we illustrate the tensions and paradoxes resulting from the mismatch of the qualitative goals and quantitative measurements. As noted, such a tendency to transform any action into numeric indicators, as well as evaluating performance through such numbers, is characteristic of the managerial logic of regulation (Novkunskaya 2020). Thus, we rely in our research on the conception of institutional logics, referring to different types of regulatory logics. These logics are assumptions and values which guide the way actors interpret organisational reality and help decide what is appropriate behaviour (Novkunskaya 2020: 52). Thus, these logics define the way organisations and institutions are regulated. Freidson (2001) distinguished three different regulatory logics: managerial, market, and professional.

The professional logic emphasises the autonomy of the professionals to make decisions and control over their professional action. It thus builds in the notion of the professional autonomy and decision-making power and authority of professionals. In this logic, professional actions and decisions are made based on professional knowledge, experience, and ethical standards. Market logic, in turn, refers to consumerism in which competitive market mechanisms are the major regulators. Market logic builds on the logic of consumers' choice (and private funding) to ensure competition between service providers and institutions, stimulating them to work more (cost-)effectively and competently. These principles are sometimes seen as empowering citizens as consumers, while consumerism is also criticised that it reduces professional autonomy and decreases the availability of services for everyone and thus increases inequality among citizens (Temkina, Rivkin-Fish 2019: 3–4.). Managerial – or bureaucratic – logic refers to the regulation by managers, which in certain cases, as Russia, are understood as state bodies (Novkunskaya 2020: 64). In managerial logic, managers and bureaucrats hold the dominant position, authority, and decision-making power. Efficiency and its measurement are in the core of this logic. Managerial logic manifests itself through the enforcement of administrative and economic efficiency, and, as Girts Racko (2017: 78–79) argued, is likely to weaken professionals' concerns with common good. Anastasia Novkunskaya (2020: 51) aptly asked about the difference of the logics in context of Russian maternity services: is the role of medical workers (doctors, midwives, and nurses) to act like as state employees, service providers, or (medical) professionals?

Similarly, as other scholars have found in the sphere of Russian health care (Litvina et al. 2020; Novkunskaya 2020), we show that Russian street-level child welfare professionals have little autonomy and decision-making power, but they remain dependent on the upper level authorities. In our explanation of the Russian child welfare reform, we find the managerial logic combined with paternalism (Litvina et al. 2020) to be dominant. This logic is a powerful means of explaining the unintended consequences in our study. In our analysis, we occupy two interrelated concepts of institutional theory – namely the 'institutional trap' and 'path dependency'. The institutional trap is defined as 'a stable but yet inefficient equilibrium in a system where agents choose a norm of behaviour (an institution among several options)' (Polterovich 2008: 3087). In other words, it is a 'lock-in situation' where institutional transformation has reached the level at which inefficient structures remain stable (Buzar 2005: 382), and inefficient institutional development can be self-supporting (Polterovich 2008: 3087). The emergence of the institutional trap is an important source of risk associated with any reform process, and thus with any institutional transformation. The concept is closely linked to the concept of path dependency, which refers to 'a system's dependence on its former path of development' (Polterovich 2008: 3089; Pierson 2000). As

Buzar (2005) noted, post-socialist transformation processes have been widely path dependent in their nature (Hašková, Saxonberg 2011). Next we present the three empirical cases of contradictions, after which their institutionalist explanations are discussed.

Case 1: status-less children: 'not because the system does not want to, but because it doesn't know how': new forms of institutional care

Our first empirical section presents an unintended consequence resulting from the need to reduce the number of children in the databank. The reduction is in many cases not done by developing community-based services, but by placing children in institutions 'without status', which means that they are not listed in the databank. 'Status' refers here to the status of 'social orphan', and being 'without status' means that the parental rights of that child have not been terminated (or limited). According to our fieldwork, the number of these 'temporarily' placed children has rapidly grown to a majority in many institutions. The Child's Rights Ombudsman of St. Petersburg estimates that 60–70% of the children in residential institutions in her region are placed in such a 'temporarily' fashion and, thus, are without official status; in other words, not visible in the statistics.[5]

As is well illustrated in the following quotation from an interview with a child protection official, these institutional placements are considered to be a type of prevention: they prevent social orphanhood as the parental rights of the birth parents remain.

I3: Excuse us, we said quite many times that this [practice] concerns small children. So [unlike earlier said] it is not the case that they would go straight to foster families?

R: I speak here about children with parents [*roditel'skie deti*].

I3: I see.

R: This is important since the issue is explicitly about prevention of social orphanhood.

The intention of the temporary placement is thus to return the child from the institution to their birth home. As the responsibility for changing family's situation is mostly placed on the shoulders of the parents, temporary placements are justified as a form of relief for the parents, i.e. giving them time and space to solve their problems: get psychosocial counselling or search for a job or an apartment without everyday caregiving responsibilities. Obviously, the idea of this being prevention can be questioned, because prevention could also have meant supporting the families much earlier to avoid the child's placement in an institution, and to organise the support in such a way that would keep the family together. Nevertheless, being able to conceptualise the placement this way is good for the system, as enhancing prevention is one of the major goals of the reform.

In the old children's homes, which have now been transformed into family support centres, there are departments responsible for prevention that are supposed to work with birth families. However, as seen in the quotation from a director of such a centre, at that point, children tend already to have been placed in an institution.

R1: As a rule, it happens like this: a family enters the services and specialists of the centre start to work with them. While working with the family, their main goal is of course to return the child to the family and to support the family. . . . So that he could, umm, live there.

I2: Which department starts to work?

R1: Our, umm, [Department of] Prevention of Family Disadvantage. Either full-time . . . . We have two departments depending on the problem. If the child has already been taken from the family, when there is some kind of socially unsafe situation, the work starts in the full-time department anyway. The child enters the full-time department. Specialists are named [to work with the child and the family]. We do everything that is possible to decrease the time spent by those children [in the institution].

As a part of these 'preventive' services, the centres might provide a combination of staying part-time in the department and part-time in the family, with a child possibly staying at home overnight or over the weekend. It is however quite evident that often these 'preventive' temporary placements in institutions are long-lasting ones – especially with children with health issues, as in the following case given as an example by a child protection official:

HIV positive children. When a parent does not understand that it [treatment] is very strict. Our medical system has its own controlling documents. They strictly monitor: if a child is not taken care of properly, that's it. She [the mother] did not understand until the end. If the child has been three months in [residential] care – of course she cannot understand. We keep continuing to work with her. We will prolong the temporary stay in the institution. . . . I explain it to her in this this way: 'You visit every day. You have a child to whom you have to pay attention. But you will not cope with two of them. Your husband comes and goes, not even officially married. It cannot be so. You don't have money for the maintenance. Let us keep the child.'

The 'temporary' placements are always voluntary for the parent(s), as they are not based on a court's decision on the termination or limitation of parental rights, but on an application (*zayavlenie*) signed by the parent, in which they ask for a temporary placement of their child into an institution, as explained by a child protection official:

We work with the parents. A parent writes: yes, he has a difficult life situation – and asks for a temporary placement. Anyhow, to recognise the family's difficult life situation – is there a need for further control and who provides this control? Among others, we have the means – I don't know if my colleagues already spoke about it – to provide assistance to such families in a difficult life situation or in a socially unsafe situation. It is called social patronage.

In the end, the parents do not have other options, as there are no community-based services available. The institutional placement is done with little or no consideration of whether the needed services could be provided at home. The family cannot get, for example, substantial financial support or assistance with housing, services at home, counselling from a psychologist or social worker, support persons, or access to peer groups. Instead, their options are either to give the child to an institution, but temporarily, or to survive with the child without sufficient support on their own. Sometimes parents are even advised and tempted to give their children temporary placement, it being explained that the parent has the right to visit the child as often as they like and to support connections with them. Meanwhile, it is emphasised how difficult it would be for the parent to take care of the child at home. At the same time, the experts often do not talk about options to provide such support services to the families which would enable a child to return to their birth home. In a more family-service-oriented model (Gilbert et al. 2011), community-based services would enable taking care of the sick or disabled child in their own homes even if the parents were single, young, or lacking the financial or other resources to solve the situation independently.

In conditions of underdeveloped community-based services, the staff of institutions have to come up with the means to support the tie between the institutionalised children and their parents. In one interview, the director of a family support centre told us proudly how they had been able to return a disabled child home by hinting that the child would be alone a lot if the mother did not visit the child regularly. As a result of this 'foxiness', as the interview participant put it, the mother developed a closer relationship with the child and in the end took the child to live at home with her. It is an important change that in these new placements, the tie between a child and their birth parents does not break down even if the child is in the institution for a longer time. Moreover, while engaging in prevention talk, professionals have shifted their thinking towards a more family- and parent-friendly direction, although they do not find working with birth parents easy and do not have sufficient tools to do it.[6]

Structurally, the situation has changed recently making it possible to open 'temporary' placements to baby homes (*dom rebenka*) (previously these children were brought to the sanatoriums and infection wards of children's hospitals). From our earlier research projects (e.g. Jäppinen 2015), we know that such hospitalisation was offered as an option to mothers of healthy small children in crisis departments for women and children, when the mother needed to go into full-time work with no access to suitable day care. In this respect, 'temporary' placements to 'usual' children's homes are a small improvement to the situation. Finally, the new category of temporary placements has not emerged only to meet the needs of children in the conditions of underdeveloped community-based support services for families, but it is also an important survival strategy for these institutions. Tragically, professionals are conscious about how traumatising and inhuman the system of institutional placements is for small children, but they cannot change it, as it has other advantageous aspects.

R2: ...These children are severely traumatised when they are left with no parental care during an extremely important period of their childhood. This is deprivation in early childhood, and at the moment these children are not counted anywhere.... They do not exist anywhere, not in the statistics, nowhere; one can only come and guess how many there are. The awful thing is that this is profitable for the state, very profitable. It is profitable for the children's homes, because, well not for all of them, I mean for the system, because the funding is per child – everything is fine, you have all the bed-places full.

I1: Well, workplaces.

R2: Workplaces are all safe. We do not terminate [parental rights], everything is well. We kind of have a facade that we do the work which the state wants us to do.

In summary, despite the official goal of preventing children entering state care, so far, the system lacks the structures, methods, tools, and skills to work with birth parents to support them to change their situations and to enable their children to live with them. This is how one of the interviewed child welfare experts from an NGO described the situation:

R1: There is practically no work with birth families. Not because the system does not want to, but it does not have the capability to. The same mothers, I see them regularly, they come to shelters for understandable reasons, they cannot raise their children. Practically no one works with them, and we do not have hands for that work. This is discussed openly. We try, but what can we do? They are so many and we have three specialists.... We are now working on an idea of a project.... We have mentoring for care leavers, but we need mentoring for these mothers.

All in all, as an unintended consequence, in these institutional placements – which are intended to serve as preventive services and to be temporary – the children remain in limbo: 'temporary' placements can last for years, but 'without status', the child has no route to a foster family, as these are only available for 'social orphans' listed in the databank. Thus, the child's right to a family is not realised in any direction: neither by living in the birth family and getting the needed support there, nor by getting a 'new family' through fostering.

The emergence of the new category of children 'without status' stems from multiple reasons. Firstly, such a category is good for the reforms, because the number of children in the bank of 'social orphans' should not increase. Secondly, the system now avoids terminations of parental rights, which was earlier the general solution for situations in which the parent was not able to take care of the child. At the same time, temporary placements are the best 'preventive' solution that the system can offer to families in conditions of underdeveloped community-based family support services and limited financial support. Thirdly, the temporary placements are affordable and beneficial for the institutions because through them they engage with 'preventive work', as they are assigned to do from above. At the same time, because these children do not proceed to foster families, there is a justification for the existence of the institutions, they still get funding, and their staff can keep their jobs.

The Russian system makes a distinction between primary prevention, meaning support for birth families, and secondary prevention, which is about working with foster parents (see more in Kulmala et al. forthcoming; Biryukova et al. 2013; Khlinovskaya Rockhill 2010). Institutional placements – even if temporary – can be considered an extreme measure, and in international comparison would hardly be considered as a preventive measure. The literature on prevention (Hardiker et al. 1991; Wattam 1999) usually distinguishes primary prevention as universal services aimed broadly at the general population (e.g. public awareness campaigns or family-strengthening programmes), while secondary prevention refers to community-based services targeted at populations at higher risk (e.g. families living in poverty or addiction or parents of children with disabilities). Tertiary prevention, in turn, would concern services for families already affected by serious problems. However, unlike in Russia, tertiary services are also typically provided as community-based services instead of placing a child in an institution.

Case 2: children in catalogues: 'a child doesn't choose a family but a family chooses a child'

Our second case presents the unintended consequence of foster parents' interests overriding the child's best interests. This results from measuring the 'success' of the reform in terms of the number of placements of children in foster families. This leads to a situation where serving potential foster parents might become more important than prioritising children's best interests. In Russia, prospective foster parents typically choose their foster children from the national online databank of children deprived of parental care (i.e. those children with the official status of social orphan). This service resembles a rude combination of a dating service and online shop. It provides a photo of each child and describes their health conditions, personality traits, and behaviour, among other aspects. The following citation presents the case of foster parents who travelled from a far-away Siberian location to a North-Western region to pick up children whom they had found in this databank.

R1:   We had a case: we got a phone call in the morning. We had people coming from [a Siberian town]. They [had looked at] the databank on their computer. They had seen photos of children whom they liked, they called to us and said: 'You know, we want to pick up these children.' In this latest case six children were taken . . . from one family. We are of course happy. But we understand that there are risks. Can you imagine. They just arrived like this. And they say that they won't have time to stay here. . . . We collect the children and prep[are] . . . the paperwork. We do the paperwork and the children are gone.

In practice, prospective foster parents browse information online and come to state whom they want to take. As in the preceding example, as the databank is national, they might come from the other end of the country just for a few days to pick up children whom they have chosen solely based on the pictures and short descriptions available on the website. In practice, it is not possible for the local officials to make any real assessment whether these people are suitable to be these children's foster parents. After a few days, the foster parents leave with their new foster children. In the preceding case, the parents took six children, which is quite a demanding situation as such – let alone without any proper adaptation period.

In situations like this, the officials have little possibility to consider the child's best interest. This is because it is inevitably good for the quantitatively measured outcomes of the reform to get six children at once out of the databank to a foster family, even if the officials were hesitant to send the children away without a period of adaptation and observing the foster parents getting to know the children before the final decision. The only option would be to invite an external expert group to assess whether the parents and children would be a good fit, but that would require a lot of time and effort, which the street-level bureaucrat of this case did not see as worth investing. In addition, the prospective foster parents could take such a denial to court, which vividly illustrates how an adult's right to foster has become more important than a child's best interests.

Importantly, the responsibility for monitoring a child's situation moves immediately after fostering to the region in which the foster family lives. The officials of a child's region of origin are not in any position to monitor how the new family life is starting and how the children are adapting to the new family and place of residence. In our data, there is also an example of the same phenomenon observed from another angle: a case in which children arrived from another, far-away location to a North-Western region with their new foster parents, who however quite soon 'returned' them to a local child welfare institution. Sadly, the children can no longer return to their place of origin, because the responsibility for taking care of them lies now with the officials of the new region, who explained that train tickets to return the children to their place of origin would be too expensive. Thus, the children were repeatedly abandoned, now thousands of kilometres from their familiar environment:

R1: A big problem was also when, a foster family from [this region] found children in the online databank. . . . Yulia, where were the children from?
R3: The Tundra.
R1: Yes, well, children from the Tundra. . . . These children, accordingly, had explicit ethnic characteristics. Well, she liked [the photo of] the children, a boy and a girl. The parents were not from [the regional capital], but from a

village. [The prospective foster mother] travelled to the Tundra and took the children very suddenly. She brought them here. Two children, two very active children. A really short period of time later, there was a total nightmare in the family, we tried to help them so much. . . . And what then? These children from the Tundra stayed here with us.

There are some examples of monitoring and observation practices with which officials are trying to improve the process. Sometimes, they require future foster parents coming from a distance to rent an apartment in the hometown of the child to be able to see how the relationship between the foster parent and the child develops.

However, overall, it seems that the street-level bureaucrats – the child protection officials and directors of the centres in which these children live – have limited discretion (Lipsky 1980) and autonomy (Freidson 2001), i.e. power to ponder the best solutions in each case. The pressure to show good statistics is higher than the power to make decisions which would prioritise the child's rights. This clearly results in the unintended consequence of placing the right of an adult to foster over the initial 'child's right to a family'. Regions are measured and ranked based on the number of family placements. Street-level bureaucrats are critical of this, but in practice, the political goal of the family placements goes ahead of the assessment of the child's best interests. Putting a child's best interests in first place would require strong professionalism and professional ethics in this context where the pressure to get children into families is so heavy. This is especially true in the political culture of Russia, in which the orders to fulfil certain goals come from above (Gel'man, Starodubtsev 2016; Paneyakh 2014). Child-friendly practices cannot depend only on individual officials, but criteria and processes for an ethical family placement process must be developed.

Both discussed cases also illustrate how in the Russian context fostering is understood as very close to what adoption usually is, as described and discussed in several chapters in this book. Our cases – including examples of parents coming from the other end of a country the size of Russia to find children with similar ethnic characteristics – in fact resemble many situations typical of international adoptions. The major difference here obviously is that in international adoption, the prospective adoptive parents do not choose children from an internationally available catalogue. Instead, the child protection services of the sending country take responsibility for seeking the best possible parent for a child according to the child's best interests, and they do it in a close and long-lasting collaboration with the adoption services of the receiving country.

Case 3: conflicting criteria: what makes an institution a home?

Our third case analyses the unintended consequences of the reform's aims to reduce the number of institutions and transform them into home-like units. This creates a contradiction again: while there should be as small a number of institutions as possible, the existing units should be small, family-like environments.

Instead of having numerous small institutions, it seems the goal of reducing the number would be more easily reached by combining the old institutions into larger units. According to the official statistics, a large number of institutions have been closed down (see Tarasenko in this volume). In the region of North-West Russia under our analysis, for example, there used to be 25–28 children's homes, and now there are only 3. This has been possible at least partly because of family placements; small, healthy children in particular increasingly find their way out into foster families (Kulmala et al. forthcoming).

Part of the progress, though, seems to result merely in playing with the numbers and types of institutions. For instance, in a regional capital in North-West Russia, the institutions there had been rather small earlier, but as a result of the reform, the number of institutions was reduced by merging the existing units into new, larger ones. Thus, the numeric goals of the reform have been reached, but one cannot speak about progress in qualitative terms. If the interest was in a qualitative change towards home-likeness, a more logical way to implement this change would be to increase the number of institutions, but decrease the number of children in each.

Another type of playing with numbers seems to be the practice of changing the type of an institution on paper to be able to continue placements of children, as in the following example given by an NGO representative:

> For example, in [a region in Southern Russia], it is ridiculous. . . . They closed institutions, because all the children were given to, well, there were families which took from eight to thirteen children with health issues, and then these institutions were reformed into boarding schools, and [the families] leave the children there and pick up . . . all the financial support for fostering twice a month.

This quotation illustrates in a nutshell the majority of the problems that we have been discussing. Firstly, playing with the numbers was made possible by the fact that the reform is not that strict when considering medical residential institutions. Secondly, at the same time, the children are living in the same old institution, now renamed as boarding school. Thirdly, in practice, they do live in an institution 'without status', while the foster families with whom they officially live, collect the benefits. The quotation also reveals that some of the foster families might have even more than ten foster children, which in fact equals already a small institution in many countries (see also Kulmala et al. forthcoming).

Moreover, monitoring has revealed examples of developments that have happened on paper but not in practice. For example, the possibility of reorganising the daily life of institutions is hindered by the old-style buildings in which they are located. It is not easy to make a corridor-style building into a family-like apartment, especially if the financial resources for the renovations are very limited. On paper, old corridor-type large institutions have been organised into small groups, but this has no accordance with the real everyday life in these institutions, as one of the experts responsible for the monitoring described:

> The federal law is a skeleton law. . . . When it says that the living should be family-like, in apartment-like groups, it is very hard to say, what 'apartment-like' means, when we have 12 numbered rooms on each floor, and a lunch room for 200 persons in the first floor. A big hall, a very big hall.

The expert expressed her concern that such institution-like arrangements will be just renamed 'apartment-like', as the law stipulates, without making it explicit what apartment-like means.

According to our conversations with representatives from different regions of Russia, the resources for renovating depend heavily on the region's economics. There are rich regions, which have really invested in the renovations, and other regions in which, for example, an ambitious renovation project of 6 million roubles dried up into a small decorative renovation that was realised with a budget of 27,000 roubles (less than 400 euros).

There are also parallel laws that hinder the renewing of the everyday practices of the institutions in the supposed direction. In addition to still eating in old-style large lunch rooms, children live without the opportunity to participate in cooking, and they may still not choose their personal belongings – or personal belongings do not exist, as the monitoring shows.[7] One of the ideas of home-likeness is that the children should be able to participate in domestic tasks such as doing grocery shopping, planning meals, and cooking them. At the same time, the ministry decides on the menus and the raw materials are delivered to the institutions centrally. The children cannot plan and decide the menus together with the staff members, let alone participate in cooking the meal, as there is a law on sanitary requirements (SanPin 2010), which complicates the process.

Similarly, while the idea of the reform promotes the practice of every child shopping for personal items like clothing and toiletries in ordinary shops with staff members, there is a law on tendering out public purchases which steers the institutions towards centralised acquisitions of 100 similar t-shirts and toothbrushes for all of the children.

> [I]f we have an institution with more than ten people, it has to live according to the law on public purchases, and there – what kind of an individual choice? You opened the tender and an unknown commission to you carried it through and an unknown company won the tender because it gave the cheapest price for the clothes of the children. And then you got some shitty, excuse me, stuff. And you are obliged to deliver those to kids – all similar because of the tender.

The intended goal of the legislation on public purchases (Federal Law 2013) is to enhance transparency in the public economy and prevent corruption. Nevertheless, here the unintended consequence of this good intention is that children living in residential institutions cannot choose their clothes and toothbrushes individually.

All in all, there are several laws that interconnect with the implementation of the reform, which are sometimes in conflict with the goals or hinder the reforming of everyday practices (Litvina et al. 2020: 15). These conflicts and contradictions become an easy tool for resisting the reform for those who want to do so. For instance, sanitary requirements and public purchases have often served as a justification for continuing with the old practices. However, as one of the interviewed experts stated, it is nevertheless possible to realise the ideas of the reform under the current legislation, if the staff try hard enough. For instance, to overcome the law on public purchases, it is possible to deliver a small amount of money for each child, which can be used individually. We have also seen promising examples of remaking old buildings into family-like environments without large-scale structural renovations. Successfully remaking old buildings clearly requires innovativeness and, importantly, a change in mindsets and the will to do things in a new way.

It is also promising that the problems caused by the conflicting laws are constantly being brought to the attention of the policymakers: because there is strong political will to implement the reform, there is always a chance that the laws can be adjusted, as described by a federal-level expert:

> We negotiated with the Ministry of Health for a long time, and worked on the sanitary requirements. And those requirements started to go along. We arrange an [all-Russian] meeting of children's home directors every year. We bring these issues to the meeting. These corrections have started to come from the regions.

Discussion

In this chapter, we have analysed the unintended consequences of the deinstitutionalisation reform. The first case, 'Status-less children', addressed those children who are at risk of remaining in a limbo – living for years in indefinite conditions, without the prospect of either returning to their birth families or getting a foster family. This new type of residential care, which can, because of its 'temporary' character, be conceptualised as the 'prevention' as desired in the reform, is also a survival strategy for still existing institutions.

The second case, 'Children in catalogues', illustrated the unintended consequences of the priority of foster parents' interests overriding the best interests of a child in order to maximise family placements. The achievements of the regions in realising the reform are primarily measured by the number of children in the databank of 'social orphans' and their placement in families. Therefore, this indicator directs the means and makes it extremely difficult for street-level practitioners to place limits on the expectations of the persons willing to foster, even if they might be hesitant as to whether the family placement is in a child's best interests.

The third case, 'Conflicting criteria', discussed the unintended consequences of the goal of cutting the number of remaining institutions and making them family-like. The goal to have as small a number of institutions as possible is not always in accordance with the goal of making the remaining institutions small and home-like. The old infrastructure and existing legislation uphold the old institutional style of organising the everyday life of the institutions and complicate moving to more family-like and individualistic practices.

Why do these contradictions and paradoxes seem to be commonplace in the reform? In each of the three cases, the unintended consequences stem from the attempt to bend a qualitative goal (better care) to a numeric indicator (increased/ decreased number). Introducing such a quantitative evaluation of the effectiveness of the performance – which is not always easily quantifiable – is typical of neo-liberally oriented new public management style reforms in many fields across the globe. In addition to social policy, we see this in education and health care, for instance. Sometimes the good causes in one policy stream might unintendedly lead to a discrepancy in another stream, as when the law on public purchases affects the practices of the child welfare institutions. Moreover, as said, sometimes it is simply impossible to show good results in terms of all the aspirations, when each is measured separately. So far, there is no model which creates a comprehensive picture of the performance of the Russian child welfare policy through a combination of quantitative and qualitative means of evaluation.

Moreover, especially concerning the case of 'Status-less children' and 'Conflicting criteria', one can very much explain the unintended consequences with a path dependency argument, when old institutional practices continue to prevail and thus hinder the completion of institutional change. For instance, in the case of 'Status-less children', the traditional prevalence of residential care continues to dominate now as a new form of 'temporary care', because the system still lacks community-based services and the local infrastructure somewhat needs the institutions to still exist for economic reasons, such as to provide a survival strategy for institutions (Chapter 4 by Kulmala et al. in this book). The same phenomenon is clearly seen in the case of 'Conflicting criteria', when it comes to old buildings and the challenges of renovating them into new home-like environments – which would require major changes in both mindsets and renovations of concrete interiors. In addition, the old basis of financing institutions according to the number of children in institutions, as described in the case of 'Status-less children', does not encourage the return of children to their birth families or their placement in foster families. These path dependencies thus seem to self-reinforcingly reproduce a given, i.e. the old institutional pattern, instead of enhancing the new principles of early prevention and/or, alternatively, care in foster families, which both could be seen as manifestations of the desired institutional change (Pierson 2000).

The situation of the funding scheme can be conceptualised as an institutional trap or even a lock-in, in which the old legislation self-supports the old institutional practice and thus hampers the implementation of the new goals and principles. As the institutional trap can be applied not only to legislative norms but also to inefficient yet stable norms of behaviour (Polterovich 2008), we can also see an obvious trap concerning the old practices of terminating parental rights. This is true in the case of 'Status-less children'. These children remain in limbo because of the aforementioned reasons concerning the survival strategy of the institutions, but, importantly, also because they cannot be temporarily placed in foster families instead of institutions due to the fact that fostering as a norm is understood as permanent (see Chernova, Shpakovskaya in this volume). This norm obviously also becomes an issue in the case of 'Children in catalogues', in which prospective foster parents search for their children-to-be. In this case, however, the greatest flaws are in an underdeveloped evaluation of the child's best interests and monitoring of the placements.

Many of the aforementioned path dependence–driven institutional traps and lock-ins interconnect with the mismatch of the reform objectives and resources to implement them. Whereas the goals are set by the federal-level government, the regions carry the responsibility for the implementation of the massive changes according to their existing resources. This general principle of social policy has resulted in remarkable regional variation (Kainu et al. 2017). Often the regions lack proper resources, and at the same time with this particular reform, the political pressure is particularly high. As Gel'man and Starodubtsev (2016: 114) have argued, reforms in Russia can only be successful if 'a certain reform is the top political priority of the strong and authoritative head of state'. Child welfare reform benefits from such top-level prioritising which makes it happen – but unfortunately, as already shown, sometimes only as an imitation and with many unintended consequences due to the lack of adequate circumstances and the pressure to demonstrate good results. All in all, this top-down led reform together with the effort to quantify the qualitative goals is a strange combination of neo-liberal and Soviet-type governing principles (Hemment 2009), which in fact both fit well with the managerial logic of regulation which is characterised first by the accent on efficiency and second by the dominating role of the bureaucratic manager. We argue that in the course of the current child welfare reform in Russia, the managerial logic obviously overrides the professional logic. We agree with the point made by Novkunskaya (2020: 53) in the context of Russian maternity care: autonomy and occupation values are likely to be undermined by bureaucratisation as 'a process of the transformation of work in accordance with the values of instrumentally rational administration' (Racko 2017: 378–379). Additionally, governmental paternalism systematically restricts professional autonomy (Litvina et al. 2020: 5).

All in all, at the level of ideas and policies, the Russian child welfare reform is to be considered as a paradigm change (Kulmala et al. 2017), which was indeed affected by an exogenous shock – the major critical juncture of the Dima Yakolev case (An, Kulmala 2020) – as mainstream theorising about institutional changes would indicate (Pierson 2000: 266). However, as we have shown, at the level of street-level practices, the changes are more slow moving, less drastic, and more gradual and incremental in their nature (Streeck, Thelen 2005). Moreover, often, as has been shown, old practices are even self-supporting and self-reinforcing, which hinders institutional change from taking place. As Torfing (2001: 306–307) has aptly asked, how is it so that 'even revolutionary reform strategies in their eager attempt to negate the old policy path reproduce traditional dichotomies and sustain what they aim to reject?' (Hašková, Saxonberg 2011: 113).

Conclusion

In this chapter, we have analysed the unintended consequences of Russian child welfare reform and discussed the causes of these consequences. We have shown that several path dependencies, institutional traps, and mismatches between federal-level goals and local circumstances have hindered implementation. We have taken a critical stance to the emphasis on quantitative measurement of the reform. Such problems exist not only in Russia; countries around the world attempt to measure reform success purely in numbers. Nevertheless, in this particular context, the emphasis solely on numbers instead of using also qualitative indicators becomes a problem. In the authoritarian environment of contemporary Russia, in which this reform is so prioritised, showing good numbers to the top-level becomes the main goal and qualitative changes remain a distant secondary interest. This produces a clash between ideals, institutions, and practices, and thus results in a particular focus solely on numbers and lock-in situations. Pathways to this situation are multiple: on the one hand, these crude quantitative approaches are related to new public management and current neo-liberalist tendencies, but, on the other hand, it is also one form of path dependency from the Soviet system. As Novkunskaya (2020: 37) argued in the context of Russian health care, the managerial–bureaucratic logic that controls professional regulation is part of an obvious continuity of the strong hierarchical relations characteristic to the Soviet administrative system. Thus, the problem is not quantitative measurement as such, but that the way it is done is inadequate. Other types of follow-ups must also be developed.

Despite the path dependencies, lock-ins, and mismatches, all of which have hindered implementation, without a doubt, the reform has been a step forward. The number of children in institutions is decreasing and simultaneously the number of children in foster families is increasing. This can be seen as a major achievement of the reform. However, we argue that the number of children in residential care has not decreased as much as is often claimed. This is because of the 'new category' of 'Status-less children', sometimes living for a long time in institutions; in such cases, the right of a child to grow up in a family environment is violated. More emphasis should be placed on the development of community-based services.

There has been a strong emphasis on placing children in foster families. This is an important part of deinstitutionalisation, but at a minimum, this should always be done in parallel with investigating and understanding the best interests of a child. In the current Russian system, this seems not always to be the case, as there is a strong pressure to place children in foster families. Moreover, black-and-white perceptions of care in a family as something that is automatically ultimately beneficial for a child and, consequently, residential care as automatically harmful, is neither analytically valid nor useful (Whittaker et al. 2016). The focus should be on finding the best solution for each individual child in order to serve their best interests. Thus, on the side of developing foster care and community-based services, it is also important to put effort into developing residential institutions to make them better places to live. As we have already shown, several issues related to funding, legislation, and norms must be solved to enable the development of the remaining institutions into home-like units.

Based on our analysis, it is possible to see certain analytic solutions to the thus far unsolved questions of the reform. Firstly, developing community-based support for birth families should become the next priority of the implementation of the reform. Consequently, the whole concept of preventive work should be reconsidered and redefined. Now, it seems rather unambitious to take 'prevention' merely as 'temporary' institutional placements, instead of developing a universal social policy to better serve those children living in vulnerable circumstances and providing non-stigmatising early support services for children, parents, and families at risk. One more solution could be to develop a portion of the existing institutions into family rehabilitation units, in which parents and children can stay together, and thereby enable effective help to the parent(s) during a temporary placement.

Moreover, the 'limbo' of 'Status-less children' could be resolved by reforming the legislation, images of fostering, and training of foster parents in such a way that children who are currently 'without status' in institutions could be placed temporarily in families. It should also be possible to place children in family care in cases where the child might return to their birth family later on. This would also require a clearer conceptual division between fostering and adoption. Now they are both regarded as permanent solutions, as discussed in several chapters of this volume. A possible solution would be to develop a new category of 'professional' foster families for those children who otherwise would not have an opportunity to be placed in families because of the temporary nature of the placements or health issues/behavioural challenges of the child.

Finally, the analysis calls for the reconsideration and strengthening of the educational background of the street-level bureaucrats responsible for child protection issues. Now, pursuing the quantitative indicators and serving the prospective foster parents seems to override the child's rights, which should always lie at the very heart of any child protection measure (UN CRC 1989). Prioritising the assessment and implementation of the child's best interests amidst multiple pressures, which are particularly high within this area prioritised by the top-level government sphere, let alone in the current political environment of Russia, requires strong professional ethics. In many systems, the professionalism and power to assess the child's best interests are with the social workers, but in our materials social workers were not usually involved in the process – or if they were, they were perceived only as bureaucrats doing all the paperwork. The professionalisation of child protection in Russia could be achieved through the professionalisation of social work and a significant strengthening of social workers' education in order to prepare them to take on such a role. Yet, the profession of social work remains underdeveloped in the Russian context (e.g. Penn 2007; Iarskaia-Smirnova 2011). Practitioners of social work have achieved – even less than Russian physicians, as Anna Temkina and Michele Rivkin-Fish (2019: 15–16) argued – the corporate autonomy and political influence associated in the West with professionalisation.

However, the most important point remains that, no matter who those professionals are by education, – the people responsible for street-level child protection must have sufficient mandate and expertise to evaluate and, importantly, act in the best interests of the child. This would require the replacement of the prevalent managerial logic of regulation with a professional one. Similarly, as Litvina et al. (2020: 15) argued concerning health professionals, in a context of a hybridisation of paternalism and managerialism, child welfare professionals' autonomy is restricted and their actions regulated by multiple and frequently contradicting rules.

Notes

1 Both authors made an equal contribution to this manuscript, so they are listed in alphabetical order.
2 Based on children listed in the national databank: www.usynovite.ru/db/
3 The record of the closing plenary can be watched online: www.youtube.com/watch?v=6 Z9YzgRMa50&feature=youtu.be [accessed 23 June 2019]
4 The project is funded by the Academy of Finland, University of Helsinki, and Kone Foundation for 2016–2020. A part of the research has been conducted also within the larger research project on youth well-being in the Arctic 'Live, Work or Leave? Youth – wellbeing and the viability of (post) extractive Arctic industrial cities in Finland and Russia (2018–2020)', funded by the Academy of Finland and the Russian Academy of Science
5 The annual report of the The Child's Rights Ombudsman of St. Petersburg in 2016, See: www.spbdeti.org/id6445 (accessed 7 November 2018).
6 More on the representations of birth parents in the child protection system is given in Jäppinen in this volume.
7 Elena Alshanskaya, a leading child rights advocate for the reform and member of the monitoring group, made a report on this subject to the Russian government. Available at: www.otkazniki.ru/events/news/elena-alshanskaya-predstavila-predlozheniya-po-reforme-detskikh-domov/.

References

Texts referred to in this volume

    Chapter 2: Biryukova and Makarentseva
    Chapter 4: Kulmala et al.
    Chapter 5: Tarasenko
    Chapter 7: Chernova and Shpakovskaya
    Chapter 8: Jäppinen

An, S., Kulmala, M. 2020. Global Deinstitutionalisation Policy in Post-Soviet Space: A Comparison of Child-Welfare Reforms in Russia and Kazakhstan. *Global Social Policy*, OnlineFirst (May 19, 2020): 1–24. Available at: https://doi.org/10.1177 %2F1 468018120913312 .
Biryukova, S., Varlamova, M., Sinyavskaya, O. 2013. *Sirotstvo v Rossii: osnovnye tendentsii i prioritety gosudarstvennoy politiki* [Orphanhood in Russia: Major Trends and Priorities of State Policy]. *SPERO. Sotsial'naya politika: ekspertiza, rekomendatsii, obzory* [SPERO. Social Policy: Expertise, Recommendations, Overviews] 18: 57–80.

Buzar, S. 2005. The Institutional Trap in the Czech Rental Sector: Nested Circuits of Power, Space and Inequality. *Economic Geography* 81 (4): 381–405.

Federal Law # 442-FZ. 2013. Federal Law of December 28, 2013 No. 48-FZ 'On the Basis of Social Provision for Citizens in the Russian Federation' (Federal'nyj zakon ot 28.12.2013 N 442- FZ "Ob osnovah social'nogo obsluzhivanija grazhdan v Rossijskoj Federacii"). Available at: www.kremlin.ru/acts/bank/38016 (accessed 30/03/2020).

Freidson, E. 2001. *Professionalism: The Third Logic. On the Practice of Knowledge.* Chicago: The University of Chicago Press.

Gel'man, V., Starodubtsev, A. 2016. Opportunities and Constraints of Authoritarian Modernisation: Russian Policy Reforms in the 2000s. *Europe-Asia Studies* 68 (1): 97–117.

Gilbert, N., Parton, N., Skivenes, M. 2011. Introduction. In: P. Gilbert, M. Skivenes (eds.), *Child Protection Systems: International Trends and Orientations.* Oxford: Oxford University Press.

Hardiker, P., Exton, K., Barker, M. 1991. The Social Policy Contexts of Prevention in Child Care. *The British Journal of Social Work* 21 (4): 341–359.

Hašková, H., Saxonberg, S. 2011. The Institutional Roots of Post-Communist Family Policy: Comparing the Czech and Slovak Republics. In F. Mackay, M. Krook (eds.), *Gender, Politics and Institutions.* London: Palgrave Macmillan: 112–128.

Hemment, J. 2009. Soviet-Style Neoliberalism? *Problems of Post-Communism* 56 (6): 36–50.

Iarskaia-Smirnova, E. 2011. *Class and Gender in Russian Welfare Policies: Soviet Legacies and Contemporary Challenges.* Gothenburg: University of Gothenburg.

Jäppinen, M. 2015. *Väkivaltatyön käytännöt, sukupuoli ja toimijuus – Etnografinen tutkimus lähisuhdeväkivaltaa kokeneiden naisten auttamistyöstä Venäjällä* [Domestic Violence, Gender and Agency: An Ethnographic Study of the Work Practices of Women's Crisis Centres in Russia]. PhD diss. University of Helsinki. Publications of the Department of Social Research, 2015: 3.

Kainu, M., Kulmala, M., Nikula, J., Kivinen, M. 2017. The Russian Welfare State System: With Special Reference to Regional Inequality. In C. Aspalter (ed.), *The Routledge International Handbook to Welfare State Systems.* London and New York: Routledge: 219–316.

Khlinovskaya Rockhill, E. 2010. *Lost to the State: Family Discontinuity, Social Orphanhood and Residential Care in the Russian Far East.* New York: Berghahn Books.

Kulmala, M., Jäppinen, M., Chernova, Z. Forthcoming. Reforming Russia's Child Protection System: From Institutional to Family Care. In: J.D. Berrick, N. Gilbert, M. Skivenes (eds.), *Oxford International Handbook of Child Protection Systems.* Oxford: Oxford University Press.

Kulmala, M., Rasell, M., Chernova, Z. 2017. Overhauling Russia's Child Welfare System: Institutional and Ideational Factors behind the Paradigm Shift. *The Journal of Social Policy Studies* 15 (3): 353–366.

Lipsky, M. 1980. *Street Level Bureaucracy: Dilemmas of the Individual in Public Services.* New York: Russell Sage Foundation.

Litvina, D., Novkunskaya, A., Temkina, A. 2020. Multiple Vulnerabilities in Medical Settings: Invisible Suffering of Doctors. *Societies* 10 (5): 1–17.

Mätzke, M., Ostner, I. 2010. Introduction: Change and Continuity in Recent Family Policies. *Journal of European Social Policy* 20 (5): 387–398.

Novkunskaya, A. 2020. *Professional Agency and Institutional Change: Case of Maternity Services in Small-Town Russia.* Doctoral dissertation. Helsinki: Faculty of Social Sciences, University of Helsinki.

Paneyakh, E. 2014. Faking Performance Together: Systems of Performance Evaluation in Russian Enforcement Agencies and Production of Bias and Privilege. *Post-Soviet Affairs* 30 (2–3): 115–136.

Penn, J. 2007. The Development of Social Work Education in Russia since 1995. *European Journal of Social Work* 10 (4): 513–527.

Pierson, P. 2000. Increasing Returns, Path Dependence, and the Study of Politics. *The American Political Science Review* 94 (2): 251–267.

Polterovich, V. 2008. Institutional Trap. In: S. Durlauf, L. Blume (eds.), *The New Palgrave Dictionary of Economics*. London: Palgrave Macmillan: 3087–3092.

Racko, G. 2017. Values of Bureaucratic Work. *Sociology* 51 (2): 374–392.

SanPin 2.1.3.2630–10. 2010. *Sanitarno-epidemiologicheskie trebovaniya k organizatsiyam, osuschestvlyayayuschim meditsinskuyu deyatel'nost'* [Sanitary-Epidemiological Requirements for Organisations with Medical Activities]. Available at: http://docs.cntd.ru/document/902217205 (accessed 30/03/2020).

Streeck, W., Thelen, K. (eds.). 2005. *Beyond Continuity: Institutional Change in Advanced Political Economies*. Oxford: Oxford University Press.

Temkina, A., Rivkin-Fish, M. 2019. Creating Health Consumers: The Negotiation of Un/official Payments, Power and Trust in Russian Maternity Care. *Social Theory and Health*, published online 4 July: 1–18.

Torfing, J. 2001. Path-Dependent Danish Welfare Reforms: The Contribution of the New Institutionalisms to Understanding Evolutionary Change. *Scandinavian Political Studies* 24: 277–309.

UN CRC 1989. *Convention on the Rights of the Child*. United Nations. Geneva, Switzerland.

Wattam, C. 1999. The Prevention of Child Abuse. *Children & Society* 13 (4): 317–329.

Whittaker, J. et al. 2016. Therapeutic Residential Care for Children and Youth: A Consensus Statement of the International Work Group on Therapeutic Residential Care. *Residential Treatment for Children & Youth* 33 (2): 89–106.

Part IV

Foster and birth families under institutional change

7 'Making' a family

The motives and practices of foster parenting

Zhanna Chernova and Larisa Shpakovskaya

Introduction

The chapter examines the discursive practices of foster parents, who have taken a child deprived of parental care in their family. We study the discursive strategies (explanations and justifications) that parents use to make sense of their parenthood and family. Foster parenthood is problematised and sometimes stigmatised at the level of wider social attitudes and media discourse in Russia (Gurko, Taseev 2006; Shpakovskaya 2018; Iarskaia-Smirnova et al. 2015). On the one hand, fostering is supported by the state policy of promoting family placement for children deprived of parental care. A wide range of public campaigns, organised by the authorities of federal and regional levels, and NGOs, have emerged in form of advertisement and mass cultural products, such as television series, novels, and media publications. These campaigns aimed to raise public awareness about fostering and children deprived of parental care while endowing fostering with the high moral value of helping the most vulnerable members of the Russian society.

On the other hand, fostering is under public scrutiny as it is suspected of neglect and sometimes even in the violent treatment of children. This theme has found its way into public scandals and trials related to foster parents. A number of media publications and television news broadcasts have accused foster parents of the inappropriate treatment of children due to their interest in state benefits instead of the altruistic motives of love and help. (For these themes in printed media, see Chapter 3 of this volume.)

At the same time, all legislative initiatives to establish professional foster families, where parents could legally work according to certain rules and receive salary from the state, were blocked at a very early stage. A moral dilemma emerged, with foster parenting seen to conduct professional work while also giving love to children. The apparent contradiction in this has proven unsolvable for the experts and opinion leaders. Those who were involved in the law development process expressed their fears that salary and the formal regulation of fostering will compromise a unique and necessary attribute of parental care: genuine love for children.

The media and legal context put parents in a situation of a need of discursive justification of their decision for fostering, relating their experience of upbringing of foster children to normative ideas about family and parenthood. In this chapter, we are interested in how foster parents talk about what family and parenthood mean for them, how they justify their decision to foster children, and what practices they mention in their narratives.

Theory: parenthood as a discourse

Parenthood is a complex social phenomenon that includes a set of practices and meanings of care, upbringing, parenting, and normative visions of the relationships between parents and children, and in couples. Parenthood is, on the one hand, governed by state policy, cultural regulations, and social norms, and, on the other hand, is defined by individuals and endowed with subjective meanings and individual experiences (McCartney, Edwards 2011: 209). Our theoretical framework approaches parenthood as a discourse, which considers 'parents' as a set of meanings, representations, images, or ideas, expressing themselves through spoken language, written text, or material practices.

Parenthood discourse is closely interrelated with discourse on the family (McCartney, Edwards 2011: 61). Parenthood and family discourses are multiple, they vary in content, place of localisation, as well as in their degree of integration into wider power structures. In this way, parenthood and family are ever-changing concepts which are very contextual and adjust to wider societal values, ideals, and practices. This definition helps to understand how family and parenthood are (re) produced at the level of subjective meanings by putting them in a wider sociocultural and political context (McCartney, Edwards 2011: 60).

Foster parenting in current Russian context is a fruitful analytical case, as the state heavily promotes adoption and fostering, which interacts with the already existing norms and ideals of care and parenting; as a result, parenting itself become modified through fostering. During the Soviet period, parenting was primarily seen as related permanent birth relations (Smirnova 2015). In the early Soviet period, there was a plurality of forms in family placement, fostering, and guardianship, all of which were promoted by the state (Zhiromskaya, Aralovetc 2018). The key direction here was the fight against child neglect and homelessness (*detskaya besprizornost'*). Although there were doubts over how appropriate the family was as a place for 'communist upbringing', family care was seen to be last resort given the shortage of public resources at this time (Smirnova 2015).

During the post–Second World War period, children deprived of parental care were defined by official discourse as 'orphans' (*deti-siroty*) (Astoyantc 2010). The term 'orphans' existed up to late Soviet time when it was transformed into 'social orphans', which described children whose parents were deprived of parental rights. Adoption as full parental responsibility was often seen as a unique form of family placement and similar to birth parenting and family relations. Family legislation contained measures allowing women to fake pregnancy symptoms when preparing to adopt a child and subsequently hide this history of adoption from the child (Shmidt 2009). Current policy of family placement contains very different forms of fostering, besides adoption, as it includes such forms as temporary fostering and paid and gratuitous fostering, with different levels of control from child protection services (*opeka*) – with low level of controls for adoption and very detailed control on the base of fostering agreement between *opeka* and parents.

We look at foster parenting as a discursive construct that contains normative ideas about parental roles, motives for foster parenting, ideas about appropriate care, and the difficulties of raising a foster child, as well as possible ways to interpret and overcome such difficulties. We understand the term 'foster parenting' to cover a wide range of legally available in Russia forms of taking care for a non-birth child (from temporary and paid fostering to full adoption). According to expert opinion, in contemporary Russia, different family placement forms are not always clearly distinguished for potential parents, who navigate through the system of social supports and benefits for foster parents, and can legally chose paid fostering which is, in practice, a kind of 'hidden adoption'.[1] Potential parents can also choose a form of temporary fostering, then take paid fostering, and finally decide to adopt a child.

In today's Russia, people who look after children deprived of parental care are in media and expert discourse called just 'parents' instead of, e.g., 'guardians' or 'foster parents' (*priemnye roditeli*). Despite their different legal statuses varying from short-term guardianship with a monetary compensation and strict control from the state to full adoption (when parents are given with full parental rights), public discourse and often parents themselves see their role as parental, which is primarily about love for children and not about 'work' (Chernova, Kulmala 2018). Following parental self-nomination, in this chapter we use the term 'parents' or 'foster parents' (*priemnye roditely*) and analyse how parents describe their motives for fostering and what parental practices emerge in their narratives.

If in the case of birth parenthood, the practices of 'making' a family and providing care are often not problematised but rather seen as natural, taken for granted, in the case of foster parenting they become spoken, as foster parents are socially forced to explain and justify their choices. For becoming foster parents, they also have to learn specialised knowledge for looking after a foster child, as education is a necessary prerequisite for fostering. Based on foster parents' written narratives, we analyse the discursive practices of creating a family and single out the following semantic areas: (1) what meaningfully constitutes family and parenthood in the context of fostering? (what is foster parenting?); (2) how is foster parenthood justified? (why is foster parenting?); (3) What everyday practices make foster parenting and family in their narratives? (how is foster parenting told to be practiced?). All these semantic areas use cultural, legislative, media, and expert discourses about parenting and fostering by adapting them in the context of their personal life stories.

The empirical data: the written narratives of foster parents

The article takes as its primary source of information a corpus of autobiographical texts written by foster parents about their fostering experiences. The texts were collected as part of a special contest 'Our Stories', organised by the Elena and Gennady Timchenko Charitable Foundation 2015–2017.[2] (http://nashiistorii. ru). The aim of the contest was to give a voice to foster parents and fight negative stereotypes of foster families. The foundation promotes family placement, its programmes aim at education and support of foster parents, sharing best practices of fostering and development of cooperation and self-help among foster parents. The participation in the contest was voluntary and free, the winners were given memorable gifts. As participants are generally not material beneficiaries of the foundation (there is no direct monetary support or cash prizes for winners), their motives were not principally about material interests. The conditions of the contest did not give the authors any direction regarding form or genre of presenting their experience of fostering. Up to 500 narratives were sent to the competition from 63 regions of Russia. Most of the collected texts were autobiographical in nature, as they tell the stories of how they decided to foster, how their search for a child went, and the specifics of family adaptation. In some narratives, parents concentrated more on the factual consequences of these events in their life. In others, more reflection was on what fostering is and its role in society. They also vary in genre from diary and life story to even poetry.

We analysed a total of 469 foster parents' written narratives published on *nashi-istorii.ru* website. The authors of the text are both men (23) and women (446). We do not have any systematic information on the sociodemographic characteristics of the authors, because not all diaries contain such information. On average, the number of foster children, in cases where they were mentioned, ranges from three to five per family. Most authors of the autobiographies have experience in raising birth and foster children, but some of them have experience of caring only for foster children. Among the latter category, we found some who used fostering to become parents due to the impossibility of birth parenting for them. These 'diaries' do not contain any systematic information about the legal forms of fostering, which would allow us to analyse the meanings and motives behind the forms the prefer. All authors use self-naming as parents (*roditeli*) or foster parents (*priemnye roditeli*). We follow their self-nominations and study what it means for them to be foster parents from their point of view.

As an additional source of information, we use data from 5 focus groups with altogether 54 foster parents in 4 different Russian regions and 9 individual interviews with foster parents which were conducted as part of the research project 'A Child's Right to a Family: Deinstitutionalisation of Child Welfare in Putin's Russia' (Aleksanteri Institute, University of Helsinki). The interviews and focus groups were used to distinguish particular meaningful features of the narratives presented to the contest and meanings of fostering which can be picked up regardless of the method of data production, as well information from 'diaries', which was verified and supplemented with interview data.

The analysed written narratives resemble an autobiography, which always have a double structure. The first relates to a broader social and cultural context of the narrative and presents the meanings of what is typical, normal, valuable in the terms of the respondent's individual life story, as well as narrations on being a member of a particular social group. Information about the 'typical' or 'normal' behaviour and life events that a researcher can obtain on the basis of an analysis of biography includes factual dimension (facts, events, and their consequences), evaluations, and justifications of actions and events in an individual life, as typical, valuable, and morally approved or disapproved.

The second meaningful structure in autobiographies is the concept of the self. In the process of creating an autobiographical narrative, the author produces a personal story and identity (Rozhdestvenskaya 2010: 8). Thus, autobiography is a discursive practice that combines the individual and the typical, based on a general semantic framework inscribed in social and political context. In the case of foster parenting in the context of contemporary Russia, an analysis of autobiographies gives access to contemporary discourses on family and parenthood in the creation of which the state, media, and experts take part, and which parents internalise in their narratives.

The nature of main materials that we analysed poses limitations on the information and conclusions which can be drawn from them. The texts were presented for the competition, which was launched by a charitable foundation. This fact encouraged their authors to share their positive experience and omit problems. For example, in the interviews, parents problematised such issues as control and fear of arbitrariness of the child protection services (*opeka*), difficulties of family adaptation, and the difficult behaviour of foster children. The authors position themselves as successful and experienced parents who were driven by absolutely moral motives and aims. At the same time, parental narratives are a unique information source as they contain normative ideas about parenting, family, motive, and practices of fostering.

Thus, our analysis is not about real parental practices; rather, it is about normative, ideal, and discursive aspects of foster parenting. Analysing discursive practices, we follow the approach developed by Ernesto Laclau and Chantal Mouffe (Laclau, Mouffe 1985), which is built around the idea that the social world is formed by discourse producing intersubjective meanings. Discourses are created by various societal actors, including mass media, state, experts, etc. (Philips, Jorgensen 2002). Data analysis was carried out according to the method of thematic coding (Flick 2006). Firstly, we coded openly semantic fragments of parental narratives. Secondly, the selected codes were compared and combined into thematic categories, which, finally, were interpreted as elements of the discourses of foster family and parenthood.

Foster parenthood in Russia: public opinion and the political and social context

The results of nationwide opinion polls in recent decades show that the family is among the most often chosen options of personal life preferences by Russians. For example, in 2000 the family was put first by 39% of Russians (between such options as security, material well-being, peace, and justice). By 2013, this number had almost doubled to 65%. According to other surveys, 99% of Russians value family above work (Lezhnina 2016: 71). The normative concept of the family as 'ideal', 'good', and 'prosperous' in the public opinion implies trust, love, and mutual respect between family members, and it also necessarily includes children (Chernova, Shpakovskaya 2010). Children in families are considered the norm, and parenting is seen as an obligatory element of life (Chernova, Shpakovskaya 2010). Foster parenting is understood by public opinion and media as one of the legitimate ways to acquire parental status (Pecherskaya 2012; Shpakovskaya 2018).

By the mid-2000s, a pronatalist turn in family policy occurred, bringing with it a consequent increase in size and number of family benefits, including those for foster parents (Biryukova, Sinyavskaya 2017; Chernova 2019). These developments contributed to the development of controversial changes in public opinion towards fostering. On the one hand, the growth of the state support and increasing promotion of fostering and family placements rose public interest in this topic and 'normalizes' fostering as a socially approved behaviour (Gurko 2015; Gurko, Taseev 2006; Ezheva, Poreckina 2004). On the other hand, at the level of everyday attitudes and media images, ideas about fostering are not only positive; they are also filled with controversial myths and stereotypes (Shpakovskaya 2018).

The motives which foster parents declare are usually divided into two groups: altruist and instrumental (Isomäki 2002). Altruist motives are usually related to self-sacrifice, help, moral and religious values, and moral duties. Instrumental motives are built around material and money benefits which parents can get as compensation for their work. Stereotypes about parents in Russia are structured alongside the similar dichotomy of altruism and instrumentalism, where both poles are seen as mutually exclusive: those who foster for love are not interested in money, or those who do this for money do not love children. Love is usually seen as the main quality of good parental care (Shpakovskaya et al. 2019); those who are interested in money cannot provide good care (Palieva, Savchenko, Solomatina 2011). Thus, negative stereotypes of foster parents include accusing foster parents of attempting to improve their own material well-being through state payments and benefits for fostering (Gurko, Taseev 2006; Shpakovskaya 2018; Chapter 3 in this volume). For example, a number of media scandals in 2017 blamed foster parents for inappropriate care and explained such parental behaviour as violence against children or giving up foster children as a result of parental material interest in receiving state benefits. One scandal was the case of a family, which had one birth, four adopted, and eight foster children. After day care workers had found bruises on the body of one of foster children, child protection services representatives came to the family's place, removed all the foster children, and placed them in institutional care. The case quickly became widely discussed in media.[3] Publications and TV messages commenting on it split into two poles. The first accused the child protection services of poorly monitoring the situation and demonstrating unprofessional behaviour. The second accused the family of bad and cruel treatment of children. The explanatory motives of cruel behaviour from the foster parents were presented as a result of their desire to gain state benefits. Another widely known case was the scandal that flared up after a family in Moscow returned seven foster children to custody when they discovered that their allowances were going to be less than they expected. The parents made no efforts to hide their discontent with money support from the state.[4] The cases were followed by a number of publications, TV shows, and analytical programmes discussing other similar cases of bad parenting and interpreting them alongside the binary of love versus money.

Results of a representative survey of foster parent opinion showed that only 2% of parents chose material interests as a motive for taking a child (Otdelkina 2013). The low rate of reporting instrumental motives can be explained by parents' desire to avoid the negative stereotypical image of public opinion of self-interested foster parents. Describing their experience of fostering, the authors of the texts that we analysed repeatedly note that they personally faced negative attitudes and misunderstandings on the part of their social environment, including their adult birth children, relatives, friends, colleagues, and neighbours:

> But I came across misunderstanding, I couldn't believe where it came from – my mum! My mother-in-law supported us, but my mother gave a lecture on the topic: 'You do not think about your [own birth] son, he will feel bad!'[5]

An analysis of the parental narratives shows that prejudices are especially articulated in cases where foster parents take children with health problems and disability into their family: 'I remember it well – the puzzled looks of my colleagues: one was silent, and one openly twisted their fingers around their temple.' Accusation of foster parents taking children for material interests is one of the most common topics in the analysed narratives:

> At first, the attitude towards our children in the village was different. Some felt sorry for them, others said that we took them to our family for money. So, we replied that there are thousands of children in orphanages in the country, that they can take several children into the family and 'get rich'.

> Often, I hear the following about foster parents: 'Yes, they take children because of money!' I personally heard this about myself: 'Got the roofing done, bought a car – it's all from children's money!' In fact, it took me several years to fix my roof and I did it myself . . . and my elder sons helped me to buy the car.

A particularly negative and cautious attitude is manifested towards foster parents who do not fit into the normative concept of the family, for example, single men, as is shown in the following:

> I am only now beginning to understand what I got myself into. Anonymous comments have already gone on the Internet – 'it's strange why he needs a boy of this age', 'he found himself a living toy', 'why he didn't he have a son of his own?'

The wider discourse of foster parenting sets the repertoire of semantic interpretations, which foster parents refer to in their narratives. The negative stereotypes and incoherence of the public discourse about fostering are built around the opposition of altruistic and material motives or dichotomous understanding of it as work and love (Chernova, Kulmala 2018). Similar discussion of ambivalent attitudes towards fostering can be found in interviews with parents and in focus group discussions with parents: 'There is a twofold [attitude from the people around]: there are people who believe that children are taken in to make profit from them. There are also those who respect us' (Interview with foster father).

Persistent stereotypes regarding foster parenthood, circulating in the media and everyday consciousness, force the authors of the analysed narratives to build their own discursive strategies to justify their choice for fostering and fit themselves into conventional and morally approved vision of parenthood as driven by altruistic motives. We will discuss in the following section how parents navigates in the dichotomy of work and love, where work is presented as an activity driven by instrumental motives and love as a purely altruistic behaviour.

Work or love? Foster parents narratives as an articulation of normative visions of parenthood

The main semantic axis along which the foster parents build their narratives is the love/work dichotomy (Chernova, Kulmala 2018). Most authors define foster parenting in the categories of love, service, and moral duty:

> I like the proverb: 'To settle an orphan is like to build a temple.' I consider the taking of these children into my family to be a noble cause since the family is a haven of refuge from the storms of life.

The moral imperative of foster parenthood, foremost motherhood, is sacrifice; a willingness to give up one's interests for the sake of a child's well-being; altruism and a willingness to take long-term action that focuses on the needs of another, as well as satisfaction from this activity. At the same time, parents mention 'difficulties': work that they have to do as parents:

> And every time I repeat that children, like trees, do not grow by themselves, they need care, affection, understanding, but children – this is time, children, they are labour. Children should not be anyone's. Children should be for mothers and fathers. And every hour and every minute, we care about somebody's life, we give a piece of our heart to someone, this is our job.

Parental work described in the analysed materials includes physical labour (cooking, washing, cleaning), emotional labour associated with establishing and maintaining relationships of trust and emotional attachment with a child, efforts to educate, keep health, socialise, and adapt a foster child (visiting children's educational and medical institutions and consultations with psychologists, speech therapists). Despite the fact that the authors describe in detail the efforts that they must make every day, they understand them in categories of altruism and intangible reward, in the form of joy and the meaning of life:

The work of a foster parent is not simple, it is responsible, but brings so much joy when you see a good result. Of course, there were sleepless nights, but what a blessing, when a child utters the first words 'mom', 'dad', takes his first steps, you see that his health is improving.

In addition to caring work, parenthood implies the cost of maintaining the well-being of the child, as well as the time resources that parents need to invest in upbringing, which potentially reduces opportunities for paid employment: 'For the sake of the kids I changed my job and chose a more flexible employment schedule, because combining maternal labour with an 8-hour working day was no longer possible'.

Despite this, foster parents do not mention financial aspects of their life, preferring to talk about moral and emotional compensation they receive:

Raising foster children is a difficult task. Parents must be trained professionals. On the other hand, becoming a mom and dad for a child is an enormous happiness. The best way to become happy is to share a piece of your heart with that person who is currently worse off than you are.

Thus, narratives of foster parents about meaning of parenting are created in a situation of suspicions about materialistic motivations, which is broadcast by media and reproduced at the level of everyday consciousness. Love and work are presented in dichotomous opposition, where one option excludes the other. In this context, parents are put in a situation of justification, which presumes explaining the meaning of foster parenting mainly in the categories of love and care. They are also reluctant to interpret their efforts as professional activity involving a specialised knowledge and competency, and, thus, something deserving of payment.

Discursive practices behind justifying the decision to become foster parents

Justifications for foster parenting are an important part of the narratives we examined. Now we turn to our second research question about how foster parenthood is justified, or how foster parents explain why they decided to foster. The articulation of the motives of foster parenting at the level of individual biographies is determined by personal meanings of family and parenthood. These meanings also allow the authors to fit their individual parenting experience into a broader sociocultural context and serve as a necessary element in building their identity. Based on our analysis of the empirical data, we identified four discursive justification strategies that foster parents use in their narrations about the reasons for their decision to take the child/children to their family: (1) to restore broken social order; (2) to normalise ones' biography; (3) to build a family; (4) to refuse to choose a child or a type of parenthood.

The first type of justification strategies we identified is related to the desire to restore broken social order. Facing a child in need, the authors present themselves as those who can correct the situation of violation and injustice concerning the child. All foster parents agree that children, regardless of their status, should live and be brought up in a family. The authors of the analysed texts are convinced that the family form of organising care for children without parental care should be the top priority over others: 'I am sure that every child should live and be brought up in a family. Not one, even the best modern state organization with very kind, responsive and attentive employees can replace a family.'

Life in a children's home and the absence of a family are considered as a wrong, disrupted order. The authors present themselves as saviours of children in critical situations. In this case, the motive for taking a child into one's family stems from the desire to help a specific child (not children in general) with whom a parent is already familiar in his/her professional activity (for example, from working at school, in an orphanage, and other social institutions, volunteering), or due to kinship, friendship, and neighbourhood relations, or other life circumstances (for example, being in a hospital where abandoned children were in care).

Such a structure of motives, as a rule, is strongly emotionally coloured. Foster parents can describe it in such terms as 'the heart could not stand it', and therefore they decided to take this particular child into the family. They write about their inability to pass by and not help a particular child. As in the following example, the emotional component of a decision is intertwined with a conscious choice:

> When we visited M., we saw in the group another girl of 3 years old with Down Syndrome, V. It was evident that the girl had a serious condition, but we consciously went to take her, it was painful to watch the child lying on bare oilcloth bitten by mosquitoes.

Foster parents who justify their choice as an attempt to restore a fair order of things often describe this situation in terms of moral duty and ethics. The categories of duty and service to the highest ideal of good are placed in the context of a personal life situation and personal biographical project:

> I decided to take the child into my family from a small children's home (*dom rebenka*) before retiring – I wanted to save at least one soul. There were many reasons: the question arose of what would I do next. I can't go to wash the floors or sweep the streets and bury the accumulated knowledge, skills, unspent love. Moreover, my son, a late child, is just finishing school. He needs to be looked after. Grandchildren – when will they come? My grandmother's syndrome is overpowering. Here the campaign for transferring orphans to families also begins. I had a son, but I also wanted a daughter. Nevertheless, the main reason was to save at least one child from the orphanage.

This quote most fully illustrates the complexity of motives for foster parenthood. It is a semantic construction of the justification of choice through linking the subjective perception of a new stage in the life cycle, the specifics of the family situation in accordance with the shared ethical category of good as a practical guide for action.

Another justification strategy is to treat foster parenthood as a way to normalise one's biography. These authors see parenthood as a mandatory biographical event. Due to the peculiarities of the individual life situation, birth parenthood becomes either impossible or problematic because of, for example, miscarriages, the death of their own birth child, giving birth to a disabled child, or having personal experience in alternative care. This type of explanatory strategy usually includes the following reasons for decision to foster: (1) reproductive health that hinders having their own children; (2) the experience of losing a birth child; (3) the personal experience of alternative care placement; and (4) the personal experience of giving birth and raising a child with disability.

One reason behind the decision to become a foster parent is often associated with the subjective perception by the authors that they can begin a new stage in their life course or family life course. For example, family life stage when children have grown up and left the parental home is problematised as a family without children. In addition, the process of growing old itself culturally questioned. These authors regret that they are no longer fertile and associated fostering with a return to the 'young' period of life, something that is a cultural norm in Russian society (Omelchenko 2015). This motive is especially relevant to women who have lost youthfulness as it is culturally prescribed by other women and wish to acquire the role of mother, which has a high symbolic status in Russian culture (Shpakovskaya 2015). In this case, foster parenthood is described in terms of acquiring the meaning of life, and the foster child is a gift that allows, as one of the authors put it:

> To become young and full of vim and vigour again', 'to get back joy of life': It happens that you are living, living and you suddenly realize that everything is useless. You get up early in the morning, make your bed, brush your teeth, drink coffee and realize that another gloomy autumn day has arrived. And then it is work and home, weekends in the country and again work and home. You are like a machine, you do your work without a goal, without pleasure, simply because it is necessary. And so, a year passes, two, three, five. . . . And then one autumn morning comes and you finally understand that you can't live like that anymore.

The use of this semantic construct to explain their motives is typical for representatives of authors, whose birth children have already grown up and left home:

> Soon the daughter graduated from high school and went to study. My husband and I were left completely alone in a big house. When he went on business trips, I could not find a place for myself. It seemed to me that from loneliness I would lose my mind. Gradually I came to the conclusion that we can take a child from an orphanage.

As in the first type of justification of the decision for fostering, the trigger that starts the decision-making process is an individual biographical event. The opportunity to become a 'normal' parent of a 'normal' child through foster parenting here is a way to normalise one's biographical project.

The third way to justify decision for foster parenting is to see it as a way of constructing a family. This type of justification could be considered as a type of biographical normalisation, but in this case, the normalisation occurs on the basis of the absolutisation of the family value and family construction as 'normal'. Normative ideas about family serve as a reference model, according to which the authors of the analysed texts build their family and parenting strategies. The positively valued image in official and mass media discourse of the large 'prosperous' family, where several children are brought up (Chernova 2012), acts as an ideal model, which can be achieved by fostering several children. The normative concept of the family determines not only the desired number of children but also their gender, to have both boys and girls. So, for example, if the family already had sons, the desire to have a daughter can be a reason of fostering.

An analysis of parental narratives shows that the family is attributed with high symbolic value. The authors describe family in such words as 'fortress', 'a castle', 'a home', and 'a support that every person should have'. The quality of the relationship between spouses, parents, and children is understood as an important condition for good family life, as one author points: 'each of us understands that everyone should build a happy family castle, build the foundation brick by brick.' Children (foster and/or birth) are considered to be a mandatory attribute of a 'genuine family'. As one of the authors wrote, 'a family cannot be without children', or another: 'a family begins with children.' The parents emphasise that they do not distinguish between birth and foster children: 'they are all mine', 'they are all my kids.' They explain, for example, why foster children should be considered as their 'own': 'There is no such thing as "someone else's children". There are only children who find themselves in difficult life situations, and they need help.'

At the same time, the authors indicate that it is foster children that make a family 'full', 'normal': 'I believe that birth children are my right hand and adopted children are the left.' Taking more foster children, according to this logic, only further improves the quality of family life and increases love: 'where love lives, all logical rules end. As more children as more love, love is not divided but multiplied.'

The fourth justification strategy sees fostering not as a conscious choice or one's own decision, but as a result of intertwining circumstances. The authors engaging with this strategy emphasised that one cannot choose seemingly with birth children whose time of birth, personality, gender, and appearance cannot be chosen. Foster parenting is represented in this case as destiny or fate. The authors of these narratives describe their decision to take a child into their families in terms of lacking choice and by emphasising that they became foster parents as a result of higher and irrational forces. Some parents elaborate this in religious terms:

Sometimes it seems to me that this fate led me exactly the way to create a foster family, by God . . . my understanding of this did not come immediately, not spontaneously. I am sure that God led us to this decision, trying to make it extremely thought out.

From the point of view of other authors, in contrast, everything happened by a chance: 'my friends ask: "How did you decide?" . . . I answer honestly: "I didn't really want to! . . . I didn't intend to do this. Somehow everything turned out this way".' We assume that this type of justification is an attempt to symbolically equalise foster parenting with birth parenthood. If birth parenthood appears as a biological fact, the description of the situation of lack of choice of a child becomes similar to a child delivery.

All of the justification strategies form different constellations of discursive practices in making a family. At the same time, parents share the ideal of family care, share with their readers their desire to help children in order to make their life better by providing the love, warmth, and care that they lack in the residential institutions or in dysfunctional birth families.

Narrated practices of fostering

The third research question which we raised in the beginning of this chapter concerns everyday practices that make foster parenting and family in the narratives (how foster parenting is told to be practiced). In their narratives, parents not only explain what fostering means for them and justify their decision for the fostering, but also often describe their daily life. We assume that the description of everyday practices included in the parental texts is an important part of the discursive creation and normalisation of foster parenting. The care and upbringing practices presented in these texts by the foster parents represent an effort to create a mundane family life environment, to involve children in the daily fabric of family life and relationships. The family practices are presented in the narratives as a joint activity which is performed by parents together with their foster and birth children. The goal of this joint activity is to 'make the child their own'. In the analysed narratives, parents almost do not mention problems of adaptation and their ways of coping with the behavioural and psychological issues. In contrast, parents in interviews talk a lot about child's problems, their own attempts to cope with them, and their difficulties in finding help from NGO specialists and state representatives, as well as their negative feelings and emotions. The following extracts from two interviews with foster mothers problematise the emotions of respondents during the period of adaptation and unsuccessful attempt to get help from the child protection services (*opeka*):

I can say that for me, the first difficulty was the biggest one: getting used to a little creature who, maybe, doesn't quite understand that he needs you. And you continue to try to love him, because when you only take a child, you still do not love him. Trying to love him, despite all his squiggles and despite the fact that he shows you in every possible way that he is not dependent on you. Although this is still a tiny creature. For me it was such a serious difficulty.

They [*opeka*] can in principle be addressed [for help]. But if they dislike you, then there will be the following reaction: They will begin to humiliate you, they will begin to show. . . . If you came with a complaint about a child, i.e. they will begin to show you that you are not so good. They will begin to put you in place of a child, i.e. they play with this, with everything. Maybe they are doing some kind of research, practicing something. But you didn't come for this! You came for 200 km in the winter in the cold, you waited no one knows how much and you need here right now. . . . You came for consolation. And they do experiments on you. Such a cruel way to gain knowledge.

In the analysed texts, such narratives are not found. All the practices described there presented as successful and unproblematic. This can be explained by the normative and normalising nature of the materials, where authors fit their narratives to the official discourse of happy and prosperous family and distance themselves from mass cultural representations of cruel and self-interested parents.

The analysis of narrated practices in this chapter has revealed the following typology of what is reported as family life: bodily practices, housekeeping, leisure, keeping and creation of family traditions, disciplinary practices, religious practices, and creating a shared family history

Bodily practices (bathing, kissing, hugging) are picked up as parents stress the importance of a body contact (usually with younger children) to accept a child as kin. The authors of the analysed texts mention, for example, that a newly fostered child 'smelled wrong'. Smell becomes the symbolic marker of a stranger. A child becomes kin when her/his smell feels pleasant. Other aspects of acceptance/rejection mentioned in the materials include the child's voice, behavioural style, and appearance:

Alyosha doesn't cry right, doesn't eat right, doesn't look right, and generally does everything wrong. And he even smells wrong! We call it a dry sponge. Just as a very dry sponge absorbs moisture, so Alyosha seems to absorb the world around him in every possible way.

Housekeeping practices include a whole range of different social activities, in which foster parents actively involve children: cleaning, cooking, shopping, caring for pets, gardening, minor repairs in the summer houses, etc., as one parent described: 'Work on the ground is not easy, but exciting, especially when you see the fruits of your labours. A very masculine job was found for the boys – to repair the fence, which was done.' Leisure practices are an important part of parental descriptions of family life. They are crucial as they imply spending time with the whole family at weekends, holidays, summer vacations, and travels. During these periods, family gets together and feels its unity. These descriptions allow parents to present their family as 'we':

The summer spent in nature in the village resembled a plot from a good Soviet film: we bathed every day, played on the lake, went to the forest, picked berries, sang songs.

We walked, skated, went to the cinema and museums, had fun in water parks, in general, we frolicked thoroughly. It seems to me that the more joint activities are practised, the easier it is to live. Time passes quickly, interestingly, positively and it was useful for everyone.

Practices aimed at (re)producing family traditions and rituals were often touched upon in the analysed diaries. Almost all foster parents noted the importance of forming ritual moments in communicating with children. Each family 'invents' its own rituals, which both parents and children love. These rituals are reproduced in everyday family communication, making the family sustainable and allowing close emotional relations. Examples of this include bedtime rituals, weekend rituals, 'evenings of revelation' (when all family get together and share their thoughts, feelings, and experiences of the day), family celebrations, and hugging when a parent and child meet.

Disciplinary practices are described as 'clear rules' of interaction between children and parents, as well as organisation of family routine. They concern the distribution of responsibilities at home as well as parents controlling their child's daily routines and educational and extracurricular activities. Many parents focus on talking about these kinds of everyday interaction, considering it important to 'work out the regime moments' as role and task distribution makes communication predictable and peaceful.

Religious practices of upbringing are actively narrated by those foster parents who present themselves as believers: 'Attending church services, the [appropriate] fulfilment of one's parental duties and praying are three steps on the path to love. And three very difficult steps.' Parents write that children in religious families regularly attend Sunday school, talk with the priest, and participate in religious ceremonies. These cases are especially interesting because parents describe community life and child socialisation going through integration not only in a family circle but also in a broader social environment.

Practices of constructing a shared family history aim at integrating the child into family, sometimes through maintaining also a child's tie to her/his birth parents and other relatives. Common ways to develop a child's identity are to make an individual photo album for each child, in which photographs reflecting the history of the child's life in the family since they met, correspondence with members of the birth family, etc., are stored.

The aforementioned descriptions of everyday practices and communication is an important part of the foster parent's narratives. The authors often use common clichés and refer to the wider political and media discourses of a 'normal' and 'prosperous' family. We suggest that parents have included these wider discourses in their narratives to stress the typical nature of their families and thus try to respond to the widely accepted negative stereotypes about fostering.

Conclusions

The aforementioned materials analysis allowed us to come to a normative vision of foster parenting. As all autobiographies, the texts contain two types of information. The first one relates to a broader social and cultural context and contains the meanings of what is typical, normal, and valuable in the respondent's story. The second is a self-concept, which the author produces in the process of narration (Rozhdestvenskaya 2010: 8).

Public opinion and media images of fostering are filled with controversial myths and stereotypes, accusing parents of wanting to make money out of foster child-care benefits. In their narratives, authors address this wider context by building self-presentations as good and normal parents. They present their activity as altruistically driven. At the same time, they omit emotional labour, physical and caring labour which is required in fostering, as well as specific difficulties which they run into while parenting a foster child. They prefer to talk about themselves as altruism-driven and neglect 'professional work' aspects, such as specific qualifications required, physical and emotional labour, and time and material investments.

Foster parents, in order to discursively normalise their experience, develop several viable strategies to legitimise their choices and experience as socially approved, meeting the claims of the larger society in regard to childcare. They present themselves as having a unique quality which they provide to children (comparing to institutional care): parental love. Love and altruism become a form of justification of their choice for fostering.

Both at the level of Russian society as a whole and at the level of individual biographies, family acts as an ultimate value and children are considered to be a necessary attribute of a 'normal' family. Foster care is often presented in parental narratives as meaningfully equal to having birth children. Parents make it clear that they regard foster children as 'their own'. Our analysis of foster parents' narratives allowed us to identify several discursive practices behind the construction of family relationships, such as emotional relationships, shared memories, and common family history. These practices are aimed at 'making the child one's own', including forging a family group and creating the family as the common fabric of everyday life.

Notes

1 'Hidden adoption' usually means that guardians use a legal fostering for family placement but actually practice adoption, describing his foster children as their "own" or even hiding from them information about their birth parents.

2 *Nashi istorii. Konkurs dnevnikov priemnykh semei.* Available at: http://nashiistorii.ru (accessed 16 March 2010).

3 Borova, I. 2017. Poboi byli privychny: novye podrobnosti izyatiya detey iz semi Del' ['Beatings Were a Habit': New Details of the Removal of Children from the Dels Family']. Moskovsky komsomoletc. 30 January. Available at: www.mk.ru/social/2017/01/29/poboi-byli-privychnynovye-podrobnosti-izyatiya-detey-iz-semi-del.html (accessed 11/12/2019).

4 Priemnaya sem'ya vernula 7 detei, ne poluchiv stolichnykh vyplat posle pereezda. 2017. [Foster family returned 7 children, without receiving capital benefits after moving]. Miloserdie.ru. 5 April. Avalible at: www.miloserdie.ru/news/priemnaya-semya-vernula-7-detej-ne-poluchiv-stolichnyh-vyplat-posle-pereezda/ (accessed 24/06/2020).

5 Despite the fact that all the texts were published on the website and open for public use, for ethical reasons in this chapter we deleted all details which could easily identify the contributors.

References

Astoyantc, M. 2010. *Politicheskij diskurs o sirotstve v sovetskij i postsovetskij period: social'naya integraciya ili social'noe isklyuchenie?* [Political Discourse on Orphanhood in the Post-Soviet Period: Social Integration or Social Exclusion]. *The Journal of Social Policy Studies* 4 (4): 475–500.

Biryukova, S., Sinyavskaya, O. 2017. Children Out of Parental Care in Russia: What We Can Learn from Statistics. *Journal of Social Policy Studies* 15 (3): 367–382.

Chernova, Z. 2012. New Pronatalism? Family Policy in Post-Soviet Russia. *REGION: Regional Studies of Russia, Eastern Europe, and Central Asia* 1 (1): 75–92.

Chernova, Z. 2019. *Nezavershennaya gendernaya revolyuciya* [An Incomplete Gender Revolution]. *Monitiring obshchestvennogo mneniya: Economicheskie I social'nye peremeny* [Monitoring of Public Opinion: Economic and Social Change] 2: 222–242.

Chernova, Z., Kulmala, M. 2018. *'Po slozhnosti – eto rabota, po sostayaniu dushi – sem'ya': profeesionalizatciya priemnogo roditel'stva v sovremennoi Rossii* [In Terms of Difficulty It's a Job, But the Heart Tells Me It Is My Family]. *Zhurnal sotciologii i sotcial'noi antropologii XXI* [Journal of Sociology and Social Anthropology] 3: 46–70.

Chernova, Z., Shpakovskaya, L. 2010. *Molodye vzroslye: supruzhestvo, parnterstvo i rodite'stvo. Diskuesivnye predpisania v sovremennoi Rossii* [Young Adults: Friendship, Partnership and Parenthood: Discursive Descriptions in Modern Russia]. *Laboratorium: Journal of Social Studies* 3: 19–43.

Chernova, Z., Shpakovskaya, L. 2016. *Professionalizatcia roditel'stva: mezhdu expertnym znaniem i obydennym soznaniem* [The Professionalisation of Parenthood: Between Expert Knowledge and Everyday Conscientiousness] *Zhurnal issledovanii sotchial'noi politiki* [Journal of Social Policy Studies] 14 (4): 521–534.

Ezheva, L., Poreckina, E. 2004. *Deinstitutionalizatcia vospitania detei bez poechenia roditelei* [Deinstitutionalisation in the Upbringing of Children without Parental Care]. *Zhurnal issledovanii sotchial'noi politiki* [Journal of Social Policy Studies] 2 (2): 203–226.

Flick, U. 2006. *An Introduction to Qualitative Research.* London: Sage Publications.

Gurko, T. 2015. *Sistema zameshchayushchej opeki nad det'mi, lishennymi roditel'skogo popecheniya vremenno i navsegda: problemy reformirovaniya* [The System of Substituting Child Guardians for Children Deprived of Parental Care Permanently: The Problem of Reforming]. In: F. Burhanova (ed.), *Professional'nye zameshchayushchie sem'i v sovremennoj Rossii: opyt, problemy, napravleniya sovershenstvovaniya. Patronatnaya sem'ya kak forma semejnogo ustrojstva detej* [Professional Substitute Parental Care in Modern Russia: Experiences, Problems, Directions to Improvement: The Patronat Family as a Form of Family Upbringing for Children]. *Materialy Vserossijskogo nauchno-prakticheskogo seminara* [Materials from the All-Russian Science-Practical Seminar (Ufa, 18–19 December 2014). Ufa: RIC Bash GU: 9–19.

Gurko, T., Taseev, V. 2006. *Priemnye sem'i v Rossii (na primere Samarskoj oblasti)* [Foster Families in Russia: The Case of Samara Oblast']. In: T.A. Gurko (ed.), *Aktual'nye problemy semej v Rossii* [Topical Problems among Russian Families]. Moscow: Institut sotciologii RAN: 74–91.

Iarskaia-Smirnova, E., Prisyazhnyuk, D., Verbilovich, O. 2015. *Priemnaya sem'ya v Rossii: publichnyi diskurs i mneniya klyuchevykh aktorov* [Foster Families in Russia: Public Discourse and the Opinion of Key Actors]. *Zhurnal sotciologii i sotcial'noj antropologii* [Journal of Sociology and Social Anthropology] 18 (4): 157–173.

Isomäki, V.P. 2002. The Fuzzy Foster Parenting: A Theoretical Approach. *The Social Science Journal* 39 (4): 625–638.

Laclau, E., Mouffe, C. 1985. *Hegemony and Socialist Strategy: Towards a Radical Democratic Politics*. London: Verso.

Lezhnina, J. 2016. *Institut sem'i v Rossii: na puti transformacii*. [The Institute of Family in Russia: In the Course of Transformation]. *Sociologicheskaya nauka i social'naya praktika* [Sociological Science and Social Practice] 2: 70–90.

McCartney, R.J., Edwards, R. 2011. *Key Concepts in Family Studies*. London: Sage Publications.

Omelchenko, E. 2015. The Solidarities and Cultural Practices of Russia's Young People at the Beginning of the Twenty-First Century: The Theoretical Context. *Russian Education and Society* 57 (1): 17–35.

Otdelkina, T. 2013. *Razvitie instituta priemnoi sem'i v Nizhegorodskoi oblasti kak professional'noi zameshchayushchei sem'i* [The Development of the Institution of Foster Family in Nizhegorodskaya Oblast as a Professional Substitute Family]. *Vestnik Nizhegorodskogo Universiteta N.I. Lobachevskogo Sociologia. Psikhologiya. Filosofiya* [Bulletin of Lobachevsky University: Sociology, Psychology, Philosophy] 6 (1): 452–456.

Palieva, N., Savchenko, V., Solomatina, G. 2011. *Motivatsiya prinyatiya rebenka v zameshchayushchuyu sem'yu* [Motivations of Taking Children into Substitute Families]. *Obshchestvo. Sreda. Razvitie* [Society, Environment, Development]: 132–137.

Pecherskaya, N. 2012. *Mifologiya roditel'stva: analiz diskursivnogo proizvodstva ideal'noi sem'i* [Mythology of Parenthood: An Analysis of the Discursive Production of the Ideal of Family]. *Zhurnal issledovanii sotcial'noi politiki* [Journal of Social Policy Studies] 10 (3): 323–342.

Philips, L., Jorgensen, M. 2002. *Discourse Analysis as Theory and Method*. London: Sage Publications.

Rozhdestvenskaya, E. 2010. *Narrativnaya identichnost' v avtobiograficheskom interv'yu* [Narrative Identity in Autobiographical Interviews]. *Sociologiya: metodologiya, metody, matematicheskoe modelirovanie 4M* [Sociology: Methodology, Methods, Mathematical Models 4M] 30: 5–26.

Shmidt, V. 2009. Orphan Care in Russia. *Social work and Society* 7 (1): 58–69.

Shpakovskaya, L. 2015. How to Be a Good Mother: The Case of Middle-Class Mothering in Russia. *Europe-Asian Studies* 67 (10).

Shpakovskaya, L. 2018. *'Podkidyshi': reprezentacii priemnogo roditel'stva v sovremennoi Rossii* ['Foundlings': Representations of Foster Parenthood in Modern Russia]. *Zhurnal sociologii i social'noi antropologii* [Journal of Sociology and Social Anthropology] 21 (3): 71–92.

Shpakovskaya, L., Kulmala, M., Chernova, Z. 2019. The Ideal Organization of Care for Children Deprived of Parental Care: Russia's Child Welfare Reform as Battle over Resources and Recognition. *Laboratitim: Journal of Social Research* 11 (1): 57–81. (in Russ).

Smirnova, T. 2015. *Deti strany sovetov. Ot gosudarstvennoj politiki k realiyam povsednevnoj zhizni 1917–1940* [Children of the USSR: From State Policy to Real Everyday Life]. Moscow, Spb: CGI.

Zhiromskaya, V., Aralovetc, N. 2018. *Rossiiskie deti v konce XIX – nachale XXI v.: istoriko-demographicheskie ocherki* [Russian Children at the from the End of the 19th Century to the Start of the 21st: A Historical and Demographic Record]. Moskva: IPI RAN.

8 No longer parents or parents in need of support?

Views of child welfare experts on birth parents

Maija Jäppinen

Introduction

The child's right to live and be raised in the family and to know their parents is one of the central principles of the United Nations' Convention on the Rights of the Child (UN CRC 1989). The Family Code of the Russian Federation (1995) emphasises the same principle. Indeed, the child's right to a family – although not necessarily their birth family – is at the heart of ongoing deinstitutionalisation reforms to the Russian child welfare system. While the family policy of the 2000s supported prosperous young families based on the pro-natalist goals of increasing the birth rate (Chandler 2013; Cook 2011), in recent years, as discussed in this volume, special attention has also been paid to children deprived of parental care. In essence, the ideological goal has remained the same: strengthening families. The state emphasises 'traditional' family values and the role of the heterosexual nuclear family, calling such a family the main social unit of Russian society.

Nevertheless, there is a strong moralistic tone in this talk about parenthood, and not all parents are regarded as valuable in their children's lives. This chapter focuses on often-silenced margins of parenthood, i.e. on the birth parents of children who have been placed into alternative care with either foster families or institutions. Their role has so far gained little attention in ongoing child welfare reforms; more focus has been given to developing the foster family system and reforming the remaining institutions into a more home-like condition (Kulmala et al. forthcoming). Work with birth parents has not yet become the object of significant attention either in the reforms or in research on Russian child welfare.

This chapter analyses the views of child welfare experts on the birth parents of children who have been placed into alternative care either temporarily or permanently. These representations are an interesting topic of analysis, because they are closely related to the system's ability – or inability – to develop family support services, preventive work with families, and support for birth parents in order to enable the return of children to their birth families after an alternative care placement, which are set as goals in the strategic documents of the reform, such as the National Strategy for Action for Children (2012), National Concept of Family Policy (National Concept 2014), and the Government Decree #481 on the Activities of Organisations for Orphans (2014).

Drawing from a constructionist research on social problems (Miller, Holstein 1993; Holstein, Miller 2017), this chapter claims that suggested solutions to the problem of 'social orphanhood' as well as possibilities to develop new methods of working with the birth families depend heavily on the representations which the child welfare experts make of birth parents. Therefore, it is interesting and important to analyse how child welfare experts view birth parents. Are the birth parents seen as important persons in their children's lives even though they have not always been able to give their children everything they needed? Are they seen as capable of change, or regarded as 'lost cases' and do they need punishments or support? The chapter asks: what kind of discourses and discursive strategies do child welfare experts use when talking about the birth parents of children in alternative care and their parenthood? How do they see the role of the birth parents in the lives of these children?

The analysis is based on expert interviews conducted in several regions of Russia with state and municipal child welfare experts, as well as with representatives of non-governmental organisations working in the field of child welfare, in 2015 and 2018.

The Russian child welfare system and birth parents

To understand the Russian child welfare system, it is important to understand how families and parents with problems are traditionally viewed in Russia. In the Russian legal system, two key concepts organising the state's concern for children in need of protection are when the child/family are in a 'socially unsafe situation' (*v sotsialno opasnom polozhenii*) and in a 'difficult life situation' (*v trudnoi zhiznennoi situatsii*). Federal Law FZ-120 'On the Prevention of Child Negligence and Youth Offences' (Federal Law 1999) considers the socially unsafe situation of a child/family as caused by parents who neglect their parental responsibilities in raising their children and who abuse or negatively impact their children. Also included are children with 'deviant', 'criminal', or otherwise asocial behaviour. The legislation underlines parental responsibility in raising and socialising a child; a child's deviant behaviour in turn is framed as a consequence of negligence rooted in insufficient parental care (Prisiazhniuk et al. 2015: 24; Kulmala et al. forthcoming).

In addition to the aforementioned concepts defined in the law, the loosely defined but undoubtedly stigmatising concept of 'unfortunate family' (*neblagopoluchnaya sem'ya*) became widespread in the 1990s. This concept was rooted in the institutional language used by the post-Soviet social workers and public authorities as well as in the discourse of wider public. The notion of the 'unfortunate family' lumps together such life situations and categories of families as one-parent families, families with many children, and families living in poverty (Iarskaia-Smirnova 2010). As Khlinovskaya Rockhill (2010: 36–37) argues, in the post-Soviet Russian context, the marginality of these families is not explained so much by socioeconomic status, unemployment, or other conditions as they would be in many other societies, but by the personal and moral characteristics of the parents, their personal failures, and deviancy.

This view has its roots in the Soviet era, during which the state – at least officially – guaranteed full employment and relative socioeconomic prosperity for all families. Thus, family problems were not explained in the light of social problems and inequality, which in official terms did not exist, but by the personal traits of the family members and their moral characteristics. In addition, when unemployment and poverty emerged as explanations in the post-Soviet discourse, there was a strong subtle classification of these people into different groups, e.g. the 'deserving' and 'undeserving' poor, again with a strong evaluation of their possible immorality, asocial characteristics, and other personal inadequacies (Khlinovskaya Rockhill 2010: 37–38). Accordingly, in the Soviet times, 'working with the family' did not mean supporting the parents, but admonishing them and expecting that, as a result, they would correct themselves. If not, the authorities could use specific sanctions towards these irresponsible parents (Khlinovskaya Rockhill 2010: 100).

Scholars classify child welfare systems into child protection–oriented, family service–oriented, and child-focusing (Gilbert 1997; Gilbert et al. 2011). In a child protection–oriented system (for example, in the United States or Canada), family intervention takes place to protect the child from abuse by their parents or other relatives. This approach is characterised by an emphasis on legal proceedings, little cooperation with birth parents, and a large number of cases of forced placement of children into alternative care. A family support–oriented child welfare system (such as in the Scandinavian countries) emphasises the importance of support to solve family problems. Families are offered therapeutic support, cooperation with parents is valued, and the emphasis is on the provision of non-residential services and voluntary removal from the family. In addition to these, in recent years a child-focused model, which emphasises the child's own agency and participation in the decision-making on their own issues, has emerged in many countries (Gilbert et al. 2011; Pösö et al. 2013; Tulensalo 2016).

Based on the aforementioned classification, the Russian child welfare system – still with strong path dependencies from the Soviet time – can so far be seen as child protection–oriented. Traditionally, the employees of child welfare authorities have intervened in the situation of problems in the child's life at a late stage, but the interventions are rigid, often based on the child's removal from the family rather than on providing support services to all family members. Parents in such a situation have been more likely to receive condemnation for neglecting their parental responsibilities than be provided with therapeutic support. After the child's placement into alternative care, parental rights may be limited or terminated. In general, the limitation of parental rights applies, for example, in cases where the parent's mental illness or difficult life situation has led to the removal of the child from the family. The basis for termination of parental rights may be a neglect of parental duties, abuse of alcohol or drugs, or the physical abuse of a child (Family Code of the Russian Federation 1995). Of the aforementioned measures, termination of parental rights is most often used (Biryukova, Sinyavskaya 2017).

One of the objectives of the reform, however, is for there to be more cases where parental rights is limited rather than terminated. In addition, as discussed by Jäppinen and Kulmala in this volume, there seems to be a growing new group of children placed 'temporarily' into institutions without the limitation or termination of parental rights. This trend can be seen at least partly as an attempt to preserve relations between the child and the birth parent, regardless of the need for alternative care. Moreover, at least baby steps have been taken to develop support services for families in order to prevent the need for alternative care. The Russian child welfare system differs from many other countries in the concepts used. Children in alternative care are usually called 'orphans', regardless of whether their parents are alive or have had their parental rights terminated by a court decision. Most of these children are 'social orphans', i.e. children whose parents are alive but do not participate in the lives of the children. Social orphans make up about 80% of all 'orphans' in the Russian Federation (Biryukova, Sinyavskaya 2017).

In the current period, new reforms aim to reduce 'social orphanhood'. This should be reached by developing family support services in order to avoid the removal of children from birth families, moving the accent of alternative care from institutions to foster families, and developing forms of support and training for foster families. Key steering documents of the reform, such as the 'National Strategy for Action for Children' (2012) and the 'Government Decree #481 on the Activities of Organisations for Orphans' (2014), speak about supporting the birth parents of children in alternative care to make it possible for the child to return to their family. However, the implementation of this aspect has so far not been given enough attention. Until now, the most significant measures have been concerned with the development of the institution of the foster family and the creation of home-like conditions in the remaining institutions. Importantly, although the reform strives to decrease 'social orphanhood', the system constantly produces new 'social orphans' through the practice of the termination of parental rights.

The effectiveness of the reform is measured not by the breadth of the range of measures aimed at supporting birth parents, nor by the number of children returned after removal to their families, but by the number of children transferred from institutions to foster care (Kulmala 2017; also Jäppinen and Kulmala in this volume). Statistics show that the return of children to their families is not a priority of the reform (Biryukova, Sinyavskaya 2017). Systematic changes can nevertheless have a positive impact on the development of preventive services aimed at early family support. If successful, these changes may be the first step towards reorienting the Russian child welfare system for providing services to families. As Kulmala et al. (forthcoming) argue, as a result of the ongoing reform, one can see that the orientation is shifting towards child-focused and family support, at least at the level of ideas.

Data, methodology, and conceptual framework

The analysis in this chapter is based on interview data produced between 2015 and 2018 as a part of an interdisciplinary research project led by Meri Kulmala entitled 'A Child's Right to a Family: Deinstitutionalisation of Child Welfare in Putin's Russia'. The project involved almost 200 interviews with representatives from federal-level, regional, and local non-governmental organisations; regional officials; directors of residential institutions for children; and foster parents; and care leavers in several regions of Russia. The empirical data used in this chapter consists of 31 expert interviews with employees of public institutions, including child protection services (*opeka*), family support centres (*tsentr sodeystviya sem-eynomu vospitaniyu*), and children's homes (*detskii dom*), as well as NGO actors and policymakers. These were conducted in one region in Central Russia in 2015 and two regions of North-West Russia in 2018[1] The first data set from Central Russia from the year 2015 has also been analysed in an article on child welfare experts' discourses on birth parents published in Russian (Jäppinen 2018).

Because of the different educational and organisational backgrounds of the interview participants, I have decided to describe them with the general concept of 'experts'. This means that they all hold some kind of expert status in the field of child welfare, but they do not represent a certain profession or a united educational background. Another important choice is to use the concept 'birth parents' instead of 'biological parents', as the latter contains in the Russian context a pejorative connotation, diminishing these parents to being merely transmitters of genes, who have never really taken care of their parental responsibilities. In Russian-language discussions, including the data of this study, these parents are often called 'blood parents' (*krovnye roditeli*), but the concept of birth parents is applied here, because with regard to the concept of the biological parent, it is the most commonly used term in the international literature on children's rights and child welfare.

Theoretically, the analysis is inspired by the ideas of constructionist research on social problems, and especially the ideas of social problems work (Miller, Holstein 1993; Holstein, Miller 2017). Social problems work refers to activities implicated in the recognition, identification, interpretation, and definition of conditions that are defined as 'social problems', and the collective analysis and understandings constructed of these problems, possible solutions to them, and necessary changes and procedures. A central idea to this is that human beings interpret and construct social problems through ongoing discursive processes (Holstein, Miller 2017).

Accordingly, the data was analysed using the tools of discourse analysis. In discourse analysis, the analytical focus is put on how speech is used to build concepts and ideas about the world around us, and we do not consider speech only as a means of transmitting information (Gee 2010). More specifically, this study relates to the tradition of critical discourse analysis (CDA), which suits well to analysis of social problems and discourse analytical examination of professional and institutional power (Van Dijk 2015), in this case on the discursive power exercised by child welfare experts' representations of birth parents. The child welfare experts of this study hold a remarkable amount of power in how they view birth parents and their parenthood. The way in which they discursively frame birth parents has consequences: the discourses affect decisions taken by child welfare officials as well as service development and delivery. The expert interviews can be viewed as speech acts in which discourses and discursive strategies are revealed.

One of the assumptions lying behind the analytical focus of this chapter is that the ideational changes to the Russian child welfare system have also led to

discursive changes among the child welfare experts. At the same time, it is important to remember that the correlation of political trends with wider social assess-
ments and perceptions is ambiguous (Murray, Powell 2009). Changes made to
political decisions are not immediately reflected in the mindset of experts, who
are also affected by the most common social attitudes and stereotypes. On the
other hand, some of the interviewed experts may be forerunners in their thinking
and ways of speaking, and their opinions may be transmitted to higher decision-
making levels. When researching child welfare reform, it is important to analyse both the leading political reform strategies and interviews with experts who
directly implement these strategies. This chapter focuses on the views of the
experts. The political documents and their strategies for updating the child welfare system serve as the starting point for the analysis, and the discourses used by
the experts are compared to the political goals set from above.

In what follows, I will elucidate the two main discourses found in the interview
data, namely the discourse of parents as 'no longer needed' and the discourse representing parents as 'in need of support', and the five discursive strategies related
to them. In the data excerpts used in the following sections of the chapter, I have
used underlining to highlight certain discursive choices made by the interview
participants. To protect the anonymity of the research participants and their clients, the exact geographical places and organisations in which the interviews have
been conducted are not indicated, and all names and other information possibly
leading to recognition have been changed or left out.

The discourse of parents as 'no longer needed'

In my earlier analysis on the first data set from Central Russia from 2015, I was
surprised by how little talk on the birth parents of children in alternative care
there was in general in the data (Jäppinen 2018). Much more attention was paid
to training adoptive parents, finding new homes and families for children who are
still being raised in institutions, and adoption as the best solution to the problem of
'social orphanhood'. Cases of the return of children from alternative care to their
birth parents were constructed as exceptions, as an employee of child protection
services (*opeka*) explained:

I: Is there a practice of returning children from foster families to birth families?
E: There are <u>practically no returns to birth families</u> unless someone returns from
   prison, but this is one out of 300 children. There are one or two children per
   year. So we know this and we arrange custody for this period. And so, in order
   to be restored in parental rights . . . <u>practically no one</u> is restored.

The rareness of the returns of parental rights still in this Central Russian region in
2015 reflects the 'traditional' way of portraying birth parents as a lost resource in
the child's life after placement into alternative care. This discourse of parents as
no longer needed is first of the two main discourses in the interview data. Next I
will present three discursive strategies used by the interview participants within
this discourse.

The discursive strategy of representing birth parents as 'former parents'

After the termination of parental rights, parents and parenthood cease to exist in both juridical terms and symbolically. The concept of 'social orphan' applied to these children emphasises this. Literally, an orphan means a child who no longer has parents. Elena Khlinovskaya Rockhill (2010), who conducted ethnographic research in children's homes in the Russian Far East before the reform in the early 2000s, has called this phenomenon the symbolic death of birth parents. In my data, this also becomes palpable in the discursive strategy of talking about these parents as 'former parents', as a policymaker did in an interview conducted in 2018:

> Contacts with close relatives and <u>former parents</u> are a problem, of course. In my opinion, there is really negative progress in this respect in our region. There are only single cases in which parental rights are returned. Nevertheless, children keep the contact. I have talked about this with many people. I see here an exploitative attitude.

By exploitative attitude, the interviewed policymaker means, in my interpretation, that the 'former parents' do not take care of their children as supposed, but leave their care to the state. Because of this withdrawal from parental responsibilities, they picture it as morally condemnable to maintain contact with the children. In this discourse, parents who do not take care of their responsibilities should just disappear from the lives of the children.

The discursive strategy of viewing contact with 'former parents' as dangerous

In the aforementioned citations, it becomes evident that according to the opinions of these interview participants, birth parents should better not participate at all in the lives of their (former) children. Exceptions to this are portrayed as dangerous to successful transition to alternative care, and keeping in contact was constructed as negative to a child's well-being. This was accompanied by an idea that a foster family can completely replace birth parents. In this discourse, the termination of communication with the birth parents occurs in the interests of the child, and the possibility of a child's return to the birth family is seen as a tragedy.

> There are these very sad (pechalnye) situations, in which, for example, foster parents take the kids, because the child protection services has offered them to these parents, and then in two or three months they are taken away from the foster family, because the birth mother appears and wants a return of her parental rights.

The preceding excerpt is from an interview with a foster parents' NGO representative, and looking at things firmly from foster parents' point of view may explain the discursive choice of representing the return of the child to their birth parents is a tragedy. Nevertheless, employees of the child protection services – those authorities preparing the decisions – also often constructed maintenance of contacts between birth parents or relatives and children as dangerous to the child's adaptation to their new family and stability in their lives. Thus, the activity of birth parents and their desire to keep in touch with their children were considered as negative and even destructive for the child. In the following citation, a director of a children's home constructed it as being in a child's best interest to cut their ties with their birth family:

> The big task here is how to find an approach to children so that they under-stand that this is done for their benefit. And we must create conditions so that they are ready to go to foster families and that they understand that the foster family may well replace the birth one. . . . The attitude of relatives of our children is sometimes negative because most children have relatives, [whose] parental rights are terminated, they even come to meet some of them: Moms and dads who are alcoholic and seem to say that they will take the child, but it is clear that they will never take it. They only disturb the further develop-ment of the child.

In this discourse, adoption was considered the best decision for the child; as the change in family ties became final, this protected the child from returning to their birth parents. Experts also emphasised that another change in family ties after suc-cessful adaptation in a foster family could be traumatic for the child.

The discursive strategy of pointing at neglected parental responsibilities

The Russian Family Code is based on the idea of the rights and responsibilities of children and parents. One of the dominating representations of birth parents in the data was to view them as persons who have neglected their parental responsibili-ties. From a statistical point of view, 'neglect of parental responsibilities' is also the most common ground for termination of parental rights (Biryukova, Sinyavs-kaya 2017: 372). This discursive focus emphasises that there are no rights without responsibilities and no parenthood without the fulfilment of parental responsibili-ties. The removal of a child from the family and the termination of parental rights in experts' views seemed to be an insufficient measure applied to parents who neglected their parental duties, and they believed that parents should be punished for this neglect accordingly.

> Most importantly, maybe what is missing is responsibility. Today, we just had a reception for citizens in the morning. We talked about the fact that, well, a mother was terminated of parental rights, a father was terminated of parental rights, they continue to party and drink, alimony is some ten roubles a month, let them pay. But we actually created all the conditions for them to continue such a way of life. They do not have a child to look after, to raise. . . . But such parents need not just to be relieved of their parental rights, but some

punishments are needed, perhaps up to imprisonment of such parents who constantly abandon their children.

The policymaker speaking in the aforementioned citation constructed birth parents' inability to take care of their children as an active choice to abandon them. This is an illustrative example of a discursive strategy that emphasises how experts hold parents responsible for their decision to neglect the needs of their children and give them to other people to be raised. The key issue in this discourse is the irresponsibility of parents and how they can be pushed to re-take responsibility for their children. One interviewed employee of the child protection services, for example, expressed hope for the emergence of legislation on parental responsibility, thanks to which it would be possible to return most children to their birth parents. Importantly, this would be done with the power of punishment, not by offering support and guidance. This view is very different from a position that emphasised circumstances that have made it very difficult or impossible for parents to care for their children. Such circumstances may be hard socioeconomic conditions, addiction to alcohol or drugs, mental illnesses, or emotional traumas, due to which the parent is not able to take into account the needs of the child and form a healthy attachment to them.

The institutional inability to see those circumstances which may have caused a birth parent's behaviour to be labelled as 'irresponsible' complicates significantly the development of support services for birth families. Being able to support these parents in a dignified way would require seeing them as human beings in vulnerable situations, because of which they have not always been able to be as good and responsible parents as expected. Similarly, a possible fear of being punished and humiliated by the service providers does not encourage birth parents to accept the new support services that may be on offer.

Putting the discursive focus on parents' need for support

The discourse of parents as no longer needed and discursive strategies to justifying this, which I analysed previously, create a rather negative and deterministic view of parenthood after the placement of a child into alternative care. Importantly, along with this discourse, the data also contains more optimistic representations of birth parents. The prevalence of these new views on birth parents in the data seems to grow over time, which signals a gradual change in the representations of birth parents by child welfare experts and the interpretations of possible solutions to the problem of 'social orphanhood'.

The discursive strategy of representing birth parents as a resource in the lives of their children

There exists also such discursive strategy in the data, in which birth parents are viewed as a possible future resource for the child. This resource can be utilised if they receive the necessary assistance to solve their problems and give them the support they need in parenthood. In this discursive strategy, the long-term goal of the work is set to return the child from alternative care to live with their birth parents, as put by a child protection services representative:

> If this is to birth parents, then this is a good indicator if you manage to restore the parents in their rights and return the child – this is good. . . . We try to work with birth parents, to convince them that enough time has passed and the situation has changed – many have begun to work, their lifestyle has changed, it is time to turn to their children, we are convinced that this needs to be done, we help to collect documents to restore parental rights. And we return the children.

Importantly, several experts phrased as an explicit goal that children need to be kept in their birth families or returned there immediately after the crisis has been resolved.

> Our priority, anyway, is to <u>keep the child in the [birth] family</u>. It is the main thing (Employee of the child protection services).
> [The main priority of the activity is] to preserve the child's birth family. When a child arrives, we not only begin to rehabilitate the child, but we also begin to work with their family – we constantly visit, talk, conduct specialist consultations, try *to restore the family*, lost connections.
> Director of a children's shelter

This discursive turn is in good accordance with the goals of the reform and the new tasks of the old children's homes now reorganised as family support centres. A major part of the work of these family support centres so far has been, however, done with children who have already been temporarily removed from their families, as Jäppinen and Kulmala discuss in this volume. Nevertheless, the priorities of the work have changed and work practices should include a new element of supporting the birth parents to be able to take care of their children at home again.

The discursive strategy of viewing parents as capable to change if supported

Importantly, parents are more often portrayed by the experts as capable of change – not lost causes, as in the aforementioned discourses. An idea is emerging that child welfare officials really are responsible for not only saving children from difficult conditions, but also trying to change these conditions by working with birth families.

> The next step, if there are kids who enter the institution, if work with parents is organised, but you know also that these parents' attitude is fickle: today I

want to return the kids, I'll do everything that it needs. For a week or two they appear actively, do everything and visit a specialist in addiction medicine. They start searching for a job and talk about arranging things at home. We think we might be able to return the children home. And then they [the birth parents] disappear. Next month they drink again. Well, it is understandable, if they have an alcohol dependency: without treatment, as a rule, it is very complicated to manage.

A director of a family support centre drew in the preceding excerpt a rather pessimistic picture of birth parents, again: they do not engage with the services in the long term, but come and go. This makes working with them very complicated and it is impossible for the children to return home. Importantly, they do not represent birth parent's possible incapability to come to the proposed meetings as a sign of their moral irresponsibility or moral degradation, but as a consequence of alcoholism, which is here constructed as an illness for which they need better treatment than is available in the region.

Until recently, a child's separation from their birth parents has not been seen as a particular problem, because what counts is not just the birth family but a good family (Khlinovskaya Rockhill 2010). Now, the worth of the birth family seems to be increasing in the eyes of child welfare experts. Birth parents are more often than earlier portrayed to be important and valuable for the child, regardless of whether they always been able to act in the interests of the child. The inability or unwillingness of the parent to commit to cooperating is considered not only as their choice but also as a consequence of their personal problems. Experts provide narratives of parents who have been able to improve the situation so that the child can return home. Seeing hope and recognising examples of change that has occurred seems to be an important precondition for the discursive change:

There are examples, though, when a girl [grown up in alternative care], who has bad relations with her mom, gives birth to a baby herself, and, all of sudden, the mom starts to help her and take care of the baby. Walks often with the baby carriage, helps her, and you think that this is a miracle. God, what has happened with that woman? Well, something has happened.

The aforementioned expert wondered, 'what has happened' with the mother, previously labelled as a lost cause, when she is able to take care of her grandchild. This kind of accounts of parents' later ability to change are interesting, because they cannot help but raise the question of whether these parents would have been able to take care of their own children, if they had received the support they needed in a timely manner.

The growing ability of child welfare experts to view parents as in need of support instead of seeing only their failures and condemning them can be of great importance and create avenues for institutional change. This citation from an interview with an NGO expert represents well the changing discourse, but also sheds light on the institutional changes affecting the discursive change:

> We have projects which focus on raising children, for example [project name] – this is a really useful project for girls, because when they end up in a shelter, not a children's home but a shelter, they most often return home to the mother, who <u>does not take care of them</u> (imi ne zanimaetsya). And there are some everyday skills, . . . well, for example, you need to change your underwear every day. Which <u>they just do not manage</u>. . . . One and the same child may leave and return [from and to home] five times in two years. . . . There is practically no work with the birth families. Not because the system does not want to, but because it is not capable of doing so. The same mothers, I see them regularly, who come to the shelter for known reasons: <u>they cannot raise children.</u> Practically no one works with them, there are no hands for that. . . . We are now working on an idea to create a project. We already have mentoring for care leavers, but we would like to provide <u>mentoring for these mothers</u>.

The aforementioned NGO expert pointed out that the structures of alternative care have changed as a result of the reform to favour temporary, short-term placements with children's shelters instead of permanent placements with children's homes and the termination of parental rights. After the acute crisis, these children are returned home to their mothers, but nothing has changed, because no one works with the mother, which is acutely needed, as nothing will change if the birth parents do not get support. The tone with which the NGO expert speaks about these mothers and their inabilities is still rather paternalistic. Nevertheless, the discursive turn to portraying birth parents' incapability as something to be solved by teaching them parenting skills, mentoring, and providing support is a major one, as often it is an NGO that is developing new services to work with birth parents (Kulmala et al. forthcoming).

Supported by whom?

As already shown, a gradual discursive change towards emphasising birth parents' need for support is taking place. In terms of neo-institutional theory, one could say that ideational change has happened, but change in institutional practices is still underway. In the aforementioned excerpt, an NGO expert said:

> there is practically no work with the birth families. Not because the system does not want to, but because it is not capable of doing so. . . . Practically no one works with them, there are no hands for that.

Similarly, in the aforementioned excerpt, in which the family support centre director discussed the inability of parents with alcohol dependency to engage with the support services persistently, the root problem was the unavailability of good-quality treatment of addictions.

Sadly, in those speech acts in which the experts construct birth parents as capable of change and worthy of support, they also claim that the system is incapable of supporting them. Despite the growing understanding that birth families need to be supported, there is still uncertainty about who should provide this support. Often, the role of family support centres is emphasised. This is quite natural, because the task of supporting birth parents has been given to these centres in the strategies steering the reform. Family support centres are usually formed on the basis of old children's homes, and they seem still to be more used to working with children removed from families than with parents.

Nevertheless, family support centres should take on this task, and also a broader role of coordinating other needed services for birth parents, for example, ensuring that parents get help in the health care system. Some experts emphasised the importance of multilateral cooperation in organising support services. One director of a children's home described a positive example of such interaction:

> Work with the birth family is carried out both by the child protection services and the juvenile commission to a greater extent, but we are also working. Because we have such cases when, thanks to our interaction with mothers whose parental rights were terminated, they were restored. We are ready to meet parents here – please come, but not all parents can or want to do this because of their dependences and illnesses. But in general, we have such cases.

As already shown, much responsibility for changing the situation lies with the birth parents themselves. The children's home director constructed it as a question of parent's will and motivation as to whether they want to engage with the offered support. This is understandable: no one can be changed from outside without their own motivation. At the same time, quite often the parents are still left alone with a demand to change the situation in six months to prove that the child can return home, and this is a problem.

> For example, a care leaver at the age of sixteen or seventeen gives birth. There is only wind in her head. She is told: 'Place the child [in alternative care] for half a year, while you get on your feet.' She places them, and after one and a half years returns and says, 'I'm ready [to take care of the child]'. They say: 'You have to prove that you are able to take the child. Prove that you are capable. Show us facts.' She, if no one helps her, cannot understand how to do that.

The example points out, firstly, how temporary placements are used in situations in which it would be more humane for both mother and child to be provided with some kind of family rehabilitation for them together to enable early attachment. Secondly, the example strikingly shows how the burden of proof of the changed situation is placed on the birth parent. She has to prove that she can now take care of the child, but no one provides any support for that care or even assists in showing the evidence of her capability as a parent.

To conclude, many of the interviewed experts note that the system lacks skills, methods, and resources for working with birth parents. Although the discursive change of talking about the need to support birth parents seems to be underway, to have real effect on how birth parents are treated in the child welfare system, it needs to be accompanied by the wider development of work practices. In addition, the accent on supporting birth families should be moved to the earlier stages and not started only after the child has already been placed into temporary alternative care. If there are no concrete services and working methods available, this may again reinforce the representations of birth parents as incapable and impossible to change, and children may end up in traumatising spirals between repeating temporary placements with institutions and returns to home, where nothing has changed.

Conclusions: discursive strategies used in representing birth parents either as not needed or as in need of support

In the preceding analysis, I have specified two discourses, namely the discourse of parents as no longer needed and the discourse representing parents as in need of support, and five discursive strategies related to them. The discursive strategies to convince that the birth parents are no longer needed in the lives of children placed into alternative care included representing birth parents as 'former parents' and thus no longer needed, viewing contact with them as dangerous to child's adaptation to a foster family, and pointing at their 'neglect of parental responsibilities'. The discursive strategies used for strengthening the discourse that represented birth parents as in need of support included viewing birth parents as resource in the lives of their children, and emphasising their capability to change if supported.

The discourse analysis of the interview data has revealed an interesting interplay between discursive change and institutional change. On the one hand, discursive change – change in ideals and representations – is a precondition for institutional change. On the other hand, certain top-down institutional changes have forced experts to change the ways in which they view birth parents. The discourses are seen here as reflections of the representations of birth parents in the changing child welfare system and the positions that are constructed to them within it.

Based on this data, it is not possible to make strong claims on how much the child welfare reform has influenced on the change of these discourses, or to measure how much change in the discourses has occurred. Importantly, the discourse representing birth parents as in need of support, which challenges the old moralistic and deterministic talk of birth parents as incapable of change and no longer needed, seems to be more common in the second data set from 2018 than in the first data set from 2015. This would speak for the strengthening of the support-focused discourse as a consequence of the reform and institutional change. Nevertheless, mindsets still need to change to enable effective and respectful work with birth families. As the experts of this study note, the question of resources, methods, and knowledge base for supporting birth parents is still open.

Towards supporting the participation of birth parents in the lives of children?

An interesting aspect of discourse analysis is to analyse what experts do not speak about. In the first data set from 2015, there was practically no talk in the data about the participation of the parent in the life of the child, if there was not seen to be a realistic chance of the child returning to the birth parents (Jäppinen 2018). In a simplified way, one can say that in the eyes of the interviewed child welfare experts, the role of parents was to provide protection and care, and if they did not cope with these roles, they could disappear from the life of the child. This is one of the issues that seem to be changing. In the 2018 data, there are promising examples of experts encouraging parents to spend time with their temporarily placed children, as we also see discussed in the chapter by Jäppinen and Kulmala in this volume, and some experts emphasise the importance of birth parents for a child and maintaining connections even if they grow up in long-term alternative care. This might be connected to the strengthening role of attachment theory in the knowledge base of Russian child welfare. At the same time, the idea of supporting ties with the birth family is complicated when it is combined with the understanding of foster care as almost adoption-like. This is an issue that needs to be solved if the system aims at promoting both fostering and the return of children to their birth families.

By definition of the UN Convention on the Rights of the Child (UN CRC 1989) and the Family Code of the Russian Federation (1995), the starting point of the child welfare system is the principle of protecting the interests of the child. The needs and wishes of the parents are secondary to the interests of the child. There are situations in which it is better for the child to be brought up outside the birth family until adulthood. It is important that the child develops an attachment to their foster parents based on safety and stability. Communication with their birth parents is nevertheless important for the child, even if they are brought up in a foster home for a long time (Hämäläinen 2012). Internationally, one of the requirements for foster parents is often their willingness and capability to maintain communication between a child and their birth parents, as well as the understanding that a child can belong to more than one family at the same time (Buehler et al. 2003; Buehler et al. 2006; Orme et al. 2007; Schofield 2002; Valkonen 2008). In the future, it would be interesting to study how such skills are supported in the training of foster parents in Russia.

According to the ideas of social problems work, which have guided this chapter, representations of certain social problems influence what kind of solutions and service designs are seen as suitable for addressing them. When it comes to the case of birth parents of children in the child welfare system, there seem to be promising baby steps towards working with them and seeing their role in the lives of their children, even during an alternative care placement. The discourse representing birth parents as capable of change and in need of support – instead of suggesting cutting the ties to the child or punishments to birth parents – is challenging the persistent discourse, in which birth parents are portrayed as lost cases and not needed in the lives of their children anymore. At the same time, much remains to be done before supporting birth families become a priority in political programmes, or before the attitudes of specialists at the local level change in full accordance with the goals of parental support for possible family reunion, as designated in these programmes. The old representations of birth parents as morally suspicious have to change to enable work with them and, even more importantly, concrete methods and practices need to be developed to work with birth families – and preferably at an earlier stage. In addition, families and parents must be able to trust that they will be treated in a respectful and dignified way if they contact support services.

To enable this, it would be important to direct research and practical interest towards collecting and analysing positive experiences of work with birth families and developing new methods for the effective support of such families. Moreover, the voices of birth parents should be included in further discussions about reforming the child welfare system. Their experiences would be valuable in developing family support services to prevent the need for alternative care as well as in developing meaningful ways to sustain family ties during placement.

Note

1 The analysis presented in this chapter builds solely on the transcripts of these interviews, which have been conducted by other participants of the research project, not on a more comprehensive and holistic personal participation in the fieldwork and ethnographic observations. I want to express my warmest gratitude to my colleagues in the project 'A Child's Right to a Family: Deinstitutionalisation of Child Welfare in Putin's Russia', led by Dr. Meri Kulmala, for the opportunity to use the interview data.

References

Biryukova, S., Sinyavskaya, O. 2017. Children Out of Parental care in Russia: What We Can Learn from Statistics? *Journal of Social Policy Studies* 15 (3): 367–382.

Buehler, C., Cox, M., Cuddeback, G. 2003. 'Foster Parents' Perceptions of Factors That Promote or Inhibit Successful Fostering. *Qualitative Social Work* 2 (1): 61–83.

Buehler, C., Rhodes, K., Orme, J., Cuddeback, G. 2006. The Potential for Successful Family Foster Care: Conceptualizing Competency Domains for Foster Parents. *Child Welfare* 85 (3): 523–559.

Chandler, A. 2013. *Democracy, Gender, and Social Policy in Russia*. London: Palgrave Macmillan.

Cook, L. 2011. Russia's Welfare Regime: The Shift Toward Statism. In: M. Jäppinen, M, Kulmala, A. Saarinen (eds.), *Gazing at Welfare, Gender and Agency in Post-Socialist Countries*. Newcastle upon Tyne: Cambridge Scholars Publishing.

Decree #481. 2014. Decree of the Government of the Russian Federation of May 24, 2014 No. 481 'On the Performance of Organizations for Orphaned Children and Children without Parental Care, and on Placement of Children in these Organizations' (*Postanovlenie Pravitel'stva Rossijskoj Federacii ot 24 maja 2014 g. N 481 g. Moskva 'O dejatel'nosti organizacij dlja detej-sirot i detej, ostavshihsja bez popechenija roditelej, i ob ustrojstve v nih detej, ostavshihsja bez popechenija roditelej*'). Available at: http://static.government.ru/media/files/41d4e0dc986dd6284920.pdf (accessed 30/03/2020).

Federal Law #120-FZ. 1999. Federal Law of June 24, 1999 No.120-FZ 'On the Basics of the System for Prevention of Child Neglect and Juvenile Delinquency' (*Federal'nyj zakon ot 24 ijunja 1999 g. N 120-FZ 'Ob osnovah sistemy profilaktiki beznadzornosti i pravonarushenij nesovershennoletnih '*). Available at: www.kremlin.ru/acts/bank/14023/ page/1 (accessed 30/03/2020).

Gee, J.P. 2010. *An Introduction to Discourse Analysis: Theory and Method*. London: Routledge.

Gilbert, N. 1997. *Combating Child Abuse: Comparative Perspectives on Reporting Systems and Placement Trends*. New York: Oxford University Press.

Gilbert, N., Parton, N., Skivenes, M. 2011. *Child Protection Systems: International Trends and Orientations*. New York: Oxford University Press.

Family Code of the Russian Federation. 1995. Family Code of the Russian Federation from December 8, 1995 (*Semejnyj kodeks Rossijskoj Federacii ot 8 dekabrja* 1995). Available at: http://pravo.gov.ru/proxy/ips/?docbody&nd=102038925] (accessed 30/03/2020).

Hämäläinen, K. 2012. Perhehoitoon sijoitettujen lasten antamat merkitykset kodilleen ja perhesuhteilleen [The Meanings Given By Children Placed in Foster Care to Their Home and Family Relationships]. *Väestöntutkimuslaitoksen julkaisusarja* D 56/2012 (in Finnish).

Holstein, J., Miller, G. 2017. Social Constructionism and Social Problems Work. In G. Miller, J. Holstein (eds.), *Constructionist Controversies. Issues in Social Problems Theory*. London and New York: Routledge: 131–152.

Iarskaia-Smirnova, E. 2010. *'Da-da, ya vas pomnyu, vy zhe u nas neblagopoluchnaya sem'ya!' Diskursivnoe oformlenie sovremennoi rossiiskoi semeinoi politiki* ['Yes-Yes, I Remember You, You Are an Unfortunate Family!' Discursive Formatting of the Contemporary Russian Family Policy]. *Zhenscshina v rossiiskom obschestve* [Woman in Russian Society] 2010 (2): 14–25.

Jäppinen, M. (2018) Krovnye roditeli detei, iziayh iz sem'i, v diskurse sotrudnikov organov zastcshiti detei [Birth Parents of Children in Alternative Care in the Discourses of Child Welfare Professionals]. *Zhurnal sotsiologii i sotsialnoi antropologii* [Journal of Sociology and Social Anthropology] 11 (3): 93–114.

Khlinovskaya Rockhill, E. 2010. *Lost to the State: Family Discontinuity, Social Orphanhood and Residential Care in the Russian Far East*. New York: Berghahn Books.

Kulmala, M. 2017. Paradigm Shift in Russian Child Welfare Policy. *Russian Analytical Digest* 200 (28 March): 5–10.

Kulmala, M., Jäppinen, M., and Chernova, Z. Forthcoming. Reforming Russia's Child Protection System: From Institutional to Family Care. In: J.D. Berrick, N. Gilbert, M. Skivenes (eds.), *Oxford International Handbook of Child Protection Systems*. Oxford: Oxford University Press.

Miller, G., Holstein, J. 1993. Reconsidering Social Constructionism. In: G. Miller, G.J. Holstein (eds.), *Reconsidering Social Constructionism: Debates in Social Problems Theory*. New York: Aldine de Gruyter: 5–24.

Murray, S., Powell, A. 2009. What's the Problem?: Australian Public Policy Constructions of Domestic and Family Violence. *Violence Against Women* 15 (5): 532–552.

National Concept. 2014. Government Order of August 25, 2014 No. 1618-r. 'National Concept of Family Policy of the Russian Federation Until the Year 2025' (*Rasporiazhenie pravitel'stva RF ot 25.8.2014 N 1618-r 'Koncepciia gosudarstvennoj semejnoj politiki v Rossijskoj Federacii na period do 2025 goda '*). Available at: https://rg.ru/2014/08/29/ semya-site-dok.html (accessed 03/06/2020).

National Strategy. 2012. Presidential Decree of June 1, 2012 No. 761 'On the National Strategy to Promote the Interests of Children in 2012–2017' (*Ukaz Prezidenta RF ot 01.06.2012 N 761 'O Nacional'noj strategii dejstvij v interesah detej na 2012–2017 gody'*). Available at: http://static.kremlin.ru/media/acts/files/0001201206040004.pdf (accessed 30/03/2020).

178   *Maija Jäppinen*

Orme, J., Cuddeback, G., Buehler, C., Cox, M., Le Prohn, N. 2007. Measuring Foster Parent Potential: Casey Foster Parent Inventory–Applicant Version. *Research on Social Work Practice* 17 (1): 77–92.

Pösö, T., Skivenes, M., Hestbaek, A. 2013. Child Protection Systems within the Danish, Finnish and Norwegian Welfare States–Time for a Child Centric Approach? *European Journal of Social Work* 17 (4): 475–490.

Prisiazhniuk, D., Markina, V., Rozhkova, O. 2015. *Analiz sistemy okazaniia pomostcshi sem'iam i det'iam v sotsial'no opasnom polozhenii v RF* [Analysis of the System of Helping Families and Children in Socially Unsafe Situations in the Russian Federation]. In: E. Iarskaia-Smirnova, E.V. Markina (eds.), *Sotsial'no opasnoe polozhenie sem'i i detei. Analiz poniatiia i metodologiia otsenki* [Socially Unsafe Situations of Families and Children: Analysis of the Concept and Methodology of Assessment]. Moscow: OOO Variant: 23–51.

Schofield, G. 2002. The Significance of a Secure Base: A Psychosocial Model of Long-Term Foster Care. *Child and Family Social Work* 7 (4): 259–272.

Tulensalo, H. 2016. *Lapsen tiedollinen toimijuus lastensuojelun sosiaalityössä* [A Child's Informational Agency in Child Welfare Social Work]. Professional Licentiate Thesis, University of Tampere. Available at: https://tampub.uta.fi /bitstream/handle/10024/98814/LISURI-1460708563.pdf?sequence=1 (accessed 17/10/2017) (in Finnish).

UN CRC. 1989. *Convention on the Rights of the Child*. Geneva, Switzerland.

Valkonen, L. 2008. *Mitä perhehoidosta tiedetään tutkimusten perusteella?* [What Do We Know about Foster Care by Research?]. In: K. Jyväskylä (eds.), *Sijoita perheeseen. Perhehoito inhimillisenä ja taloudellisena vaihtoehtona* [Place in a Family: Family Care as a Human and Economic Option]. Jyväskylä: PS-Kustannus: 99–120 (in Finnish).

Van Dijk, T.A. 2015. Critical Discourse Analysis. In: D. Tannen, H.E. Hamilton, D. Schiffrin (eds.), *The Handbook of Discourse Analysis*. Hoboken, NJ: Wiley-Blackwell Publishing. doi:10.1002/9781118584194.ch

Part V
Children in care
Social adaptation and aftercare

9 The successful transition to foster care

The child's perspective

Larisa Shpakovskaya and Zhanna Chernova

Introduction

Foster care leavers form one of the most socially deprived groups of Russian society. Managing the successful transition of this group into adulthood is considered in public opinion as a key problem. Media discourse defines graduates of foster care as being at risk of poverty, crime, alcoholism, drug addiction, poor parenthood, family distress, etc. At the same time, the social position of this group is controversial. On the one hand, the system of state support for children deprived of parental care provides them with a wide range of different types of assistance aimed at their successful adaptation to adulthood. On the other hand, despite a large package of material, educational, housing, social, and psychological support, experts in the field note the extremely low effectiveness of pursued policies (Abramov et al. 2016). An articulation of this problem is reflected in the current deinstitutionalisation reform, aimed at reducing the number of children's homes and developing family placements (Kulmala et al. 2017). Moreover, the family is reckoned to be an instrument that will help make the transition to adulthood successful for this group of young people.

Despite the fact that the process of deinstitutionalisation of the child welfare reform in Russia has frequently been a subject of analysis (see, for example, Abramov et al. 2016; Kulmala et al. 2017; Shpakovskaya et al. 2019), children have almost never been involved in it, and their voices have rarely appeared in analysis. We still know little about how children experience growing up in foster families in Russia. In this chapter, we analyse how foster care leavers perceive their experience in a foster family in the context of their biographies. The chapter examines the narrative identity construction of children experiencing family placements in the process of transition to adulthood. In the analysis, we pay special attention to the barriers that children face in the process of transition into foster care, as well as the resources which helped achieve successful transition.

The analytical framework: transition to foster care through the eyes of children

Sociology views childhood as a social construct, studying specific historical forms of childhood and ideas of childhood (Aries 1965; Zelizer 1994; Dudenkova

2014). As the new sociology of childhood suggests, as a methodological principle, childhood should be studied through the eyes of a child (Jenks 2005: 47; Pufall, Unsworth 2003: 2; Dudenkova 2014: 51). This approach highlights an agency of a child and studies it as an active participant in social relations, who can adapt, cope, and resist even being in a very vulnerable and dependent position (Reimer, Schäfer 2015). The process of transition to foster care is a very contextual phenomenon, which depends on the cultural and social policy background. Studies of foster care experience from the child's perspective can be found in international research, which show favourable and unfavourable circumstances for successful transition to foster care, as well as examine the transition to adulthood for foster care leavers (Schofield et al. 2000; Reimer 2010; Reimer, Schäfer 2015; Sinclair et al. 2005). The process of transition and adaptation to foster families in Russia remains an unexplored area from the point of view of the new sociology of childhood.

In addition to the aforementioned theoretical perspective, our analysis utilises the life course approach. It studies individual biographies as institutionalised in a particular context as an age-based sequence of life events, which poses constraints on individual agency. It also looks at how individuals are enabled with opportunities, focusing on specific events that significantly affect lives of the individuals (Cuconato, Walther 2015: 286). We include the subjective aspects of children's experiences and are interested in how children in their narratives construct their identities. Based on a biographical approach, we explore the ways in which children and young people manage their own lives and legitimise their decisions, both for themselves and others. We focus on how children living under difficult circumstances forge their identities and develop interpretations that enable them to cope with challenges, explain events, and take action. Analysing the process of transition to foster care, we distinguish typical biographical trajectories which lead to foster care. These trajectories are structured with critical life events: biographical circumstances that change everyday life and require new knowledge, habits, and resources. Examples include the death of birth parents, the removal of the child by child protection services from their birth family, moving to a new institution, and family placement. These events often represent turning points in a biography and significantly change its flow (Reimer, Schäfer 2015: 8).

Foster care in the life course of children deprived of parental care in Russia

Adolescence and youth are phases of life course where the transition from child to adult status occurs. In contemporary societies, the family plays crucial role in the process of transition to adulthood, which is one reason why children deprived of parental care are at risk of social exclusion (Abramov et al. 2016). The Soviet system of institutions for children deprived of parental care offered an institutionalised path of transition to adulthood. This path was a rather standardised trajectory from the orphanage through vocational training to a blue-collar job (Smirnova 2015; Volohatova 2005). It was complemented by correctional comprehensive

schools, as well as correctional vocational training institutions for 'difficult' adolescents, who constitute a visible part of children's home graduates (Krivonosov
2003; McAuley 2009). However, in the post-Soviet period, this system experienced a crisis not only due to criticism from society and expert practitioners
(Kulmala et al. 2017; Iarskaia-Smirnova 2015), but also as a result of a crisis in
vocational training (Cherednichenko 2011: 101–102) and the loss of the economic
and symbolic value of the blue-collar professions (Walker 2012: 54). Leavers of
institutional care were described as a youth group at a high risk of social exclusion, deviant behaviour, and poverty (Chapter 10 by Kulmala et al. in this volume; Schmidt 2010; Semia 2016; Shpakovskaya et al. 2019; Iarskaia-Smirnova,
Sadykov 2015). As a result of the child welfare deinstitutionalisation reforms, a
trajectory of transition through foster family has become available for many children deprived of parental care (Biryukova, Sinyavskaya 2017). New systems of
support for transition to adulthood among children deprived of parental care were
added by the services of psychological, social work and peer aid to foster families
provided by state organisations and NGOs. The outcomes of the DI reform in
terms of future successful transition of foster care leavers to adulthood have not
yet been analysed, but it is obvious that a wider range of work and life trajectories
have opened up as a result of family socialisation, including upward social mobility through higher education to middle-class positions (Chernova, Shpakovskaya
2019). We now shift attention to how the role of the family is perceived in the
process of socialisation and future educational trajectories.

In our chapter, we use the term 'fostering' to refer to all forms of family placement available in Russia. Despite that from the legal point of view there are
various family placement arrangements, social actors do not always see similar difference between them. According to legislation, a range of legal forms are
available today for Russian citizens, from adoption to paid and unpaid guardianship, permanent or temporary (Khlinovskaya Rockhill 2010: 257). Children
deprived of parental care, in any form of institutional and foster care, who did not
enter to adoption, are given certain privileges and benefits, such as allowances,
privileges in entering vocational training, and housing provision after reaching
adulthood (Chapter 10 by Kulmala et al. in this volume; Chernova, Shpakovskaya
2019: 11). The forms of paid fostering imply benefits together with tough control
from the state. Thus, the system of social support leaves space for foster parents
to choose the most suitable legal type of fostering, navigating between the support
and control of the state.

The status of fostering and foster children in Russia also is formed by a policy on 'unfortunate' (*neblagopoluchnye*) families and birth parents who do not
meet their parental duties. When parents are officially recognised as 'unfortunate'
and dangerous for their children, they can be limited in their parental rights and
later fully deprived of them by a court decision. For the children, this means
that they lose their connection with their birth parents, as the full deprivation of
rights removes any legal basis for further contact (Khlinovskaya Rockhill 2010:
257). Actors in the system of child welfare protection, including foster parents
and NGOs specialists, are not always aware of the need to maintain a child's

ties with their birth parents. In fact, some specialists consider contact with birth parents to be dangerous or believe the child's negative experience in the birth family prevents them from building attachment in a new family. All these aspects of legal regulation and widespread stereotypes about fostering produce a situation when different forms of fostering and even adoption are not always meaningfully distinguished by social actors (Chernova, Kulmala 2018). Everyday perception of different forms of family placement, as well as the rationalities behind choosing them, requires separate detailed research, which is beyond the scope of our study.

Autobiographical memoirs of childhood

Our analysis draws on memoirs written by adolescents and young people about their lives in foster families. These memoirs were collected in the framework of the 'Our Stories' autobiography contest for foster parents and children launched by the Elena and Gennady Timchenko Charity Foundation in 2015–2017 (http:// nashiistorii.ru). The aim of the contest was to give a voice to foster children and, in this way, fight negative stereotypes about foster families. The foundation promotes family placement; its programmes aim at the education and support of foster parents and the adaptation of foster children to families. Participation in the contest was voluntary and free, and winners were given memorable gifts. Not all participants were beneficiaries of the foundation, and did not receive prize money. The conditions of the contest did not give authors any direction with regard to a form or genre of presenting their experience of fostering, but most authors chose the form of autobiographical narration, structuring their stories as a historical consequence of the life events, although a few authors chose the genre of poetry for their stories. The autobiographies were sent to the organisers both electronically and by post, but they became available for analysis only in electronic form after their publication on the website of the foundation.[1] Publishing the memoirs on the foundation website was one of the conditions of contest participation.

In total 238 autobiographies were analysed. The authors were 14–25 years old and the greatest number of authors were between the ages of 14 and 18 (not all diaries contain information about the age of the authors). Of the texts, 151 were written by young women and 87 by young men. The geographical coverage of the texts is very wide. While the authors live all over Russia, the overwhelming majority of them reside in small cities, towns, villages, and rural settlements. Of them, 25 authors reported a disability or a permanent illness. The narratives do not contain any systematic information about legal status (type of fostering or adoption) of children in their families that can be used for the analysis. From the point of view of their content, the stories sent to the contest cover different periods of children's lives – from particular episodes (for example, only the period of meeting their foster parents or several episodes of life in a foster family) to a detailed description of their entire biography from birth to the moment of the actual writing of the text.

The analysis of the data was carried out according to the method of thematic coding (Flick 2006). At the first stage of the analysis, we performed thematic coding, including such categories as critical life events, problems and difficulties in the process of transition to foster care, positive experience, resources and barriers in the process of transition, and descriptions of the role of adults, peers, and institutions. At the next stage of analysis, the selected codes were compared and combined into broader thematic categories, which, finally, were interpreted as biographical trajectories of transition to foster care and the stages of narrative identity formation into foster children.

We analysed children's autobiographical narratives as sharing particular features, which make restrictions to the information available for our studies. Firstly, as with all biographical narratives, the texts present an attempt to build the identity of the authors, an answer to the question 'Who am I?' (Rozhdestvenskaya 2010). Stories of childhood, birth, and relationships with significant adults are key to building children's and adults' identity (Nurkova 2010). Thus, the memoirs of foster children can be viewed as the biographical work of building a narrative identity for the authors who participated in the contest.

Secondly, biographical narratives are an attempt to fit personal experience into wider semantic constructs: normative notions, common semantic clichés, social expectations, common values, etc. (Golofast 2006). The authors of the memoirs rely on these typical meaningful constructions and strive to present children's lives as stories of gaining their place in society, inscribing themselves in such commonly shared concepts as 'family', 'mother', 'father', 'relatives', 'friends', 'school', 'personal achievements', 'happiness', etc. While narrating their life, the authors also use typical cultural tropes, analogues of which can be found in fiction, films, TV series, and media on orphanhood (Shpakovskaya 2018).

Thirdly, the fact that the analysed autobiographies were sent to a contest with the intention of publication and it was known they would be read by a large audience influences their content. They differ from intimate personal diaries and biographies that are written for oneself, close friends, or relatives (Churilova 2016). Perhaps that is why in the analysed narratives, the authors emphasise their success and luck ('I got a lucky ticket') and describe mostly positive personal features of their foster parents and foster families, sometimes not disclosing personal negative experiences and conflicts. Moreover, all children who took part in the contest performed a successful transition to foster care; they all describe their experience of life and adaptation to their current family as positive, despite a few examples of problems and conflicts in previous families. Apparently, authors perceive their participation in the contest as being about telling the story of their successful transition into family. This circumstance is especially important for our analysis; as using these materials we cannot detect successful and unsuccessful scenarios of transition to foster care, as well as factors which contribute to successful and problematic transition, we limit our analysis mostly to positive experiences.

Fourthly, work of memory of child recollections makes the specificity of documents content. The work of memory, such as forgetting, or, conversely, false memories, structures the narratives. Some events in children's lives are so traumatic (for example, physical violence and neglect in a birth family, the process of withdrawal from a birth family, or the death of parents) that the authors consciously or subconsciously do not describe them and write that they do not remember these events. From this assumption, we understand that only a part of the story is told and brought into focus in a narrative identity which links unique stories, traumatic personal experiences, and the specifics of the child's cognitive and psychological perception of the events with broader meaningful categories of normative order.

All these particularities of children's autobiographies do not cancel the fact that they are texts written by individuals with unique personal stories and perceptions of life events. Most biographies are written by children and teenagers and contain memories of early childhood experiences. They are childishly sincere, often talking about the most intimate matters, and about what caused the most vivid emotions: love, fear, disappointment, grief.

Thus, the memoirs can be viewed as documents of life, first-hand evidence of experience, individual voices, which together tell us a general story about what it means to be a child without parental care, as well as how to grow up to be an adult in a foster family in Russia. However, because these autobiographies were not written as personal diaries 'for oneself', but as a public self-representation of a 'family career', it is not possible to fully understand where the authors are using conventional clichés and where they are writing about their personal experience. Taking into account this complex interplay between the personal and the common, we analyse intersubjective meanings of narratives about growing up.

Losing and finding personal identity in the stories of transition to foster care

Current Russian cultural and social conventions represent childhood as a happy stage in the human life cycle. It is also understood as a preparatory period for adulthood. Family is considered a necessary prerequisite for a happy and prosperous childhood. Cultural ideals about childhood discern successful growing up through warm, personalised, close relationships with parents (Maiorova-Scheglova 2018; Maiorova-Scheglova, Kolosova 2018; Kulmala et al. 2017). Although in the analysed memoirs we are dealing with the subjective evidences of life experience, it is possible to single out a set of structuring biographical events. Their authors appeal to the commonly used cultural models of childhood, trying to fit their biographies into the semantic framework of family and happy childhood. Sequences of events in the memoirs can be described as biographical trajectories of growing up (McCartney, Edwards 2011). In general, permanent life in a 'normal' family (e.g. answering to current ideas about family and family care, where the parents satisfy the whole range of needs for the child's well-being from physiological and emotional aspects to social recognition and success) is presented as a key meaningful element of biography that structures life history as 'before' and 'after' gaining such a family.

We have identified three main biographical trajectories, structured by a number of critical events serving as turning points in biographies, in which the foster family is the end and climax point: (1) life in a birth family – the death of the birth parents – foster care of close relatives (grandparents, aunt); (2) abandonment of the child by birth parents at birth – life in an institution – life in a foster family is described; (3) life in a dysfunctional birth family – removal from the family – life in an institution – life in a foster family is stressed. These scenarios describe the general course of foster children's lives prior to their current foster family. The number of displacements between institutions and families can be different, and variations in these scenarios are possible. For example, among the autobiographies, there is the story of a young woman who was left immediately by her birth mother in the maternity hospital and was immediately adopted there by her foster mother who was a patient of the hospital at the same time. In other stories, the death of the parents is not followed by the care of relatives (as it is in most cases), but the children end up in an institution. In general, stories of kinship fostering are described in more positive terms compared with the stories of those adolescents who were removed from a dysfunctional, neglectful family.

The overall semantic motive of events in the biographies of those children who lose their birth family (if this event is described in autobiographies), prior to the moment they enter foster family, can be presented as a story about the loss of their memory, identity, and ultimately, their personality. The authors write about what they are losing, consciously forgetting, or cannot remember what they are losing:

> I remember nothing. I do not want to remember anything. I want to forget what sometimes flashes in my head. I was born at the age of four. For a long time, I could not understand what was happening to me. Some grey veil shrouded and hid my early childhood. Everything is foggy, gloomy, evil . . . a constant feeling of helplessness and the constant cry of my little brother. He wants to eat all the time. And crying . . . and crying . . . And this crying haunts me now.

Autobiographies mention the loss of personal belongings, for example, when moving from institution to institution, photographs taken from home are lost, loss of contact with birth brothers and sisters or relatives. The moment of losing one's birth family is recalled as a period of confusion, fear, uncertainty, and misunderstanding of what is happening. The next period of residence in an orphanage, if it appears in the memoirs at all, is described extremely scarcely and in little detail, which might be explained by the absence of permanent significant adults with whom these memories could be shared. This period is also often described as a period of waiting for a meeting with birth or foster parents.

Analysing the memoirs, one gains the impression that children lose their sense of self in a situation when there are no significant permanent adults (whose role is played by parents or other adults who take care on an ongoing basis) as key social agents for the production of children's identity. The vacuum of identity becomes especially noticeable in the case of those children whose parents could not cope with their parental duties and were recognised by the state services as dysfunctional.

Meeting their foster parents is a meaningful turning point in all the memoirs. Some authors begin the narration from this very moment. The emotional tone of the story becomes positive. This event is interpreted by children as a possibility of finding the conditions of a happy childhood, building a 'normal' identity and future adulthood. The meeting and acquaintance with the foster parents are circumstantially described with many details, which speaks of their subjective significance. Children immediately notice the 'kind eyes', 'gentle voice', 'good hands' of their future foster parents. The authors mention details of what their new parents looked like, what they were wearing, what they said, and how they behaved: 'On the day when we first met, my mother was wearing a beautiful purple dress, and amber beads adorned around her neck. My mother's appearance, [her] kind eyes, I will remember all my life.'

Description of life in a foster family is transformed into a story about finding one's 'self' through relationships with foster parents, with other children in the family, as well as through success in the 'big world' (school grades, sports victories, participation in study groups and clubs, acquisition of various socially relevant skills) that are made possible by the family unit. The story of living in a foster family is also a story of overcoming the social stigma felt by children who have experienced the loss of their birth family. The authors of the diaries use such metaphors to describe the changes that happened to them in the foster family: 'a light turned on inside of me', 'I discovered so much love and affection in myself', 'an anchor in life, a safe haven' appeared, 'opened for me new world'. From this moment the construction of a new identity begins as the story of entry into a family.

In some cases, the stories of entering the new family are presented as trouble-free and happy:

> I got used to my parents almost immediately and began to call them mum and dad.

> You know, I quickly got used to my mother, I instantly fell in love with her, we found a common language, I was extremely glad that now we wouldn't have to separate even for an hour.

In other cases (most often in teenagers' stories), the process of adaptation to a new family is described as a process of getting acquainted with the rules of family life, changing everyday habits, and acquiring new social skills:

> It is now we have become truly relatives, but then these were years incomprehensible to us. At first, we called our parents by their names and only a year later we began to call them mum and dad, which our parents perceived with a smile. You can ask, what were the difficulties? There were a lot of them, I don't remember everything. I will never forget how Oleg couldn't find the key to the front door and went to the drawing circle, leaving the door unlocked, because in the orphanage there was no need to do that. We studied everything like people who have gone into civilisation from a desert island.

Sometimes children mention mistrust, emotional closedness, and constraint in relation to foster parents. The authors explain this distrust by the fear of being rejected again by their new parents. In other cases, the authors write about a period of 'constraint' which was due to the desire to please the foster family, the fear of doing 'something wrong'.

Thus, biographical trajectories at the subjective level are divided into 'before' and 'after' meeting their foster parents and entering their family. Events 'before' are presented as stories of the loss of one's 'self', one's own personal history as the result of a loss of communication with one's birth relatives. Stories 'after' are presented as stories of the formation of self through communication with the family.

Building narrative identity in foster care

Family as a category in autobiographical narratives acts as a source of identity and status normalisation. The memoirs contain detailed descriptions of family practices. These descriptions are read as stories of an ideal family. They completely reproduce the cultural conventions of a heterosexual family with a large number of children. The authors write practically nothing about conflicts and difficulties (except for few descriptions of adaptation to the foster family), but they describe in detail the positive qualities of their parents, family rituals, holidays, good relations with parents and siblings, and so on. On the one hand, such family representations in the autobiographies can be explained by the nature of the documents analysed, as we are dealing with texts submitted to a competition. On the other hand, the repeated detailed descriptions of family practices and declaration of love for foster parents show the high value of the family for the authors, and the importance of representing it as 'normal' and happy.

The following quote is a typical description of family practices as family traditions. The text contains a number of categories which emphasise the usualness of the family, its permanent, timeless nature (through the description of family rituals, constantly repeated actions), as well as the integration of the family into a wider cultural and political semantic order (mention of holidays and socially approved lifestyles practised by the family):

> As in any other family, we have traditions: Our family has a healthy lifestyle and – [supports] environmental protection. Every year, on 1 May, we go hiking. On 9 May, we go to the Nameless Heights, to pay tribute to the memory of the fallen soldiers of the Great Patriotic War. Every summer, for a whole month, we go travelling to interesting places and new cities. We always celebrate the New Year at home, in the circle of our family, and on 1 January, guests always come to us and Mum bakes duck with apples. At Christmas and Easter, we go to church. Our weekends begin with baking a cake and inviting our grandmother to visit us for tea. Every night before bedtime, we always read out loud.

In addition to describing family 'traditions', the children's autobiographies have the common trope of travel stories undertaken with families. The meaning of the descriptions of these travels is similar to the stories of family rituals. Adolescents try to inscribe their identity into the family as a significant semantic category, and through this, they present themselves as part of broader kin relationships, as well as part of broader categories, such as 'Motherland' or 'our country':

> Next we travelled around Moscow, we have relatives there too, Aunt Oksana, she has two sons, we also met them, she has a big and beautiful apartment and small decorative dogs, she also cooks very tasty food. We went to the Exhibition of Economic Achievements, took amusement rides, went by bus around Moscow at night, visited Red Square, I really liked it. Our capital is very beautiful. And this summer we were in Sochi.

Thus, foster family in autobiographies is described as having a high subjective value. This allows the biography to be normalised through the ability to relate to the main cultural attributes of family life, to fit individual history into broader kin structures, as well as into broader cultural and political contexts.

Adaptation to family life: barriers and resources

Foster children after being placed in family encounter with social stigmatisation in educational institutions or form the part of their new social environment: peers, neighbours, or relatives. The stigma is produced by the attitude to the foster children as having experience to live in poor and 'socially unfavourable' (*sotcial'no neblagopoluchnye*) families and orphanages, who have a great risk of experiencing developmental delays, psychological and behavioural disorders, of being aggressive and morally spoiled. Barriers on the institutional level include the formal rules and informal principles of the work of educational and medical institutions that deal with children from foster families. For example, schools are extremely reluctant to accept children whose documents contain notes about living in a socially dysfunctional family or in an orphanage or having a medical diagnosis (as other chapters in this volume show, children in orphanages often have poor health). These patterns are significantly enhanced in the case of elite schools that seek to maintain their exam indicators at a high level. Having the status of a foster child or a child with a disability becomes a barrier to accessing educational institutions:

> When my sister and I went to school, I was excluded from the first grade as learning disabled, but my parents managed to get me reinstated.

> Since there was a diagnosis of 'severe developmental delay' on my medical card, there was a question about whether I would go to school at all. We had to go through very many commissions to prove that I could go to the first grade and that I could study according to the regular programme.

The authors of the memoirs mention that the programmes of schools that they attended in the orphanage had low requirements for the level of knowledge of students. Adolescents from 'socially dysfunctional' families recall that they attended school irregularly. As a result, children recall as the first experience in comprehensive school after family placement, their inadequate level of knowledge, inability to cope with the school curriculum, and low academic performance:

> I started to study badly; I don't understand much. I came to fourth year, but there, in my 'old' home, I went to the first year, and rarely went to the second and the third because they [birth parents] didn't buy the necessary clothes and everything for the school, they drank all the money. . . .

> Autumn came, and we went to a new school. From the first day of school I realised that all my fives and fours [school grades] received at the Centre [children's home] are 'fake' and that I'm lucky to get at least three. In the fifth grade I didn't know how to work with fractions, didn't know the English alphabet, and I'm ashamed to even recall [my performance in] the Russian language.

At the level of interpersonal communication, the status of a child from an institution or a dysfunctional family becomes the basis for stigmatisation in the educational social space. School teachers are low on the knowledge of the specificity of such children, ignoring their life situation. There is evidence that foster children have been subjected to bullying in the classroom, stigmatised as a 'stepchild' or 'orphan'.

> Soon I went to school, I liked to study so much, everything seemed to be fine, but then it began. . . . In some sense it was 'hell': they started calling me an 'orphan', and it was painful for me to hear this. After school I would go to my room and cry.

> In the first grade, children began to tell my sister and me that we were stepchildren, that our parents had brought us from the orphanage.

In general, the memoir authors problematise their experience of social communication outside the foster family – in kindergartens, schools, yards, and on the street. For example, they write about uncontrolled aggression which overwhelmed them in the period of socialisation in a comprehensive school:

> It was harder and harder, when the summer ended, mother Faina took us to the local day care centre. Here my harmful character began to show little by little. For some reason, I was angry at everyone and everything. It seemed to me that Christine [sister] and I could be insulted here, they might somehow call me bad names. There was none of this, but I was on my guard all the time. . . . I began to feel even worse when I went to school. The fact that Christina is now in kindergarten, and I'm at school, made me angry. I was often rude to teachers, I called children names, I could beat my head against the table for 10–15 minutes. I did not understand what came upon me. I had bursts of evil, bad behaviour.

In their autobiographies, adolescents recall difficulties associated with finding their place in the peer groups and social space of a school. Some authors mention that they got into the bad company, were inclined to antisocial behaviour, or did not attend school. If parents are not able to cope with these problems, children risk being taken into an orphanage again:

> I began to be late from school, hang out with my friends, drank, smoked and did not want to go back at all, to hear how bad and underdeveloped I was. I was too lazy to learn. All day long I was thinking about where to find cigarettes and where to spend the night. The lady, who I don't feel like calling mother, beat me for vagrancy, insulted me, now I understand what it was for. But it was terribly insulting, and again I felt deeply unhappy and abandoned.

Thus, the institutional environment and communities are not sensitive to the educational and emotional needs of these children. The current reform of the child protection system aiming at the inclusion of children deprived of parental care into comprehensive schools and communities, as the memoirs show, has not led to overcoming the social stigma of being an orphan. In this context, it is important to understand how children cope with institutional and social forms of exclusion, what resources allow them to compensate for the situation of a hard start to life and normalise their biographical trajectory.

First of all, a good-quality education that becomes available as a result of family support helps to break institutional barriers. The authors of the autobiographies write that their foster parents were deeply involved in school life and the educational process. They helped with homework and hired tutors to bring the child's knowledge in line with the requirements of the school curriculum. Foster parents pay a lot of attention to extracurricular education: art, music clubs, sports, etc. Children are proud of their merits and achievements (prizes, certificates, victories in contests and academic Olympiads). In describing educational achievements, the role of parents is also presented as the role of significant adults who form positive value of educational success:

> Now in my arsenal, there are ten medals, 25 certificates and diplomas. But behind each medal is not only my work and the work of a coach but also the experiences, faith, tears and joy of my family, my mum and dad. Thank them for that! My mum and dad deserved even more medals: they are my champions and my beacon which shows me the right path in life.

One child also writes that the family, through inclusion in their social networks, endows them with social capital, which they later use to organise their daily lives and solve various problems. The texts mention the assistance of foster parents, as well as older step-siblings, in choosing educational institutions, finding work, arranging housing, and organising care for their own children. The description of foster family practices that contribute to successful social inclusion, in this case, does not substantially differ from similar practices of birth parents and children. However, foster children demonstrate high reflexivity with regard to the importance of the family in their lives as a source of socially significant resources.

Some memoirs show the history of the family life of the children as stories of total transformation, as a result of the educational efforts and support of parents, for example, from a developmentally delayed child into a talented, educated young woman. This transformation begins with socially significant resource allocation: in particular, education and social connections.

At the level of interpersonal communication, the role of the family in overcoming the stigma of an orphan child lies in the production of the skills of socially normal behaviour, communication, self-control, and the ability to cope with emotions. These skills form the habits by which adolescents are not identified by their surroundings as 'orphanages' or 'foster care'. Children feel socially competent fully-fledged participants in their communication with peers and adults.

Emotional support, the feeling of 'being loved', and the possibility of open communication with parents in the family become the basis for their psychological stability: 'Support for the person is needed throughout the life path. Just talk sometimes is worth a lot. I am very glad that I have close people who respect and love me.' The ability to manage the household and self-service skills is mentioned among the skills of social competence. Residents of rural areas mention farming skills: taking care of pets, cultivating plants. All these home practices are described by the authors in the context of their ideas about gender social competence. Foster mothers and grandmothers teach the girls women's work. Foster fathers are described as agents of male socialisation. In general, parents, as well as older siblings, become role models. Children believe that parents determine their professional choice, setting behaviour patterns in the field of family and parenthood.

Thus, in the family, children receive a repertoire of communicative, emotional, and behavioural skills that allow them to acquire social competence, knowledge of the rules for presenting themselves, and their ability to carry out daily emotional work and maintain psychological well-being. Thanks to the family, children acquire resources that are in demand in the 'big world'. These include education, social capital, communication skills, and general social competence.

Conclusion

In this chapter, we have analysed how children build their identity in the process of transition to foster family in the context of their biographies. Foster families are represented by children as absolutely ordinary, normal families. The vocabulary used to talk about experience of being fostered is very similar to those which can be used by birth children to describe their family life. The authors of autobiographies use the typical categories of 'family', 'mother', 'dad', 'brothers', and 'sisters', and the everyday life of foster families is presented as the everyday life of a typical family. Perhaps the authors of our materials were more attentive and reflective in describing the significance of the family in their lives, and the use of normative categories to describe family life was existentially more significant for them than for children living in birth families. At the same time, the legal and cultural status of fostering makes children do discursive work to avoid its meaningful controversies and ambiguity, presenting their life in the family as usual and ordinary.

The analysis also shows how the identity of children deprived of parental care is built in the foster family. Family and family life give them a sense of belonging to a kin group, though this is connected up to other meaningful identity categories, such as a peer group, religion, or motherland. Children also mention the process of building their gender identities and professional identities which they present as the wish to resemble their foster mothers and fathers or older siblings in their new families. The perceived barriers and resources of successful adaptation to family life and to broader society were also analysed. The barriers are stigmatisation and bullying in educational institutions and peer groups, which are presented as being overcome by the efforts of their parents to make their foster children 'normal' through education success, sport, art, and personal education in 'normal' behaviour. Thus, in general, the process of the successful identity-building of foster children can be described as the process of normalisation.

The histories of children from foster families also demonstrate the process of the socialisation in childhood, which is described by researchers as a global phenomenon (McCartney, Edwards 2011). A family is considered as a necessary condition for a happy childhood: personalised warm care provided by parents, as well as friendly, supportive family relationships (Du Bois-Reymond 2001; Chernova, Shpakovskaya 2010). The family allows the institutional barriers of a successful transition to adulthood for orphans to be broken and the stigma of a foster child to be overcome. Family education allows children to acquire the skills of communicative and social competence that help overcome social stigma. Thanks to the family that the formation of identity and the normalisation of the status of orphans, the subjective overcoming of social stigma, and the formation of a positive identity all occur.

Note

1 See the official website of the Elena and Gennady Timchenko Charity Foundation where the results of the contest can be found: http://timchenkofoundation.org/grants/stories/index.php?sphrase_id=174970 (accessed 25 February 2020).

References

In this volume

Chapter 10: Kulmala, Chernova and Fomina

Abramov, R., Antonova, K., Il'in, A., Grach, E., Liubarskii, G., Chernova, Z. 2016. *Traektorii social'noi i professional'noi adaptacii vypusknikov detskikh domov v Rossii* [Trajectories of Social and Professional Adaptation for Graduates of Children's Homes in Russia]. *Obzor issledovatel'skogo otcheta* [Review of Research Results]. Moscow: SB Grupp.

Aries, P. 1965. *Centuries of Childhood: A Social History of Family Life*. Oxford: Vintage Books.

Biryukova, S., Sinyavskaya, O. 2017. Children Out of Parental Care in Russia: What We Can Learn from the Statistics. *The Journal of Social Policy Studies* 15 (3): 367–382.

Cherednichenko, G. 2011. *Obrazovatel'nye i professional'nye traektorii rabochei molodezhi.* [Educational and Professional Trajectories of Working Youth]. *Sociologicheskie issledovaniya* [Sociological Research] 9: 101–110.

Chernova, Z., Kulmala, M. 2018. *'Po slozhnosti – eto rabota, po sostayaniu dushi – sem'ya': professionalizatsiya priemnogo roditel'stva v sovremennoi Rossii* ['In Terms of Difficulty It's a Job, But the Heart Tells Me It Is My Family': The Professionalisation of Foster Parenting in Modern Russia]. *Zhurnal sotciologii i sotcial'noi antropologii* [Journal of Sociology and Social Anthropology] 21 (3): 46–70.

Chernova, Z., Shpakovskaya, L. 2010. *Molodye vzroslye: supruzhestvo, partnerstvo i roditel'stvo Discursivnye predpisaniya i praktiki v sovremennoi Rossii* [Young Adults: Friendship, Partnership and Parenthood: Discursive Descriptions and Practices in Modern Russia]. *Laboratorium* 3: 19–43.

Chernova, Z., Shpakovskaya, L. 2019. *Trajectories of Successful Transition to Adulthood of Residential Care Leavers: Resources and Barriers of Resilience.* Analytical report of research results. Moscow: Arifmetika Dobra.

Churilova, E. 2016. *Representaciya samosoznaniya v lichnykh dnevnikakh sovremennykh devushek* [Representation of Self-Awareness in Personal Diaries of Modern Women]. Moscow: Izdatel'stvo 'Prometei'.

Cuconato, M., Walther, A. 2015. Doing Transition in Education. *International Journal of Qualitative Studies in Education* 28 (3): 283–296.

Du Bois-Reymond, M. 2001. Negotiating Families. In: M. du Bois-Reymond, H. Sünker, H. Krüger (eds.), *Childhood in Europe: Approaches, Trends, Findings.* New York: Lang Publishing: 161–179.

Dudenkova, I. 2014. *Detskii vopros' v sociologii: mezhdu normativnost'yu i avtonomiei* [The Children Question in Sociology: Between Normativity and Autonomy]. *Sociologiya Vlasti* 3: 47–59.

Flick, U. 2006. *An Introduction to Qualitative Research.* London: Sage Publications.

Golofast, V. 2006. Tri sloya Biograficheskogo povestvovaniya. In: O.B. Bozhkov, V.B. Golofast (eds.), *Sociologiya sem'i. Stat'i raznykh let* [Sociological Family: Articles of Differing Years]. St Petersburg: Aleteiya: 407–441.

Iarskaia-Smirnova, E., Prisyazhnyuk, D., Verbilovich, O. 2015. *Priemnaya sem'ya v Rossii: publichnyi diskurs i mneniya klyuchevykh aktorov* [Foster Families in Russia: Public Discourse and the Opinion of Key Actors]. *Zhurnal sociologii i social'noi antropologii* [Journal of Sociology and Social Anthropology] 18 (4): 157–173.

Iarskaia-Smirnova, E., Sadykov, R. 2015. *Problema opredelenia sotcial'no opasnogo polozhenia semei i detei v sovremennoi Rossii* [The Problem of Socially Dangerous Conditions amongst Families and Children in Modern Russia]. In E. Iarskaia-Smirnova, V. Markina (eds.), *Sotcial'no opasnoe polozhanie sem'i i detei: anaiz poniatia i metodologii otcenki* [Socially Dangerous State of Families and Children: An Analysis of Concepts and a Methodological Survey]. Moscow: OOO Variant: 7–22.

Jenks, C. 2005. *Childhood.* Second edition. London, New York: Routledge.

Khlinovskaya Rockhill, E. 2010. *Lost to the State: Family Discontinuity, Social Orphanhood and Residential Care in the Russian Far East.* New York, Oxford: Berghahn Books.

Krivonosov, A. 2003. *Istoricheskii opyt borby s besprizornost'u*. [Historical Experience of the Struggle against Child Homelessness]. *Gosudarstvo i pravo* [The State and the Law] 7: 92–98.

Kulmala, M., Rasell, M., Chernova, Z. 2017. Overhauling Russia's Child Welfare System: Institutional and Ideational Factors behind the Paradigm Shift. *The Journal of Social Policy Studies* 15 (3): 353–366.

Maiorova-Scheglova, S. 2018. *Deti i detsko-roditalskie otnoshenia kak resurs razvitia sovremennogo obschestva* [Children and Child-Parent Relations as a Resource for Developing Society]. *Vestnik NNGU* 4: 55–61.

Maiorova-Scheglova, S., Kolosova, E. 2018. *Deti kak ob'ekt sociologicheskih issalovanii*. [Children as the Object of Sociological Research]. *Sotciologicheskie issledovania* [Sociological Research] 3: 62–69.

McAuley, M. 2009. *Children in Custody: Anglo-Russian Perspectives*. London: Bloomsbury Academic.

McCartney, R.J., Edwards, R. 2011. *Key Concepts in Family Studies*. London: Sage Publications.

Nurkova, V. 2010. *Avtobiograficheskaya pamyat' v optile kul'turno-istoricheskoi i leyatelnostnoi metodologii* [Autobiographical Memory in the Optic of Cultural-Historical and Latent Methodology]. *Psikhologiya. Zhurnal Vysshei Shkoly Economiki* 7 (2): 64–82.

Pufall, P., Unsworth, R. 2003. Introduction: The Imperative and the Process for Rethinking Childhood. In P. Pufall, R. Unsworth (eds.), *Rethinking Childhood*. New Jersey: Rutgers University Press.

Reimer, D. 2010. 'Everything was Strange and Different': Young Adults Recollections of the Transition into Foster Care. *Adoption & Fostering* 34 (2): 14–22.

Reimer, D., Schäfer, D. 2015. The Use of Biographical Narratives to Explain Favorable Outcomes for Children in Foster Care. *Adoption & Fostering* 39 (1): 5–20.

Rozhdestvenskaya, E. 2010. *Narrativnaya identichnost' v avtobiograficheskom interv'yu* [Narrative Identity in Autobiographical Interviews]. *Sociologiya: metodologiya, metody, matematicheskoe modelirovanie 4M* [Sociology: Methodology, Methods, Mathematical Models 4M] 30: 5–26.

Schmidt, V. 2010. What Legal Regulations Provide Efficient Child Protection Policy: Russian and Czech Cases Comparison. *Argumentum* 2 (1): 150–178.

Schofield, G., Beek, M., Sargent, K., Thoburn, J. 2000. *Growing Up in Foster Care*. London: BAAF.

Semia, G. 2016. *Formirovanie roissiskoi modeli preodolenia sotcial'nogo sirotstva* [The Formation of the Russian Model for Overcoming Social Orphanhood]. *Psihologicheskaya nauka i obrazovanie* [Psychological Science and Education] 21 (1): 67–82.

Shpakovskaya, L. 2018. 'Podkidyshi': reprezentacii priemnogo roditel'stva v sovremennoi Rossii ['Foundlings': Representations of Foster Parenthood in Modern Russia]. *Zhurnal sociologii i social'noi antropologii* [Journal of Sociology and Social Anthropology] 21 (3): 71–92.

Shpakovskaya, L., Kulmala, M., Chernova, Z. 2019. The Ideal Organization of Care for Children Deprived of Parental Care: Russia's Child Welfare Reform as Battle over Resources and Recognition. *Laboratitim: Journal of Social Research* 11 (1): 57–81 (in Russ).

Sinclair, I., Baker, C., Wilson, K., Gibbs, I. 2005. *Foster Children: Where They Go and How They Do*. London: Jessica Kingsley Publishers.

Smirnova, T. (2015). *Deti strany sovetov. Ot gosudarstvennoj politiki k realiyam povsednevnoj zhizni 1917–1940* [Children of the USSR: From State Policy to Real Everyday Life]. Moscow, Spb: CGI.

Volohatova, V. 2005. *Sirotskie uchrezhdenia sovetskoi Rossii: istoria stanovlenia i problemy funkcioniroivania* [Orphan Institutions in Soviet Russia: The History of Formation and Problems of Functioning]. Candidate of Science Dissertation. Moscow: Moscow State Open Pedagogical Sholokhov University.

Walker, C. 2012. *Klass, gender i sub'jektivnoe blagopoluchie na novom rossijskom rynke truda: zhiznennyj opyt molodezhi v Ul'janovske i Sankt-Peterburge* [Class, Gender and Subjective Well-Being in the New Russian Labour Market: The Life Experience of Young People in Ul'yanovsk and St. Petersburg]. *Zhurnal Issledovanij Sot'sialnoi Politiki* [Journal of Social Policy Studies] 10 (4): 521–538.

Zelizer, V. 1994. *Pricing the Priceless Child: The Changing Social Value of Children.* Princeton: Princeton University Press.

10 Young adults leaving care

Agency and educational choice

*Meri Kulmala, Zhanna Chernova,
and Anna Fomina*

Introduction

Young people's transition to adulthood is generally considered to be a pivotal window of both opportunity and vulnerability in terms of their future life. This is especially true when it comes to the particular group of young people under our investigation: young people leaving care. Their journey into adulthood is 'both accelerated and compressed' (Stein 2006: 274). It has been noted (Hiles et al. 2014: 1) that care leavers 'undertake this journey against a backdrop of difficult life experiences, sometimes amidst unsupportive family relationships and, and with little time to allow psychological adjustment to these changes'. 'They make the transition to independent living far earlier and more rapidly than their peers generally without the option to return', the authors continue. If more generally the literature on youth-adult transitions now speaks about yo-yo transitions, meaning that these transitions have become less linear, more complex, and also reversible (Biggart, Walther 2006), young adults leaving care might not have a place to return to. Thus, they might have fewer chances to 'make mistakes' in making decisions and choices concerning their later life, including their education and future profession.

According to the widespread notion of the typical educational trajectories of children deprived of parental care, these children globally face problems in learning at school, show low motivation to receive education, and have low grades, which significantly limits their access to higher education and, consequently, might lead to employment in low-prestige and low-paid sectors (Arnau-Sabatés, Gilligan 2015; Hiles et al. 2014; Pinkerton, Rooney 2014; Stein 2006; Törrönen et al. 2018). Many countries have proceeded with efforts to improve the quality of care in order to promote better social inclusion of this specific group of young people. The development of aftercare services is also in the essence of the Russian recent child welfare reform (Chapter 4 by Kulmala et al. in this volume). In the Russian context, this group of young people is of particular interest, because, on the one hand, it is considered to be a low resource, excluded from the general Russian trend of people getting higher education, while the prestige of secondary education is declining (Walker 2012). On the other hand, they are provided with a rather large package of state support, including an opportunity for professional education, both secondary special and higher. At the same time, the forms of support provided are not always effective in terms of overcoming stigma and social exclusion (Ilyin 2015).

This chapter analyses the educational strategies of young people leaving alternative care.[1] We focus on young adults' experiences of their transition from different forms of care to independent living in one industrial region of North-West Russia. Interviews were conducted with 22 young adults. We consider education as a factor structuring the individual life biography and thus as highly crucial for later life inclusion (Gilligan, Arnau-Sabatés 2017). Therefore, understanding the choice of education and what factors affect this choice is important from the viewpoint of its impact on the later professional trajectory, and, thus, even income.

We explore the decision junctures in education by analysing how the studied young adults narrate their choice of education and future prospects. The central concept in our analysis is 'agency'. As Hitlin and Elder (2007: 185) state, the 'sociological issue is not whether agency exists but the extent to which one exercises it and the circumstances that facilitate or hinder that exercise'. In our understanding, young adults who are about to leave care make a choice (of education) – i.e. exercise agency – and they do it within both enabling and constraining structures. Through our modification of Hitlin and Elder's conceptualisation of agency (2007), we ask: (1) what modes of agency do care leavers exercise in their choices of education and (2) what factors affect the modes? In order to fully answer the first question, special attention is paid to the temporal dimension of decision-making, professional identity, and individual sense of agency, while the second question is structured by the analysis of the macro-, meso-, and micro-level factors affecting agency. This allows us to understand how agency is formed at the level of individual life histories. However, individual choices are made under certain structural conditions that determine opportunities and set limits.

The study of young care leavers' transition to adult life is not new to social research. However, our focus on agency makes it possible to take a fresh look at this transition, moving beyond the so-called problem-oriented frame which largely focuses on studying the problems this group of people face. It also helps us to focus on the active position of the individual who is able to make (rational) decisions and achieve short- and long-term goals instead of, for instance, the concept of adaptation. The latter rather involves a reactive strategy of an individual who is forced to adapt to a new situation and learn the new rules of social interaction, while agency focuses on strategic action and the ability of an individual to build their own life project. We focus on the studied care leavers' goals, expectations, feeling of control over one's life, and (in)dependent ability to do things and make choices.

By focusing on agency, instead of hardships, we pay attention to their resources and resilience, which are also connected with the concept of subjective agency involving (a) perceived capacities and (b) perceived life chances or expectations of what life holds in store. Such self-efficacy and sense of agentic possibility have important life-course consequences (Hitlin, Kirkpatrick Johnson 2015). Such feelings are themselves resources that can be utilised in the face of difficulties and contribute to mental and physical well-being (Andersson 2012). Thus, a person with strong conviction and the ability to control various aspects of their daily life, who believes that their efforts will pay off in the future, will have greater persistence and will more successfully cope with various challenges (Hitlin, Kirkpatrick Johnson 2015). In this chapter, we aim to understand the conditions, in particular the kind of support, that could facilitate the development of such subjective agency among these children in vulnerable life situations in the given Russian context.

We first discuss the federal social policy concerning this particular group of children with a focus on education. Next, we introduce our data and conceptual framework to build the scheme for our analysis of agency. After our empirical analysis of the modes of agency, we discuss the different-level factors that affect the modes.

Care leavers, education, and state support

As this volume discusses, Russian child welfare policy has undergone dramatic changes in the 2010s. The deinstitutionalisation reforms – with its emphasis on family(-style) care and community-based services – stem from the common understanding that residential care leads to weak social adaptation and social exclusion. In this regard, one of the priority areas of reform has been to develop aftercare services for young people, aged 18–23, transitioning from care into their independent life, by providing them with many kinds of support during this transition, including counselling and help with paperwork for entering educational institutions. The family support centres (*tsentr sodeystviya semeynomu vospitaniyu*) are former children's homes now assigned with this new function, but as Kulmala et al. show in Chapters 4 and 6 of this volume, the input of NGOs is significant, with many kinds of supplementary and complementary support services for care leavers. For instance, the NGO-run (and often state-funded) programmes recruiting volunteers who act as an individual support person for a young person in alternative care (*nastavnik*) are currently widely spread throughout the country.

The transition to independent living is surrounded by many expectations of a certain kind of path, the deviations from which are usually seen as concerning (Furlong 2012). In Russia, the notion of individual well-being is viewed in the traditional sense as having education, paid work, residence, marriage, and children (Glendinning et al. 2004). Such an understanding is clearly seen in the social policy tools designed for children deprived of parental care. Generally, the benefits that young people leaving care receive from the state include one-off and monthly payments, the right to get an apartment (of one's own property, which is quite unusual in the international terms), subsidies for housing and communal services, and compensation for public transportation costs. In the sphere of education, care leavers have the right to free-of-charge vocational and compensated higher education.

The Russian primary school system consists of three levels: primary education (four years), basic general education (five years), and secondary education (two years). Primary and basic general education of nine grades is compulsory for everyone. Upon completion of a nine-year programme, the student has a choice of either completing the remaining two years at a normal school or of a transfer to a specialised professional training school. The first option is the so-called high school–type optional upper secondary education (or complete secondary general school) with 11 years in total. Alternatively, the student may enter vocational education institutions (professional secondary education), which have been traditionally divided into low-prestige ones (PTUs) and better-regarded technical schools (*tekhnikumy*) and medical schools (with nurse level), for instance. If after having completed 11 years of general school the student takes the Unified State Exam (USE), this enables them to enrol at universities or any other higher educational institutions (tertiary education). One can continue to higher education without the USE with a vocational degree.

According to the OECD (2019), most adults in the Russian Federation attain at least upper secondary non-tertiary education: 47.7% complete secondary education with the full 11-year course, while 26.5% complete 9 years. The proportion of young adults (25–34 year olds) who did not take an upper secondary degree is just 4%, much lower than the average across the OECD countries (15%). Post-secondary non-tertiary levels are very well established in Russia and provide opportunities to gain further vocational qualifications. Russia has the highest proportion of adults (25–64 year olds) with a post-secondary non-tertiary qualification (20%) among the OECD countries. Most graduates have studied engineering, manufacturing, and construction (58% compared to 19% on average across the OECD countries). Russia has one of the highest tertiary attainment rates across the OECD countries, at 63% of 25–34 year olds compared with the OECD average of 44% (and the G20 average of 38%). Vocational and higher education are provided by state and non-state institutions. In all non-state educational institutions, all students have to pay tuition fees, whereas approximately half of students in state educational institutions pay for their studies.

According to the Russian law, children without parental care have the right to two secondary vocational degrees and to free training in the preparatory programmes of higher educational institutions, up to 23 years of age.[2] The right to receive free-of-charge vocational education is accompanied by a full package of benefits and is thus obviously one of the important opportunities offered to children deprived of parental care. Young people transitioning from alternative care have the right to study full-time and free-of-charge twice at the vocational level of education. In addition, when studying in higher education – which one can enter either after having completed 11 grades of general school or a vocational degree – care leavers receive more benefits than other students. The state support for (vocational) education is viewed by experts, including government officials, NGOs, and social scientists, as an important element of a successful transition to adulthood and independent living (Abramov et al. 2016).

However, research has revealed many problems concerning the practical implementation of this right. As a rule, care leavers have a lower level of knowledge from elementary school in comparison to children brought up in their birth families. As a result, children deprived of parental care do not usually continue to upper secondary school (with 11 grades) and thus do not pass the Unified State Exam, which is required for admission to higher education, which significantly complicates their access to higher education (Abramov et al. 2016); however, they can continue there without the USE after vocational education. The importance of education as a factor structuring the further life trajectory is recognised by NGOs, which might offer special tutoring programmes aimed at increasing the level of knowledge and training for the USE.

Studying is basically the only provided option. It is widespread among young people in alternative care to obtain nine grades and continue to vocational school. Even with this opportunity, strongly encouraged by the support system, young people encounter a number of restrictions that limit their options for choosing a profession that is interesting for them, as we show in this chapter. Against the background of often difficult life histories, it can be assumed that these young adults would need a more supported and individualised strategy in their transition to adulthood, including information and counselling to support their choices. Some research (Abramov et al. 2016; Chernova, Shpakovskaya 2019) has argued that increased benefits would contribute to the lack of motivation to consciously choose a future profession. It is more like the primary way to provide for themselves financially. It is also important to note that all the state benefits for education – as for the other benefits – are dependent on the status of having been in alternative care. Thus, even if much-needed, they can be seen as stigmatising to this particular group of young people.

Theoretical framework: agency within limits

In our understanding, the educational choice of a young person is an individual action in a world of social structures. Educational choice is a critical juncture in the biography of any individual, having a significant effect on their later life trajectories, as discussed previously. As Hitlin and Elder (2007: 177) state, vulnerability obviously somewhat limits agency, but 'even those without power have the ability to make decisions though they face severe consequences for those choices'.

Therefore, what matters to us is to what extent the studied young adults exercise their agency when making their educational choices and what circumstances enable or restrict this practice. Even if the choice of education is an individual decision, it is structured by social and educational policies, social norms and values, and individual preferences, which all contribute to a set of repertoires of possible choices. To analyse the various modes of agency, we use the conceptualisation by Hitlin and Elder (2007), modifying it in accordance with the objectives of our study. Hitlin and Elder distinguish four modes of agency: existential, pragmatic, identity, and life-course agency. They put a particular emphasis on the temporal dimension – a long- or short-term orientation in action to understand an individual's ability to make independent and informed decisions combined with the planning horizon of certain actions. Existential agency is the fundamental premises for any ability to take independent action and initiative and the ability to control one's behaviour. By pragmatic agency, the authors refer to individuals making choices in everyday life that are temporally proximate and do not involve planning, while life-course agency refers to the actions that aim at exerting influence on the formation of their life trajectory. The life-course mode contains two elements: situational agency with implementation of an action with long-term consequences, and a self-reflective belief in one's ability to achieve important life goals in the long run (self-efficacy). Thus, unlike pragmatic agency, this mode involves orientation to the future in accordance with certain expectations, aspirations, and goals. As Hitlin and Kirkpatrick Johnson (2015) note, this is 'the power of looking ahead'. According to these authors, identity agency, in turn, interconnects with social norms that determine the behaviour of individuals as they intentionally seek to assimilate and comply with these norms recognised in a society as conventional patterns of behaviour. Individuals build their identities, and these identities determine subsequent behaviour.

By our modification of Hitlin and Elder's conceptualisation, we developed a conceptual scheme for our analytical purposes. This scheme is based on two criteria. One is the time horizon: either short-term planning in the case of the pragmatic mode of agency or long-term and strategic planning in life-course agency. Another criterion is our modification of identity agency, by which we refer to an individual's ability to form a (positive) self-image in connection to their future professional life. Based on such an understanding, we included in our scheme a mode of identity agency with strong or weak identity construction in terms of sharing the value of education for further career plans. Weak identity is connected with a negative attitude towards education in general and the lack of a clear idea of the relationship between education and future career. With the strong mode, a young adult knows with whom and where they want to work in the future and the educational choice is a step in that direction – especially when combined with the life-course mode of agency. In the combination of the weak mode with the life-course type of planning, a person plans ahead, for instance, knowing that having vocational or higher education is crucial and is striving for that, yet without a concrete choice of profession. In the case of the strong identity mode and pragmatic agency, one might have a dream job but with no concrete efforts to strive in that direction, while in pragmatic agency with weak identity in terms of profession, a person – for one reason or another – is lost with their individual choices. In our analytical scheme we thus distinguish four types of agency with the previously explained dimensions (see also Figure 10.1):

1   Pragmatic agency with weak identity construction in terms of future profession
2   Life-course agency with weak identity construction in terms of future profession
3   Pragmatic agency with strong identity construction in terms of future profession
4   Life-course agency with strong identity construction in terms of future profession

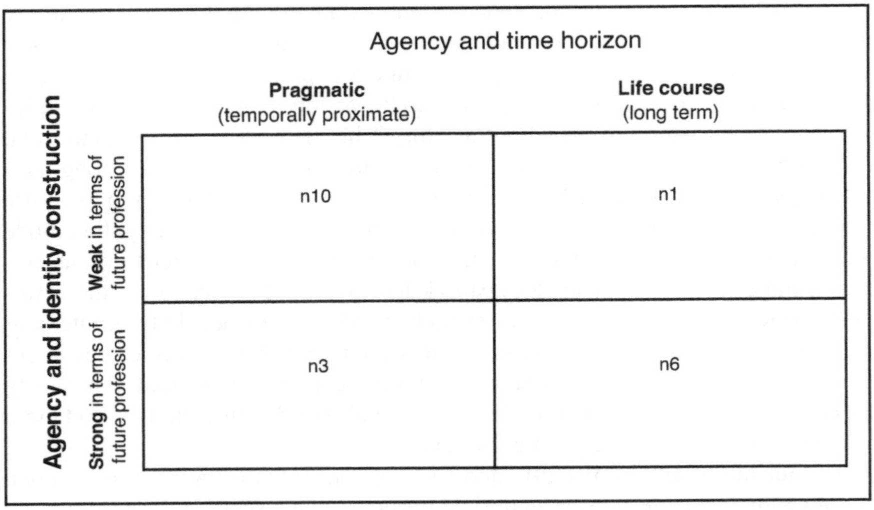

Figure 10.1 Agency, identity construction, and time horizon.

The previously explained criteria were not chosen by chance. Considering the planning horizon and professional identity as accelerated and compressed (Stein 2006: 274), the transition of this particular group of young people is perhaps more linear than of their peers growing up in birth families. Despite the fact that the state provides these young care leavers with the opportunity to obtain two secondary vocational or one vocational and one higher education course for free, they have less opportunity to 'make a mistake' and 'try again' compared to their peers. Based on the fact that these young adults often lack the 'option to return' (Hiles et al. 2014: 1), we tend to think that they are in a position to 'choose right' in the first place when making a decision concerning their education and consequently their future profession.

In our analysis, we also pay special attention to care leavers' own perceptions of their agentic possibility, i.e. their own view of how much influence and control they have over their own future. Following Hitlin and Kirkpatrick Johnson (2015), we assume that belief in the ability to influence events in one's life, as well as positive expectations from decisions made, are crucial for building a long-term life strategy. One of the practical goals of our work is to understand what types of support which are most significant and in demand by young people in the transition to adulthood will have a positive impact on the formation of their subjective well-being. Importantly, none of the modes represents the 'success' or 'failure' of a care leaver themselves, but the mode is structured with multiple external factors, as will be discussed in our analysis. As Hitlin and Kirkpatrick Johnson (2015: 3–4) note, 'people differ in their individual abilities, as well as structurally determined advantages which provide them with more active options for action'.

In our analysis, we paid particular attention to interviewed care leavers' narrations of their educational choice(s), which we then categorised through the aforementioned two dimensions of the ability for future planning and identity construction and their possible combinations. After having distributed all the interviews by their modes of agency, we considered which factors influence the practised modes of agency. We identify several explanatory factors at three different levels of analysis: macro, meso, and micro. The macro-level structural conditions include the system of social support. The meso-level refers to the regional and local-level infrastructures, including the specificities of labour markets and availability of different educational institutions as well as the presence of different forms of alternative care and availability support services. Micro-level factors are more related to the individuals themselves and their close circles (birth and foster parents, staff of the residential institutions, school teachers, social workers and pedagogues, mentors, and friends and peers). This level of analysis will allow us to study an individual's subjective value towards education, and make a subjective assessment of their available resources and their ability to use them.

Data and analysis

The empirical materials of the study consist of 22 thematic interviews with young people aged 18–24 (20.5 years in average), living in one region located in the North-Western Federal District of the Russian Federation. Of these 22 adults, 14 are females and 8 males. All the interviewed young adults had experience of living and being brought up in a form of alternative care (children's home, foster family, children's village, or a combination of these). Thirteen grew up in a children's village, three in residential institutions, and the other six had first been in residential institutions and later re-placed in foster and guardian families. Some of the informants had also returned to the institution from family placement.

We partly implemented our research as co-research in the following manner. We first interviewed seven young adults, who were found and volunteered to participate in our research through our earlier contacts and collaboration with a local child welfare NGO.[3] As a response to our request to find co-researchers, three of these young care leavers were recommended by the director of an NGO. We talked with them and they were willing to engage as co-researchers to peer-interview their fellows. The co-researchers conducted 15 peer interviews with their peer care leavers whom they searched and contacted by themselves. Thus, the care leavers interviewed by the co-researchers remained anonymous to us, the adult researchers. All the interviews were recorded and transcribed.

Because the topic is very sensitive and the interviewees and interviewers involved have most likely experienced severe hardships in their lives, we considered it of the utmost importance that the young people – both interviewers and interviewees – had a local focal point that they trusted and with which we have a confidential relationship. In this region, our partner was a children's village, which explains the dominance of this form of alternative care in our study.[4] The local coordinator, employed by the NGO, assisted the interviewers. Her contact information was delivered to each of the interviewed persons, indicating that informants can turn to her with any issues or feelings related to the interviews. For the sake of sensitivity, we do not name the studied Russian region here. Moreover, all the people and organisations referred to and cited in this chapter have been anonymised.

Any research with children or young adults involves ethical issues that need to be addressed, including concerns about possible exploitation, child protection, informed consent, and gatekeeper issues (Törrönen et al. 2018). We have tried to be sensitive and reflective to any issues raised by the young adults involved in the process and spent time going through our research design and providing, alongside the needed research skills, training on numerous ethical issues, such as principles of confidentiality, anonymity, and voluntary participation. These principles needed to be shared with everyone they interviewed, and everyone's consent was recorded at the beginning of the interview. We have discussed – and will continue discussing – in more detail elsewhere why we engaged in such a research design and introduced the different phases of our collaborative project (Kulmala, Fomina 2019).

As our research focused on young people's agency, we found it impossible to carry out the research without the involvement of young people in the research process. As usual for participatory research methods (e.g. Kilpatrick et al. 2007; Bradbury-Jones, Taylor 2015), we wanted to involve young people as active agents in our knowledge production and hopefully thus support their sense of agency. Our purpose has been to highlight young people as experts in their own life and the alternative care system in question through their personal experience, while providing some tools that can be useful in their work and study life: we, for instance, trained them in qualitative interview and interaction skills and gave certificates for their participation (Kulmala, Fomina 2019). We wanted to give young people a voice in understanding the forms of support that have been useful to them during and when leaving alternative care. Ultimately, we hope our research will bring improvements to these forms of support, which is why we emphasise the importance of collaboration with practitioners. However, as admitted earlier (Kulmala, Fomina 2019), the processes within which knowledge is being constituted, starting from research interests to full research designs, have been adult-led, which obviously creates the potential to exploit young people for the adult researcher's ends (Kilpatrick et al. 2007: 352). In our focus group discussion with the co-researchers afterwards, these young adults reported many kinds of benefits and learning processes they had gained during the process (Bradbury-Jones, Taylor 2015: 163–165; Kilpatrick et al. 2007: 367–368).

We have sought to overcome the asymmetric power relationships between the researchers and researched (Bradbury-Jones, Taylor 2015; Kilpatrick et al. 2007). Anyone can recognise multilayered asymmetries in the situation where we, middle-class (and partly middle-aged) academically educated women, interview 20-year-old young people who have experienced situations leading to alternative care replacements. Through peer-to-peer talk, we have hoped to also open new perspectives on the studied issues. For example, similar experiences bring to interviews mutual understanding and language that perhaps allow for better communication and a more accurate reflection of young people's own thinking in our research materials (Törrönen et al. 2018; Kulmala, Fomina 2019).

Both groups of interviewers used the same interview guide. The interview questions followed a sort of life-cyclic logic, including topics, such as birth family, placement in alternative, school and studies, working life, housing, leisure time, close relationships, satisfaction with one's life, and future plans. At all stages of life, we have tried to understand the involvement of the young person in the decision-making over their life and the kinds of support they have received around this. Special attention was paid to possible preparatory programmes and support for transitioning to independent life. All interviews were conducted in December 2018–May 2019.

Analysis of the interviews was conducted using thematic coding. Codes, combined into categories and thematic units of text, were arranged chronologically, in accordance with the interviewed young adults' life trajectories. Concerning the educational choice such as making decisions on education and interpretations of one's choices, we analysed and arranged the narrations of the young adults through paying attention to: (1) the school trajectory (starting from elementary school); (2) the desired level of education; (3) the decision to enter a specific educational institution for a particular speciality; (4) the attitude towards education in general and subjective assessment of their experience in school and vocational education; (5) the influence of the family and close circle regarding the adoption of a particular educational decision; and (6) taking into account the regional profile of the educational space and the employment market. This made it possible to track, on the one hand, the influence of various factors on the formation of the agency of young people in different forms of alternative care, and on the other hand, their subjective perceptions of education and their own abilities and skills. After the thematic coding and biographical organisation of the interview data, each of us individually placed each of the young adults into one category of the previously presented four different modes of agency, created by us based on the theory, after which we compared and explained to each other our choices in terms of the categories. Both the coding and categorisation results were discussed several times by the authors, which helped to reduce the amount of influence of the subjective interpretation of one researcher on the data. Based on these conversations and our theory-driven analysis of the modes of agency, we resulted in agreeing upon the modes, as presented in Figure 10.1 (n indicating the number of young adults in each category). Each of the modes is next discussed in more detail in light of our empirical materials.

Studied young adults and modes of agency

As already stated, we consider education to be a structuring factor for further life trajectories. It is highly connected with the well-being of an individual and also an important element of their identity. Importantly, all 22 young care leavers from different forms of alternative care were studying or had studied at the time of the interviews: 16 people had received or were receiving secondary vocational education and 6 people were studying at universities. As a rule, the typical educational trajectory is to complete 9 years at school and then to continue to vocational school; only one of the studied young adults chose to take 11 grades which allowed them to continue straight to university.

When we look at the educational choices of the studied care leavers, the pragmatic mode of agency with weak professional identity construction turned out to be dominant, appearing in 10 out of 22 care leavers. Pragmatic agency with strong professional identity construction was identified in three cases, while six showed life-course agencies with strong identity construction. Life-course agency with weak construction of professional identity in turn appeared to be rare: we categorised only one young adult into this mode.[5] We now turn to a more detailed discussion of each of the combinations.

'Who knows how life will turn out?': pragmatic agency with weak professional identity construction

This mode of agency is characterised by the young person's short-term horizon for planning their education and life course more generally. For young adults who demonstrate such a pragmatic mode with weak identity construction, education is not related to acquiring skills that can be used in future work; instead, it is considered as an opportunity to make use of the available benefits for studying. They have no strong opinion on the field of study and often might change their speciality when obtaining the second vocational education they are entitled to, as seen in the following interview quote: 'Well, I want to study, because up to 23 you can do it for free and if there is such a chance, I do not want to miss it. Why would I later pay to do it if I can study for free?' (F_21_1). Almost as a rule, these young adults go for the so-called standard choice of sphere of vocational education: for instance, girls for beautician or confectionary jobs, and boys for car renovation. Usually young people who implement this mode tend to get two, often somewhat unrelated, degrees, the choice of which is often influenced by advice from someone in their close environment (social pedagogues or foster parents, for instance) or due to the ease and guaranteed admission because of quotas for including care leavers or knowing that there are easy exams, as one of the interviewed young adults explained her, rather haphazard, decision to study medicine:

> I went to study to be a nurse, I don't know, it somehow happened that my [foster] mother told me: ' . . . you need to become a doctor, a doctor, it's very suitable for you, since you have such a petit shape and a white coat suits you . . . .' And you know, I stuffed it in my head after that, well, why not?
> (F_22_3)

Later, explaining the choice of her second profession, social work, she explained that the choice was partly made because of its connection with medicine, and also because there were easy entrance exams: 'And social work . . . is still, you know, closely connected with medicine, with communication with people, that is, something like that. . . . Well, plus the entrance exams were easy [laughs]' (F_22_3). Later, when thinking about future work, the respondent concluded that working in a sanatorium would be a good option.

The stability of the everyday life plays an important role in how young people choose educational institutions. Having friends and support networks (foster parents, social pedagogues, mentors) as well as housing in the area where they have lived become important criteria for choosing educational institutions in order to stay in the same place. In such case, the available educational infrastructure obviously influences the choices available. One young adult had a dream job in mind but such, quite rare, education was not available where she lives and she did not want to move:

> When we went to study, I generally wanted to become a car mechanic, . . . or an animal attendant. There was no animal attending here close to us anywhere. So decided to study to be a car mechanic. We only had this course in [city name]. When I went there, they told me, 'We don't take girls'. This was, damn it, it was just such a disappointment. As a result, in short, the only profession left available was cook-confectioner.
>
> (F_24_4)

As seen in the quotation, her choice was restricted not only by the unavailability of a certain school in her place of residence but also by a highly stereotypical understanding of the gendered division of labour, which is to be considered as a structural constraint.

The weak discursive construction of professional identity is often also characterised by a negative attitude towards education in general. These young adults often also lacked any concrete plans to work in the acquired profession, but they were more concerned about finding some job with a stable income. One of the young adults described her choice of working in the public sector as a social worker: 'that is, I can work everywhere – [social workers are needed] in the police, and they're in kindergartens, schools, everywhere' (F_21_1). Weak identity construction in terms of future career is also expressed in the rejection of strategic planning of their life project/strategy because not much has an effect on it. Such a not-planning strategy is sometimes seen in a somewhat more optimistic light: 'Everything will be fine' (M_21_8), as one young adult saw his future life. However, more typically it was expressed through lack of trust in one's own ability to make change because everything can just change, as seen in the following quote from a young adult who did not believe that there is need to make plans for the future: 'who knows how life will turn out?' (F_22_3).

'I was attracted to car repair ever since childhood': pragmatic agency with strong professional identity construction

Unlike the previous mode, pragmatic agency with strong identity construction in terms of future profession is characterised to a certain extent by the young adult's own desires of future profession, yet they lack the strategic planning for how to get there, as one young care leaver addressed his long-time wish to work with cars: 'For me, as if from childhood, I was drawn to car repair, and the like. Well, yes, I wanted to learn to drive too' (M_20_2). However, these young people did not typically describe concrete efforts and educational plans to achieve the job in question. Young people who demonstrate this mode of agency often receive a second vocational education in a related field. The influence of the surrounding community on the choice of educational institution and occupation of research participants does not always occur directly, but indirectly. A young adult, having chosen for himself to study carpentry and glass work, says that he decided to follow in his father's footsteps:

I: And why did you decide to go to the school you are currently attending?

R: Well, I decided to follow in my father's footsteps. He is a carpenter.

I: Well, did you want it yourself, or did your dad advise you?

R: No, no, I wanted to, I had a lot of options where I could go. In principle, my entry grades allowed me to enrol in all the colleges. But I decided to go to this college.

(M_20_21)

However, in the end, he did not end up with any direct educational path. Even despite the fact that often these paths of this type are not linear, but intermittent, young people might face difficulties with their studies, they might even quit but then anyhow return to the initially selected programme or similar/related fields. Education is anyhow seen as an integral, obligatory part of their life, the experience that structures their further biography, as one put it: 'because if there is no education, but education is needed' (M_20_2).

Young male research participants often had experience in military service between receiving two degrees. This experience is usually seen as beneficial: on the one hand as a resource that temporarily provides an opportunity to think about life trajectories, and, on the other hand, because it can also be converted into education and a future profession: 'In fact, with the service in the army – you served, came back – you have more opportunities, in the end, with getting a job too, there is something else' (M_20_2). Strong identity construction in terms of future profession combined with pragmatic agency was usually seen in the situations when the educational choice was one's own, yet this decision was taken within a short-term horizon, if any. In these situations, the choice of professional field was usually narrated through the positive perception of education generally. The supportive attitude of the close environment of a care leaver plays an important role for young people to learn about available educational institutions and gain support for their own desires and ability to act. Combining the pragmatic mode of agency with a strong construct of professional identity is quite rare. Most often strong professional identity is connected with another mode, namely life-course agency.

'At my home, there lies a branching plan – the development of my life': life-course agency with strong professional identity construction

Life-course agency can be characterised by the general orientation of graduates to design a life path in which education is a highly significant part of life. This mode connects the choice of an education with long-term planning in regard to future work, other personal life, and place of residence. Young people engaging with this mode often go for higher education believing that through it they will be able to build a good professional trajectory. Life-course agency with strong construct of professional identity implies that young adults have a clear life plan and a long planning horizon with a particular speciality in their mind combined with a desire to work in the chosen sphere. When choosing educational institutions, these young adults know well what they want and what is needed to acquire the related goals, as one pointed out:

> Well, only because we have the technologist profession, here, though, when I was admitted, someone told me why would you go to a university when there is a college [where I live] for technologists? I said, 'Hey people, you do not understand that there are higher education and vocational education'. That's it. And I didn't like the other specialities.
>
> (F_22_22)

For young people engaged with this mode, higher education is a logical and natural continuation of the vocational level of education and immersion in the chosen profession:

> And so I chose the job of a technologist because it's interesting: I'll study the other side of cooking, that is, I studied to be a cook for three years, that is, this is one step, the inside, this is the kitchen, there, the workshop, that's it, the technologist he looks at it all from above and controls it all. This is also interesting, because I have this commanding tone in me, so to speak. It is necessary to control someone, to direct someone somewhere, to move.
>
> (F_22_22)

Some of the young adults wanted to make it explicit that it is their own achievement to be proud of being admitted to higher education universities, instead of any quota or other benefits, which are often considered as somewhat stigmatising:

> But I was admitted because of my knowledge, not just because of privileges, and that is also pleasing. So, to speak, a reason for pride, because many acquaintances asked 'did you get in because of your privileges?' I say, 'No, not because of it'. They were so surprise.
>
> (F_22_22)

Long-term life-path planning is the hallmark of life-course mode agency with strong professional identity. People make plans to achieve their educational and other specific goals, as well illustrated in the following quote from an interview with a young adult who had carefully thought through her options – even drawing a chart with those different options:

> I drew a chart with different options of the course of my life. That's it. To finalise my studies now study, then go on to a Master's programme. Then stay at home [with kids] if my husband's salary allows. If not, then I'll go on maternity leave and then come back to work. I will try to find job with as good salary as possible because having family and children requires money. So, if I'm not able to work at all, then I'm going to become a home baker, making cakes by order. That's what I like and doesn't distract me too much from the child. If I don't have a family then I'll work hard. Exactly. I will work in a company or at home, as a self-employed pâtissier. I would probably like to finish my studies, stay home and then open my own pastry shop for a while.
>
> (F_22_22)

Life-course agency with strong professional identity construction was also sometimes expressed through refusal of the standard trajectory of certain professions that care leavers might typically (be advised to) choose, as one young adult reflected on her choice:

> In general, I didn't want to go into nursing, I didn't want to be a chef, any of those professions . . . which I had to choose from. I didn't want to continue at school either. I wanted to go to a pedagogical college where all the best would go. It's a demanding sphere. I got in easily. And I long ago promised to myself that I will finish university.
>
> (F_21_6)

As illustrated also in the preceding quotation, life-course agency with strong identity construction in terms of future profession was usually connected with a developed understanding of the utility of their efforts. They showed pretty strong self-belief to achieve the set goals and importantly concerning personal control, mastery over one's life course.

'The most important thing is that I graduate': life-course agency with weak professional identity construction

Life-course agency with weak identity construction in terms of profession of identity by profession was a rare case. This mode was characterised by the notion of the importance of having education along with showing efforts to achieve and finalise it, unlike the earlier described pragmatic modes. Studying and consequently having the degree constitutes the value itself, while the sphere and future professions did not seem to matter that much, as illustrated by the following quote: 'I graduated successfully. Then things went well – I met a young man. That's it, I got married, now I'm working. Thanks to my studies, everything also went well, everything is fine with me' (F_21_9).

All in all, education is an important structural factor in the entire biography of young adults leaving different forms of alternative care. As our empirical analysis shows, two opposite modes of agency turned out to be dominant: pragmatic agency with weak professional identity construction and life-course agency with strong professional identity construction. In order to understand and explain the factors that influence the modes and their combinations, we must discuss certain explanatory factors.

Why certain modes of agency?

As already stated, we understand that the educational choice of care leavers is an individual action in a world of social structures which either facilitate or hinder the exercise of agency. In the context of Russia, the state stimulates education, the choice of which still requires a personal decision, which again can be affected by many factors ranging from macro-level policies to micro-level personality traits. As people vary in terms of their individual capacities and their structural advantages that allow for more agentic options (Hitlin, Kirkpatrick Johnson 2015), in this section, we aim to understand the factors at the macro-, meso-, and micro-levels that either enable or constrain the individual choice of the studied care leavers.

Macro-level explanations

It is important to emphasise that all of the young adults who participated in our research (had) studied at the moment of the interviews. Thus, we can conclude that most Russian care leavers use the opportunity provided by the state and choose to study, which is not something that is obvious in international comparisons (Gilligan, Arnau-Sabatés 2017). Furthermore, several of the studied young adults, again quite atypically in the wider comparison, have continued to university. Thus, state policy is obviously an enabling macro-level structural factor. Studying also allows some more time before the 'full transition' to independent living, because many colleges and universities provide living in dormitories and support services from the social pedagogues of those educational institutions. Obviously, one crucial factor is that completion of a degree as such opens up new opportunities in the labour market that one would not have without any education; in other words, education serves as a major institutional pillar of social inclusion.

However, the choice of education is socially channelled. In the Russian context, the state heavily directs care leavers to receive vocational education, because many privileges and benefits are targeted at care leavers having formal student status at such educational institutions. In sum, the care leavers receive financial support until the age of 23 if they enrol in vocational educational institutions.

Leaving school after nine grades, young people can have the full package of state support for two degrees of secondary vocational or one secondary vocational and one higher vocational education programme up to 23 years of age.

According to our study, children without parental care, as a rule, finish 9 grades (instead of the possible 11 grades), after which they receive one or two degrees of vocational education, while 11 grades would open up the possibility of higher education (although only once). According to our interviews, most young adults had not even considered – let alone been encouraged by the official support system – to take the full 11 grades; moreover, not all were even fully aware of this option. We consider the widely spread stereotypical picture of children deprived of parental care as 'bad students' (Chernova, Shpakovskaya in this volume) as a structural-level restricting factor. Furthermore, it seems that young adults leaving care are limited to the 'standard choice' – the choice of 'traditional' professions such as nursing, hairdressing, cooking, car mechanics, etc., the choices of which also follow very gendered patterns.

On the other hand, though, this system of two supported degrees (in different spheres if desired) provides some flexibility to rethink that this group of young people might not have because of the lack of a place to return to. If choosing for themselves the educational trajectory of 11 grades and admission straight into higher education, these young people deprive themselves of the 'right to make mistakes' and the opportunity to make other choices.

Meso-level explanations

The studied young people's dominant engagement with pragmatic agency with weak identity construction in terms of future profession is influenced by the regional labour market and local educational infrastructure, which we define as meso-level. As shown, at this level, the lack of or presence of an educational facility strongly influences the choice of these young people, who often have few options to move to study further away, which is also dependent on the state policy on the provision of housing. The regional specificities of available industries and thus the labour market obviously affects which educational institutions are available and, consequently, also the standard professions that might be more easily accessible to this group of young people. Thus, the accessible and standard choices vary from region to region.

In our understanding, the meso-level also includes the availability and use of different forms of alternative care. It became obvious that young adults who live in residential institutions are less informed about their options, as one peer-interviewer reflected to us in a focus group discussion:

> In one interview, I realised what some people lack – not necessarily monetary support but a person who would tell them what can be done without money. . . . We [from a children's village] know our rights better, we know what we can or cannot do.
>
> (P1, focus group discussion)

In the residential institutions, care leavers are more often advised to choose certain educational institutions as the standard professions, as one explained:

> I was told that it was possible to go to a college. . . . At that moment, they were youth workers in [place]. They came, told me that I could go to [town] to study, that they would help me with this choice of a profession and arrange everything.
>
> (M_21_8)

In NGO-supported facilities there seem to be more seminars and training dedicated to the choice of education and profession. This is in line what Kulmala et al. show in Chapter 6 of this volume: despite the new formal requirement of the family support centres to provide aftercare services for young people leaving care, these centres often fail or fulfil this obligation to a minimum. This being the case, the existence of an active NGO community in the region in question and the availability of its work for particular care leavers seems to be a significant enabling factor. According to our research, it clearly seems that it is the NGO-run children's villages or certain other projects targeted at care leavers which do better in this sphere by putting emphasis on individual support, counselling, and encouragement – which brings us to the importance of the micro-level factors.

Micro-level explanations

The micro-level is connected with young adults themselves, their family, and their close environment. At this level, the support of significant adults – be they foster parents, social workers, or volunteer support persons – crucially affects the attitude to education in general as well as the choices of the educational trajectories of a young adult. As one young adult, with strong life-course agency combined with strong professional identity, said:

> First, my mother's support, because my [foster] mother always helped with my studies, and I finished my studies well enough. That is, if I had finished my studies poorly, I would not be able to go on to study as I wished, that is pedagogical college. I was able to enrol, the competition that year was huge, even among those who have benefits. I could do it. And also, the university – if I didn't have that knowledge throughout school and college, I would not have been able to enrol most likely. . . . My mom helped us a lot with our studies; that is, she followed what we did, so we were good students. And they were able to go to further colleges, and, here, for everyone who lived in our family, all graduated from college for sure.
>
> (F_21_6)

Or, vice versa, it can lead to the formation of pragmatic mode with weak identity construction in terms of future work, as seen in the following quote: 'My guardians (*opekuny*) here . . . did not inform me. They just suggested to me that it is better to do such a speciality' (M_21_17).

It does not have to be a family member; the important point is that a young person trusts someone to discuss their future plans (Pinkerton, Rooney 2014). This person should guarantee that the young person in question has all the necessary information to make a decision concerning their education. This requires knowing the young person well enough and carefully listening to their needs and wishes and a realistic (not underestimating!) understanding of their capabilities. Importantly, it requires efforts to strengthen the perceptions of the possibility of agency. It is a question of the self-efficacy of a young person, about a sense of control over their own life to believe that they have the ability to make decisions and that those decisions can have an effect over their future. Developing such a mastery is a resource in its own right, because a person with strong control believes that their efforts will pay off in the future and will tend to persevere in the face of hardship (Hitlin, Kirkpatrick Johnson 2015). Our analysis shows that residential care in state institutions is less likely to provide such a positive outcome which would positively contribute to the self-efficacy and resilience of these young adults.

Conclusions: not-to-plan vs. mastery over one's life

As shown, two modes of agency were dominant: on the one hand, pragmatic agency with weak construction of professional identity, often combined with the so-called not-to-plan strategy; on the other hand, life-course agency with strong professional identity construction, often combined with strong self-efficacy, i.e. a sense of control over one's life through own choices and decisions. Both modes result from the combination of factors at all three levels. Even if the macro-level structures are in principle enabling, without strong individual support and planning at the micro-level, the majority of the studied care leavers fail to build their desired life course at once. However, this cannot be considered as a 'success' or 'failure' of the young adult themselves, as there are external factors that affect the modes.

Obviously individual life trajectories and experiences also contribute to the overall picture of planning. Among the care leavers practising pragmatic modes of agency (with weak or strong professional identity), we saw quite a few cases of 'not-planning' (Appleton 2019: 10–11) intertwined with a sense that planning would be worth it. These young adults could not believe that their plans could come true. Instead, their understanding was that planning does not matter because life goes as it goes. In fact, based on the severe hardships that these young people have experienced in their lives, such a perception can be considered as a consistent, logical continuum of 'ending up doing what (s)he has most reason to do' (Appleton 2019: 7; Morton 2011: 577). The life experience of young people leaving care is nothing like stable; perhaps only inconsistency is the stable thing. Life has most likely brought up endless occasions that the person has not planned or even wanted to happen. In such a context, it is of the utmost importance that these young people have a trusted person to plan together with (consider the concept of 'shared agency' (Bratman 2013 cited in Appleton 2019: 5–6).

However, we would argue that is it is not only a question of care leavers but partly also a generational issue. The research on the Y and Z generations to which these young care leavers belong show more widely a more fragmented process of transition to adulthood (Biggart, Walther 2006) and that the conventional markers of adulthood are not necessarily the same any more as they were for the older generations (Radaev 2018). As Radaev (2018) argues, millennials seem to appreciate formal education to a lesser extent and are less oriented towards choosing their profession and workplace for 'forever'. Instead, this generation can be characterised as being in a constant search for work and to develop themselves. This approach includes rejecting routine work that would guarantee a stable income and ensure a mundane life. Thus, in addition to the 'not-planning' strategy clearly connected to the personal, sometimes hard, life experience that clearly would not promote trust in the future, these young adults are also representatives of a certain generation which more widely refuses to make long-term plans. However, in comparison to their peers who live in their birth families, the transition to adulthood of this particular group of young adults is sped up and they are forced to make early decisions that have crucial consequences for their later life trajectories (Hitlin, Kirkpatrick Johnson 2015), often without the necessary support. Often this happens with no option to return (Stein 2006). Unlike their peers, who might have better chances to return to their birth parents in the case of a 'wrong decision', these young adults are in a weaker position in terms of the previously described self-search.

However, we did also identify careful planning through the several cases of life-course agency with strong identity construction in terms of future profession. Here we can confirm that there are truly enabling structures at the macro (and meso)-levels, but they are not enough as such; it still requires a great positive influence of external factors at the micro-level such as the presence of an encouraging foster parent, an accompanying teacher, and strong connections (see aforementioned shared agency; Gilligan, Arnau-Sabatés 2017). Usually this mode was combined with strong self-efficacy, a strong sense of control over one's life, and the ability to see the causal influence of one's own decisions and choices. Providing support and care that promote the development of such agency is highly important because, as research shows (Andersson 2012), strong feelings of control accumulate in many spheres of life and thus contribute to overall well-being. But it seems that this is something one can achieve only through highly individualised care, which still appears to be an underdeveloped approach in Russian official aftercare services. However, as in many other fields, here Russian NGOs are the forerunners in developing new practices and approaches (Kulmala et al. forthcoming).

All in all, our investigation of care leavers' agency with a temporal dimension clearly helps us to see the intertwined nature of individual agency, circumstance (local cultures) and social structure, and how they come together to impact on vulnerability, social divisions, and inequalities (Pinkerton, Rooney 2014). Despite significant measures of state social support in the field of education, young care leavers remain in a vulnerable situation in contemporary Russian society. One can also see a certain discrepancy between the formal rules and the practice of realising the right to education. Moreover, their public image as a marginalised and stigmatised group limits their opportunities at the practical level and must affect their subjective perception of their own educational opportunities and more widely of their mastery over their own life (Hitlin, Kirkpatrick Johnson 2015). The studied young adults indeed talked quite a lot about stigmatisation and discrimination related to their status, starting from the first grades and consequently affecting later educational strategies at the level of school education associated with their social status. Targeted support for this specific group might also end up being stigmatising. In our conversations with our co-researchers, it became clear that the provided support is needed and appreciated, even if there is some ambiguity in this regard. During our excursion to learn about youth services in neighbouring Finland, these young adults started to think about the possible benefits of the One-Stop Guidance Centres operating on the principle of anonymity and available to all youths (Määttä 2017). However, the Russian system can be considered generous in terms of material support (owned housing, free education), although it often fails to provide much-needed individual (emotional) support to young adults considering their available options.

Notes

1 Our research is a part of the larger research project on youth well-being in the Arctic, 'Live, Work or Leave? Youth – wellbeing and the viability of (post) extractive Arctic industrial cities in Finland and Russia' (2018–2020), funded by the Academy of Finland and the Russian Academy of Science.
2 Federal Law of 21 December 1996 N 159-FL on Additional Guarantees for the Social Support of Orphans and Children Deprived of Parental Care.
3 Meri Kulmala leads an international, interdisciplinary research project 'A Child's Right to a Family: Deinstitutionalisation of Child Welfare in Putin's Russia', funded by the Academy of Finland, University of Helsinki and Kone Foundation, within which we have conducted 43 interviews with representatives of Russian child welfare NGOs. We have also participated in and arranged five research-practice seminars with mainly Russian child welfare street-level practitioners, including NGOs, during which we have engaged in close dialogue with these practitioners (See details in Chapter 4 by Kulmala et al. in this book).
4 We are conducting similar participatory research with young care leavers as co-researchers in another region of Russia where we have more variation in terms of the forms, which allows for more valid comparison between different forms.
5 In addition, we had two interviews which could not be easily included in only one of the categories. One is somewhat a combination of life-course agency with the features of both weak and strong identity construction. The second combines the characteristic features of both pragmatic and life-course agencies with weak identity construction.

References

In this volume:

Chapter 4: Kulmala, Shpakovskaya and Chernova
Chapter 7: Chernova and Shpakovskaya

Abramov, R.N., Antonova, K.A., Il'in, A.V., Grach, E.A., Lyubarskiy, G.Y., Chernova, Z.V. 2016. *Trayektorii sotsial'noy i professional'noy adaptatsii vypusknikov detskikh domov v Rossii (obzor issledovatel'skogo otcheta)* [Trajectories of Social Adaptation of Care Leavers of Children's Homes in Russia (Review of the Research Report)]. Moskva: SB Grupp.

Andersson, M.A. 2012. Identity Crises in Love and at Work: Dispositional Optimism as a Durable Personal Resource. *Social Psychology Quarterly* 75 (4): 290–309.

Appleton, P. 2019. Anchors for Deliberation and Shared Deliberation: Understanding Planning in Young Adults Transitioning from Out-of-home Care. *Qualitative Social Work*. https://doi.org/10.1177/1473325019869810

Arnau-Sabatés, L., Gilligan, R. 2015. What Helps Young Care Leavers to Enter the World of Work? Possible Lessons Learned from an Exploratory Study in Ireland and Catalonia. *Children and Youth Services Review* 53: 185–191.

Biggart, A., Walther, A. 2006. Coping with Yo-yo-Transitions: Young Adults Struggle for Support, between Family and State in Comparative Perspective. In: E. Ruspini, C. Leccardi (eds.), *A New Youth? Young People, Generations and Family Life*. New York: Routledge: 41–62.

Bradbury-Jones, C., Taylor, J. 2015. Engaging with Children as Co-Researchers: Challenges, Counter Challenges and Solutions. *International Journal of Social Research Methodology* 18 (3): 161–173.

Bratman, M.E. 2013. *Shared Agency: A Planning Theory of Acting Together*. Oxford: Oxford University Press.

Chernova, Z., Shpakovskaya, L. 2019. *Traektorii uspehsnogo perehoda k vzrosloi zhizni vypusknikov detskikh domov: resursy i bari'ery rezil'entnosti* [Care Leavers' Trajectories of Transition to Adult Life: Resources and Barriers of Resilience]. Unpublished research report by the Charity Foundation Afirmetika Dobra. St. Petersburg: Afirmetika Dobra.

Furlong, A. 2012. *Youth Studies: An Introduction*. London and New York: Routledge.

Gilligan, R., Arnau-Sabatés, L. 2017. The Role of Carers in Supporting the Progress of Care Leavers in the World of Work. *Child & Family Social Work* 22 (2): 792–800.

Glendinning, A., Pak, O., Popkov, I.V. 2004. Youth, Community Life and Well-being in Rural Areas of Siberia. *Sibirica* 4 (1): 31–48.

Hiles, D., Moss, D., Thorne, L., Wright, J., Dallos, R. 2014. 'So what am I?'–Multiple Perspectives on Young People's Experience of Leaving Care. *Children and Youth Services Review* 41: 1–15.

Hitlin, S., Elder Jr., G.H. 2007. Time, Self, and the Curiously Abstract Concept of Agency, *Sociological Theory* 25 (2): 170–191.

Hitlin, S., Kirkpatrick Johnson, M. 2015. Reconceptualizing Agency within the Life Course: The Power of Looking Ahead. *American Journal of Sociology* 120 (5): 1429–1472.

Ilyin, V.I. 2015. *Professiya kak individualnaya zhiznennaya koleya: kontseptualizatsiya kategorii* [Profession as an Individual Life Track: Conceptualisation of Categories]. *Zhurnal issledovanij socialnoj politiki* [Journal of Social Policy Studies] 13 (2): 515–528.

Kilpatrick, R., McCartan, C., McAlister, S., McKeown, P. 2007. 'If I am Brutally Honest Research has Never Appealed to Me . . . ': The Problems and Successes of a Peer Research Project. *Educational Action Research* 15: 351–369.

Kulmala, M., Fomina, A. 2019. *Luoteisvenäläiset nuoret kanssa- ja vertaistutkijoina* [North-Western Russian Young People as Co- and Peer-Researchers]. *Idäntutkimus* [The Finnish Review of East European Studies] 4: 96–102.

Kulmala, M., Jäppinen, M., Chernova, Z. Forthcoming. Reforming Russia's Child Protection System: From Institutional to Family Care. In: J.D. Berrick, N. Gilbert, M. Skivenes (eds.), *Oxford International Handbook of Child Protection Systems*, toim. Oxford: Oxford University Press [in print].

Määttä, M. (ed.) 2017. *Uutta auringon alla? Ohjaamot 2014–2017.* [New under the Sun? One-Stop Guidance Centres 2014–2017.] Jyväskylä: Kohtaamo-hanke (ESR), Keski-Suomen ELY-keskus.

Morton, J.M. 2011. Toward an Ecological Theory of the Norms of Practical Deliberation. *European Journal of Philosophy* 19 (4): 561–584.

OECD 2019. *Education at a Glance 2019: Russian Federation.* [Online]. Available at: www. oecd.org/education/education-at-a-glance/EAG2019_CN_RUS.pdf (accessed 17/12/2019).

Pinkerton, J., Rooney, C. 2014. Care Leavers' Experiences of Transition and Turning Points: Findings from a Biographical Narrative Study. *Social Work & Society* 12 (1): 1–12.

Radaev, V.V. 2018. Millennials Compared to Previous Generations: An Empirical Analysis. *Sociological Studies* 3 (3): 15–33.

Stein, M. 2006. Young People Aging out of Care: The Poverty of Theory. *Children and Youth Services Review* 28 (4): 422–434.

Törrönen, M., Munn-Giddings, C., Gavriel, C., O'Brien, N., Byrne, P. 2018. *Reciprocal Emotional Relationships: Experiences of Stability of Young Adults Leaving Care*, Publications of the Faculty of Social Sciences 75. Helsinki: University of Helsinki.

Walker, C. 2012. Class, Gender and Subjective Well-being in Russia's New Labour Market: Experiences of Young People in Ul'ianovsk and St Petersburg. *Zhurnal Issledovanii Sotsialnoi Politiki* [The Journal of Social Policy Studies] 10 (4): 521.

Part VI
Conclusions

11 In conclusion

The fragmented implementation of the new child welfare policy

Meri Kulmala, Maija Jäppinen, Anna Tarasenko, and Anna Pivovarova

Employing a rather broad (encompassing) neo-institutionalist framework, in this volume we used in-depth investigations for a wide variety of empirical phenomena. These included formal and informal institutions ranging from families, associations of foster families, and self-help groups, to the former residential care institutions that, for long time, dominated the sphere of the Russian alternative care system. We have also considered emerging new public support services for birth and foster parents and children themselves. The chapters of the volume have analysed the implementation of the ongoing child welfare reform in Russia. In our empirical investigations, we have asked how the reform is affecting the institutions and practices of Russian child welfare, especially alternative care. What kind of institutional change has followed the shift in the ideals (i.e. ideational change)? What are the intended and unintended consequences of the reform at the level of (institutional) practices and how can we explain them?

Incremental institutional change and nested newness

The paradigm change – which we argue has happened in Russian child welfare policy – was furthered by an exogenous shock (the Dima Yakolev case) which initiated ideational changes at the level of policies. Yet, our empirical investigations of the implementation of the new ideas show that ideational change has not been always straightforwardly translated into practice at the level of concrete institutions and daily practices. At those levels, instead of rapid changes, the changes are more slow-moving, less drastic, and more gradual and incremental in their nature. One can see different types of 'more organic' transformations, such as conversions, when new institutions are directed to a new purpose. As has been shown, there are wholly new tasks that were previously assigned to children's homes (now called as family support centres). Despite the reforms, many institutions continue to stick to their old ways: fighting for their existence and keeping children in their care. In such cases, the new tasks layer on the top of the old ones. It is obvious that many legacies and continuities with the past profoundly affect the operation of care providers – be they organisations or families. Such interconnectedness with the previous practices can be labelled as 'nested new-ness', which occurs when, according to Mackay (2014: 22),

> new formal institutions are neither blank states nor free-floating. Rather they are indelibly marked by the past institutional legacies and by initial and on-going interactions with already existing institutions (formal structures and rules, informal practices, norms, and ideas) within which they are nested.

In contrast to the new ideal of family care on show in Russia's DI reforms, resi-dential institutions have proven their durability. Sometimes institutional change is constrained because of these continuities. Many old practices are self-reinforcing, which is why we see even non-transformations and lock-ins due to severe path dependencies both in formal and informal institutions. This includes formal and sometime contradicting laws, which for instance hamper the reorganisation of the previous large children home's into smaller family-like units, and more informal cultural norms which we see in the case of understanding fostering as an adoption-like family formation. Often though, the boundaries between institutional repro-duction and institutional creation are blurred which leaves room for innovation as well. As we have shown through our investigation, many kinds of changes are nevertheless possible if there is a strong will combined with innovativeness. As this volume shows, institutional change in Russian welfare reform contains several layers, from the rapid change especially at the level of policies to more organic layering and even lock-ins at the level of concrete services and practices. In the Russian child welfare reform, periods of institutional reproduction overlap with moments of institutional creation in partial and often unpredictable ways and with unanticipated outcomes. Thelen (2003) labelled such institutional change as 'bounded innovation'.

The competing interests of the many actors involved translate into scattered practices. The reorganisation of the system according to the new ideas and ide-als of care is debated and negotiated among the key actors involved, including regional officials, street-level practitioners, non-governmental actors, and fami-lies themselves. Limited resources at the disposal of different actors produce a battle for resources, which produces fragmentation in the implementation of the new ideas imposed by the reform. This variation in reform outcome is particularly visible at the level of Russian regions. A lack of socioeconomic resources seems to be an important explanation for regions to resist the implementation of the new principles, including the reduction of residential facilities. Such resistance is typi-cal to any institutional change and it was obvious also in many of the analysed cases of this volume.

Despite the tensions and challenges, one can witness progress towards the goals of the reform. The number of children placed in foster care has increased significantly, and the number of residential facilities has declined. Nevertheless, despite the key goal of the reform – to prevent children entering the alternative care system – the focus of the efforts of the reform has been on the reorganisa-tion (or faking the reorganisation) of the alternative care arrangements instead of developing preventive measures. Preventive services are obviously still less developed. In our view, in order the new ideas to be properly implemented, developing community-based support for birth families should become the next priority of the implementation of the reform. Consequently, the whole concept of preventive work should be reconsidered and redefined, as it now mostly refers to 'temporary' institutional placements, instead of developing a universal social policy to better serve those children living in vulnerable circumstances and providing non-stigmatising early support services for children, parents, and families at risk.

Our key empirical conclusion is that the implementation of the new DI ideology and thus the Russian child welfare reform is sporadic and fragmented. The multilevel analysis has revealed unintended consequences that often derive from the mismatch between the qualitative goal of better care and its measurement in quantitative terms. This mismatch gets multiplied in the current political system of Russia. Whereas the goals are set by the federal-level government, the regions carry the responsibility for the implementation of the massive changes according to their existing resources. Often the regions lack proper resources to implement the federal policy. At the same time, with this particular reform, the political pressure to implement the new principles – or to show good results concerning proceeding with the reform – is particularly high. In such situation, regional actors, who are in charge of executing the changes, play with the numbers and invent sometimes rather questionable strategies to imitate the institutional change. Sometimes this 'massaging of numbers' is more strategic, although this can be seen more as an unintended consequence of 'good intentions', competing interests, and contradicting rules.

Relying on our exploration, we identified a set of reasons for these features of the DI reform in the Russian context. Firstly, we argue that the Russian political regime – which we call electoral authoritarianism – on the one hand forces lower level governments and actors to proceed with this top-priority reform, which, on the other hand, leads these lower level players to imitate reform. Secondly, we argue that the traditionally low level of trust in Russian society prevents the adoption of the new ideals on many levels. Families – both birth and foster – lack trust in officials and each other; the state (and NGOs) lack trust in families; against a backdrop of difficult life experiences, children and young people have multiple trust issues to carry through. Thirdly, we discuss the ways in which family is understood in the current child welfare system and how it affects the possible structures and solutions and hinders the fulfilment of certain goals. Fourthly, even if the reform – following the global deinstitutionalisation ideology – brings along a new rights-based approach to Russian child welfare, we argue that it is not always evident that children's rights are at the forefront during the stages of practical implementation.

An authoritarian political regime

We argue that the Russian political regime – i.e. electoral authoritarianism –forces lower level governments and actors to proceed with this top-priority reform. As Gel'man and Starodubtsev (2016: 114) argued, reforms in Russia can only be successful if 'a certain reform is the top political priority of the strong and authoritative head of state'. The implementation of the new child welfare ideology thus benefits from top-level prioritising, which makes things happen. Yet, unfortunately, these changes happen sometimes only as an imitation and with many unintended consequences due to the lack of adequate circumstances and the pressure to demonstrate good results.

In an authoritarian regime, there is a strong incentive for the lower levels of the government to implement the new policy. For instance, the measurement of the efficiency of regional leaders by the number of family placements (practised in 2013–2017) in the current political environment obviously directs the prevailing practices. In the current non-democratic, top-down led political environment, such incentives obviously create pressure on the lower level officials, and this might encourage them to fake their performance (Paneyakh 2014). Managerialism coupled with paternalism and authoritarianism and insufficient resources at the disposal of the regional authorities contribute to this manipulation with numbers.

The dominance of quantitative measurement and top-down regulation, as well as the consequent faking of the outcomes, obviously bears their legacy in history as well. In the Soviet times, social or health institutions were often monitored by according to the number of beds or patients in medical/care institutions and their funding was made dependent on this point. It was prestigious for the administration to have more money and more beds, all of which led to inefficient administration. We still see similar heavily path-dependent situations in the current child welfare system, such as when children's homes (now renamed public family centres) might receive their funding based on the number of children living in those institutions – even if there should be less and less children placed in institutional care. Again, we see a contradiction with the new goal and the existing regulatory logic (funding mechanism).

All in all, this top-down led reform together with the effort to quantify the qualitative goals is a strange combination of neo-liberal and Soviet-type governing principles (Hemment 2009). The neo-liberally oriented new public management principles of efficiency of services according to the performance-based budgeting are based on assessing the cost of services and their results: for instance, assessing how many patients (by diagnostic groups) are cured (and not just lay in bed) vs. the cost of the cure. This requires both new thinking and new capacities. A crude quantitative approach is often visible and represents one form of path dependency, not related to the principles of new public management or neo-liberalism as such – even if they can be also criticised in many ways. A paternalist and top-down led governmental system adds to the picture by creating heavy pressure to those who are in the charge of the concrete implementation of the new principles and who are put under obligation to show good results of their work.

The low level of societal trust

The low level of interpersonal and societal trust in the Russia society (Avdeeva 2019; Gibson 2001) is an issue that effects all levels of implementation in the new DI policy. Trust is a cultural resource necessary for the stable and predictable operation of social institutions (Temkina, Zdravomyslova 2008: 279). Seeing trust as an individual's understanding on how their fellow people would perform on a future occasion (Good 1988: 33) or as a 'bet about the future contingent actions of others' (Sztompka 1999: 25), we refer to societal trust as those expectations that the actors being involved in child welfare might have towards the other actors in the sphere and their ability to act in the best interest of a child. Here, however, we see more distrust than trust. This becomes a crucial obstacle for the implementation of many changes. Piotr Sztompka (1999: 26) defined distrust as the 'negative mirror-image of trust', which 'involves negative expectations about the actions of others (of their harmful, vicious, detrimental actions toward myself), and it involves negative, defensive commitment (avoiding, escaping, distancing myself, refusing actions, taking protective measures against those I distrust)'. In our case, in the massive, top-down led DI reform, such mistrust, being present almost anywhere, as many of the chapters show, results in multiple miscommunications and the inability to collaborate between different actors involved in the implementation of the new ideals of care.

Each actor, at each possible level of the implementation of the new policy, is believed to be the one who acts in the best possible ways in the interests of children, while the other actors involved are most likely – according to those beliefs coloured by suspicion – guided by a misconception about the interests of the child, or by personal interests. As shown in this volume, public opinion towards foster parents is highly suspicious in the Russian society. Within the reform, the federal government has increased financial support for foster families which have become a source for criticism according to which foster families make money at the cost of children in vulnerable situation. Public opinion – as well as the attitude of professionals – is negative also towards the birth parents who are often seen as those to blame for the abuse of their children. No one tends to trust child protection services (*opeka*) who are seen to practice control instead of providing support. In particular, people do not trust the *opeka*, and do not wish to get in touch with them. This has to do with the concrete work practices at the *opeka* but also with generalised mistrust in state institutions in post-communist Russia (Offe 1999: 27). In the end, both birth and foster parents are often reluctant to request assistance from state services and authorities. Birth parents are distrusted by foster parents, and the vice versa. A sort of buffer role in this context is played by child welfare NGOs, which, on the one hand, have up-to-date expertise in working with families (foster ones in particular) and, on the other hand, have experience in cooperation with the authorities and state institutions. This, however, cannot fill all the gaps between the different levels of the system. Even if the state outsources some of the support services to the non-state actors, namely socially oriented NGOs, it allows almost no autonomy in practising these functions. Also, the other street-level practitioners lack autonomy in the current environment. NGOs, as well as parents, do not always trust public service centres. Additionally, NGOs tend to question the ability of the parents to cope with the foster kids without their interference and expertise. In the end, children themselves who are placed in alternative care still tend to carry a strong stigma in the Russian society, which seemingly affects the implementation of new ideas for child-centred and child-focused approaches. Similarly, as Anna Temkina and Elena Zdravomyslova (2008) argued concerning the Russian reproductive care system, we argue that distrust remains one of the most significant dilemmas of the Russian child welfare system.

Permanent and kinship-like understanding of alternative care

What makes the Russian case of deinstitutionalisation reform exceptional in international comparisons is, first, its focus on alternative and foster care instead of preventive work and support for birth families. A second feature is the understanding of foster family as something that completely replaces the birth family. Once a child is placed to foster care, little if any, support is provided to birth parents in order to enable family reunification. This lack of support for birth families leads to a situation where only a few children return to their birth families. Additionally, the tie between the child and the birth family may break for good, as support services do not particularly encourage the foster parents to keep ties with birth parents. Foster parents themselves also tend to see fostering as permanent, almost as an adoption-like solution. What seems to be steadily changing is the understanding of institutional care as temporary, yet not always in the practice, as seen in several chapters of this volume. Indeed, in respect to family placements, there is little change in the attitude, except in some specific contexts like children's villages.

Both in the biographical stories of foster parents and in the media discourse, kinship and relatedness are often used as the dominating concepts for describing relations between children and foster parents. This understanding of foster care as kinship-like permanent relationship creates challenges when it comes, firstly, to the public discussion on the legal status of foster care as paid work, and secondly, to the development of support services for birth families and the possibility of a child's reunion with the birth family. All these conditions make Russia different from how alternative care is seen in international child rights norms, according to which foster care is in most cases provided for a fixed period of time (UN CRC 1989; UN Guidelines for the Alternative Care of Children). Thus, the prevalent norms of fostering as permanent family-making and similar to 'birth parenthood' hamper the implementation of the global DI ideology.

Child rights as the guiding principle?

The reforms are obviously inspired by the international child's rights movement and international child's rights norms that the Russian Federation has committed to by ratifying (UN CRC 1989). The reform can be seen as a leap forward in child's rights situation of the country. During the years prior to the reform, Russia was repeatedly criticised by the UN's Child's Rights Committee about the large number of children in institutions and insufficient efforts to change the situation.

Now, there is clear evidence of less children living in institutions than earlier, as shown in Chapter 2 of this volume by Biryukova and Makarentseva, and at least baby steps taken towards better support services for families to prevent need for alternative care.

At the same time, as we have shown in the chapters of this volume, other issues in the implementation of the reform sometimes override child's best interests, although they should always be the leading principle of all action considering children. For example, the child's right to a family as the core goal of the reform translates sometimes to foster parents' right to get a child. Another perspective overriding child's best interests can be regional authorities' will to have as many family placements registered in the statistics as possible – i.e. the sole need to make the statistics look good in the eyes of the top-level authorities and politicians is more important than the right of an individual child to be placed in the best possible solution of alternative care for them. On the other hand, little attention is so far paid either to child's right to know their birth parents and to maintain personal relations and direct contact with birth parents on a regular basis even during the alternative care placement or to child's right to family reunification. The idea that a foster family can completely replace the birth family, as chapters of this volume show, is somewhat contradictory to Article 9 of the UN Child's rights convention (UN CRC 1989),

Another child's rights issue that has got little attention in the implementation of the reform so far is child's right to participation. Traditionally, children are treated rather as the future of the nation than as agents of their own lives. In the reforms, the understanding of children seems to be still rather objectifying, which means that they are seen as objects of measures taken by child welfare authorities and other adults rather than individuals participating in the decision-making over their own lives.

What can we learn from the Russian case – and what next?

DI of child welfare is a global policy. Its application and implementation in the context of Russia have brought along multiple unintended, even paradoxical consequences. The challenges found in the Russian case may not be very unique, but different kinds of problems and mismatches between the goals and implementations are most likely to be found in any context. Yet, our investigation and findings in the Russian context may shed light also on processes going on in other contexts. In-depth analysis of one country case also opens eyes and interest towards international comparisons, which would be needed in the field of academic research on child welfare systems. Similarly, we hope that the analyses of this volume may be fruitful also for the future investigations of DI in other spheres than child welfare. Services for people with disabilities and mental health issues are crucial spheres for deinstitutionalisation in the post-Soviet space.

At the same time, several topics for further investigation can be identified in the Russian child welfare system. One important task would be bringing child perspective and children's agency and right to participation as well as the voices of birth parents to the forefront. We still know very little about their experiences and about the existing and developing 'preventive' support services for birth families, which should be the next focus of the service development. Interesting topics for analysis would be also the role and practices of monitoring of the services, as well as how the different actors of the system – professionals, foster and adoptive parents, for instance – are trained to their tasks.

References

Avdeeva, D. 2019. *Doverie v Rossii i ego svyaz' s urovnem ekonomicheskogo razvitiya* [Trust in Russia and Its Connection with the Level of Economic Development]. *Obshchestvennye nauki i sovremennost* [Social Science and Modernity] 3: 79–93.

Gel'man, V., Starodubtsev, A. 2016. Opportunities and Constraints of Authoritarian Modernisation: Russian Policy Reforms in the 2000s. *Europe-Asia Studies* 68 (1): 97–117.

Gibson, J. 2001. Social Networks, Civil Society, and the Prospects for Consolidating Russia's Democratic Transition. *American Journal of Political Science* 45 (1): 51–68.

Good, D. 1988. Individuals, Interpersonal Relations, and Trust. In: D. Gambetta (ed.), *Trust: Making and Breaking Cooperative Relations*. Oxford: Basil Blackwell: 31–48.

Guidelines for the Alternative Care of Children: Resolution/adopted by the General Assembly. UN. General Assembly (64th session: 2009–2010).

Hemment, J. 2009. Soviet-Style Neoliberalism? *Problems of Post-Communism* 56 (6): 36–50.

Mackay, F. 2014. Nested Newness, Institutional Innovation, and the Gendered Limits of Change. *Politics & Gender* 10 (4): 549–571.

Offe, C. 1999. How Can we Trust our Fellow Citizens? In: M. Warren (ed.), *Democracy and Trust*. Cambridge: Cambridge University Press: 42–87.

Paneyakh, E. 2014. Faking Performance Together: Systems of Performance Evaluation in Russian Enforcement Agencies and Production of Bias and Privilege. *Post-Soviet Affairs* 30 (2–3): 115–136.

Sztompka, P. 1999. *Trust: A Sociological Theory*. Cambridge: Cambridge University Press.

Temkina, A., Zdravomyslova, E. 2008. Patients in Contemporary Russian Reproductive Health Care Institutions: Strategies of Establishing Trust. *Demokratizatsiya* 3 (3): 277–293.

Thelen, K. 2003. How Institutions Evolve: Insights from Comparative Historical Analysis, In: J. Mahoney, D. Rueschemeyer (eds.), *Comparative Historical Analysis in the Social Sciences*. Cambridge: Cambridge University Press: 208–240.

UN CRC. 1989. *Convention on the Rights of the Child*. United Nations. Geneva, Switzerland.

Index